KT-492-825

PENGUIN BOOKS

# THE PSYCHOLOGY OF
# INTERPERSONAL BEHAVIOUR

Michael Argyle, D.Sc., D.Litt., Hon. D.Sc. Psych., is Emeritus Reader in Social Psychology, Emeritus Fellow of Wolfson College, and Emeritus Professor of Psychology of Oxford Brookes University. He was born in 1925, went to Nottingham High School and Emmanuel College, Cambridge, and was a navigator in the RAF. He has been teaching social psychology at Oxford since 1952. He has been engaged in research in various aspects of social psychology and is particularly interested in the experimental study of social interaction and its application to wider social problems. He has been a visiting professor at a number of universities in the USA, Canada and Australia, and has lectured in thirty-four countries. He established the Oxford Social Psychology group, which produced seventy D. Phils, some of them now professors elsewhere.

His recent books have been *Psychology and Social Class*, *The Social Psychology of Everyday Life*, *The Psychology of Happiness*, *The Anatomy of Relationships* (with Monika Henderson) and new editions of *Bodily Communication* and *The Social Psychology of Work*. He has written numerous articles in British, American and European journals. He helped to found the *British Journal of Social and Clinical Psychology* and was Social Psychology editor (1961–7). He was editor of the Pergamon Press *International Studies in Experimental Social Psychology* and Chairman of the Social Psychology Section of the British Psychological Society (1964–7 and 1972–4).

He is married and has four children; his hobbies are travel, interpersonal behaviour, Scottish country dancing, Utopian speculation, theological disputation and playing the goat.

MICHAEL ARGYLE

# THE PSYCHOLOGY OF
# INTERPERSONAL BEHAVIOUR

*Fifth Edition*

PENGUIN BOOKS

PENGUIN BOOKS

Published by the Penguin Group
Penguin Books Ltd, 80 Strand, London WC2R 0RL, England
Penguin Putnam Inc., 375 Hudson Street, New York, New York 10014, USA
Penguin Books Australia Ltd, 250 Camberwell Road, Camberwell, Victoria 3124, Australia
Penguin Books Canada Ltd, 10 Alcorn Avenue, Toronto, Ontario, Canada M4V 3B2
Penguin Books India (P) Ltd, 11 Community Centre, Panchsheel Park, New Delhi – 110 017, India
Penguin Books (NZ) Ltd, Cnr Rosedale and Airborne Roads, Albany, Auckland, New Zealand
Penguin Books (South Africa) (Pty) Ltd, 24 Sturdee Avenue, Rosebank 2196, South Africa

Penguin Books Ltd, Registered Offices: 80 Strand, London WC2R 0RL, England

www.penguin.com

First published in Pelican Books 1967
Second edition 1972
Third edition 1978
Fourth edition 1983
Reprinted in Penguin Books 1990
Fifth edition 1994

14

Copyright © Michael Argyle, 1967, 1972, 1978, 1983, 1994
All rights reserved

The moral right of the author has been asserted

Filmset by Datix International Limited, Bungay, Suffolk
Printed in England by Clays Ltd, St Ives plc
Set in 10.5/12 pt Monophoto Bembo

Except in the United States of America, this book is sold subject
to the condition that it shall not, by way of trade or otherwise, be lent,
re-sold, hired out, or otherwise circulated without the publisher's
prior consent in any form of binding or cover other than that in
which it is published and without a similar condition including this
condition being imposed on the subsequent purchaser

ISBN-13: 978-0-14-017274-4

# CONTENTS

# LIST OF FIGURES AND TABLES

## FIGURES

## TABLES

Man is a social animal: he collaborates with others to pursue his goals and satisfy his needs. It is well known that relations with others can be the source of the deepest satisfactions and of the blackest misery. Moralists, novelists and others have written about these things, but the detailed analysis of social interactions and relationships has been lacking. Recent research by social psychologists has made these phenomena very much clearer. In particular there have been important advances in the experimental analysis of social encounters at the level of such things as eye movements, the timing of speech, and non-verbal communication.

This research has a number of possible applications. The work of many people consists of dealing with people rather than with things – teachers, psychologists, air hostesses, managers and many others; research has been done into the social techniques which are most effective, and into how such skills can be taught. Many people are lonely and unhappy, some are mentally ill, because they are unable to establish and sustain social relationships with others. Many everyday encounters are unpleasant, embarrassing or fruitless because of inept social behaviour. Conflicts between different social classes and different cultural groups are partly due to the difficulties of interaction. Many of those difficulties and frustrations could be eliminated by a wider understanding of and better training in the skills of social interaction.

# PREFACE TO THE FIFTH EDITION

This book has been part of my life for years. I originally wrote it in the first flush of enthusiasm produced by the early work on non-verbal communication and social skills. I thought that it would solve everyone's problems, by showing the way to more effective social behaviour and better relationships. Perhaps it has helped a bit; there have been large sales – more than the rest of my books put together – and translations into many languages, and it has been prescribed reading for many courses.

It was never intended to be an elementary textbook of social psychology; it is about research which is directly relevant to successful performance in everyday situations and relationships.

It is ten years since the last edition, and a great deal of new research and ideas in social psychology have been produced since then. I have tried to include the main new developments which are related to my central theme.

'I love Social Psych.' was printed on a badge once given me by a grateful student. Indeed I do, but I particularly love rigorous and well-designed research on real social behaviour, rather than on subjects sitting in 'booths' trying to make money out of or give shocks to other subjects, who may or may not be there in other booths.

Some areas have been particularly strengthened in this edition, such as:

verbal and non-verbal communication;
social competence;
close relationships;
social behaviour of mental patients.

I am indebted to many members of the Oxford social psychology group, past and present, and particularly to Peter Collett, Adrian Furnham, Yair Hamburger, Monika Henderson, Mansur Lalljee and Luo Lo, to my son Nicholas Argyle, to Sonia Argyle for her work on the index, to Ann McKendry for typing yet another manuscript, and to the ESRC and Leverhulme Trust for research support.

MICHAEL ARGYLE
Oxford
June 1993

## CHAPTER I

# SOCIAL MOTIVATION

Most people spend a great deal of their time engaging in some kind of social interaction. They live together, work together and spend spare time with their friends. Why do they do this? Why don't we all behave like hermits, living and working alone? In fact for most individuals solitary confinement, or other forms of isolation for more than short periods, are very unpleasant indeed. Loss of 'face' in the Far East is a cause of suicide, and rejection by friends in our own society is a common source of distress.

People seem to seek a number of goals in social situations: to be approved of and to make friends, to dominate or to depend on others, to be admired, to be helped or given social support, to provide help to others, and so on. Different people seek different things in social situations. In the present state of knowledge it looks as if social behaviour is the product of at least seven different drives. A 'drive' can be defined as a persistent tendency to seek certain goals. As well as directing people towards goals, a drive is a source of energy; when the drive is operating there is a general increase of vigour. Much the same is true of biological drives, such as the need for food: when a person is hungry he will seek food with increased effort. Furthermore the drive can be subdivided into a number of more specific ones, for salt, sugar and so on; animals deprived of one of these substances will select a diet which makes good the deficit. It is necessary to postulate these various forms of motivation to account for variations in the behaviour of the *same* person on different occasions, for example when hungry and not, and to describe differences between *different* people in the goals they pursue and the energy with which they do it.

There is as yet no final agreement on how social motivation should be divided up. What will be done here is to offer a provisional list of motivational sources of interpersonal behaviour. These are sufficient to account for the phenomena described in this book, and each has been extensively studied by psychologists and others. Later in this chapter some account will be given of how these drives function, and of their origins in childhood experience or innate tendencies. Here, then, is the provisional list, together with a note of the goals which are sought in each case. Except for biological needs these are either responses from, or types of relationships with, other people:

1 *Biological needs* – eating, drinking and bodily comfort;

2 *Dependency* – help, support, protection and guidance, at first from parents, later from people in positions of power or authority;

3 *Affiliation* – warm and friendly responses from, and social acceptance by, peers, shown by physical proximity, smiles and gaze;

4 *Dominance* – acceptance by others, and groups of others, as the task leader, being allowed to talk most of the time, take the decisions and be deferred to by the group;

5 *Sex* – physical proximity, bodily contact, etc., eye contact, warm, friendly and intimate social interaction, usually with attractive peers of the opposite sex;

6 *Aggression* – to harm other people physically, verbally or in other ways;

7 *Self-esteem and ego-identity* – for other people to make approving responses and to accept the self-image as valid;

8 *Other motivations which affect social behaviour* – needs for achievement, money, interests and values.

This list is provisional but moderately well established: drives 1 to 6 have all been studied in animals, and their biological and evolutionary basis is understood; they have also been studied in humans, and we know how they are affected by childhood experiences, how they are aroused and how they affect social behaviour.

*The biological functions of social behaviour in animals* A lot of human social behaviour has close parallels with animal social behaviour, and can be explained to some extent in terms of the evolutionary origins of this behaviour. Sociobiology can offer such explanations of non-verbal communication, social relation-ships, helping behaviour and social motivation.

During the last few years studies have been carried out on apes and monkeys in the wild; these studies have shown clearly how their social behaviour is important for the biological survival of these animals. A set of partly innate social drives has emerged during the course of evolution; these drives produce a pattern of partly instinctive social behaviour that enables groups of apes and monkeys to eat and drink, defend themselves against enemies, reproduce themselves, and care for and train their young.

1 Apes and monkeys need access to water and to suitable vegetables and fruits to eat. They occupy a territory which contains these resources, and may defend it against rivals. The patterns of social behaviour described below vary considerably between species. They also vary between groups of the *same* species, depending on the ecology, for example the availability of food and nesting sites; such 'cultural' patterns are perpetuated by socialization (Crook, 1970).

2 Most species live in groups, with a fairly stable dominance hierarchy which is established by aggressive displays between adult males. Certain adult males provide leadership in defending the territory and keeping internal order.

3 There is a definite family structure, which can vary from one species to another. Opposite-sex pairs mate in order to continue the species, while adult males look after their females for a time and act as generalized fathers to the infants in the group.

4 Mothers feed and look after their young, and provide socialization experiences which complete the partly 'open' instinc-tive systems. They have maternal patterns of behaviour which are aroused by the sight of young; the young have dependent patterns of behaviour which are aroused by the sight, feel and sound of the mother.

5 Aggressive behaviour is used to defend group and territory; it may also occur between males of the same group who are competing for dominance or for access to the same female. However, such aggression is usually limited to ferocious

displays in which the most terrifying animal wins; it would not be in the interests of the group for much real fighting to take place.

6 Young apes and monkeys engage in play, adults in grooming; these are two examples of affiliative behaviour which probably have the functions of restraining aggression inside the group and making co-operation easier. Like other animal species they exhibit a lot of co-operation and help, especially of close kin.

Social behaviour in lower animals is almost entirely instinctive: the whole pattern of social behaviour is innate and has emerged during evolution because of its biological survival value. The apes and monkeys are different in that their instinctive systems are more open, and remain to be completed during socialization experiences. There are also components of culture, perpetuated in particular groups of animals; these include washing food in sea water, in one group of Japanese macaques, and swimming in another.

The behaviour of apes and monkeys is quite illuminating for understanding human social behaviour; they are certainly more helpful than rats. However, there are some very important differences between men and monkeys: we use language, and our behaviour is more affected by plans and social rules. In humans innate factors are less important and there is a longer period of socialization. Human groups build up a far more elaborate culture, which is passed on to later generations, so that we live in an environment which is not only physically constructed by us but has been given meanings by us – as in the case of clothes, cars and everything else around us. Much of this is made possible by language, which enables us to accumulate and pass on culture, and which also makes our social behaviour entirely different.

*Biological and other drives* The best-understood drives are those aroused by hunger and thirst. There seems to be a self-regulating system which keeps the levels of food and water in the body at an equilibrium level. For example, when the level of water is low, thirst is experienced and the drive is aroused, leading to behaviour which makes good the deficit and restores the equilibrium. (The self-regulation of eating or drinking can go wrong, as in cases of obesity.)

The social drives, which we are interested in, do not work like this. In the drives for affiliation and money, the contents of the bloodstream are not involved; whatever physiological basis they have must be in the brain. There is no deficit, so that satisfaction of the need does not lead to a cessation of activity. These drives still resemble hunger and thirst in that relevant internal states and external stimuli result in autonomic arousal and the direction of behaviour towards the goals in question.

Sex is an interesting intermediate case. In lower animals sexual arousal depends on the level of sex hormones in the bloodstream – though there is no deficit here. In higher mammals and in man there is little connection between hormones and sexual arousal and activity; castration after puberty leads to no loss of sexual desire.

People are not hungry all the time, and the momentary strength of this drive depends on how far it has been recently satiated. It is now known that the activation of all drives involves a similar pattern of physiological arousal. This consists of electrical activity originating in the hypothalamus, and of activity in the sympathetic nervous system, producing higher blood pressure, a faster heartbeat and perspiration – though the physiological pattern varies between individuals and drives. Arousal is stronger when the expected reward or 'incentive' is larger, when it is greatly desired and when its probability of being attained appears to be greater. The effect of incentives varies with the drive strength, and may vary between different cultural groups. For instance, working-class children are aroused more by cash incentives, while middle-class children are more affected by hopes of 'success'.

We turn now to the conditions under which needs are satisfied. The hungry person is made less hungry by eating; the hunger drive builds up gradually with time until it is satisfied again. The drives behind social behaviour do not seem to work quite like this. A person who seeks money or fame does not cease to do so when he receives some gratification. Indeed the reverse is more likely: a person who seeks fame and never receives any is likely to give up and seek different goals instead. In other words, gratification seems to reinforce rather than satiate the goal-seeking tendency. There may still be some parallel to biological drives, in that there might be temporary satiation before further goals of the same type are sought.

Motivation can be looked at in terms of the goals people are seeking. The pattern of people's lives, in which they move from one event or situation to another, can therefore be explained in terms of the goals they seek. Goals are associated with positive affects, with cognitions about how they can be attained and with patterns of behaviour. People enter situations because they anticipate that they will enable certain goals to be attained (p. 104). Personalities can be studied by sampling the goals pursued, discovering the categories into which they fall and investigating their hierarchical structure (Pervin, 1989).

*The origins of motivation* Hunger and thirst are due to innate bodily needs, though the way they are satisfied is partly learnt from the culture; sex and aggression also have an instinctive basis. In other words human beings have an unlearnt tendency to pursue these goals in certain ways when suitably aroused. Other social motives, like dependency and affiliation, may have innate components but are mainly due to early relations with parents. Some social drives may be wholly learnt, as is the need for money. Drives may be acquired in childhood in a number of ways. A pattern of behaviour may become a drive because it consistently leads to other kinds of satisfaction; the origin of the need for money is probably that it leads to gratification of hunger and then becomes a goal which is sought for its own sake. Drives may be acquired through other learning processes, such as attachment to or identification with parents: a child who takes a parent as a model is likely to acquire the parental pattern of motivation.

There are great variations between cultures in the typical strength of these drives. Some cultures are very aggressive, some are greatly concerned about status and loss of face. These variations can sometimes be traced to the environmental setting; tribes which are constantly having to defend themselves against enemies need to have aggressive members, and so aggression is encouraged in children (Zigler and Child, 1969).

*The restraint of motivation* In the case of sex, aggression and probably affiliation, there are restraining forces which often prevent the goal being attained. When the drive is aroused there is also arousal of inner restraints, probably because of punishment in the past. These are cases of approach–avoidance conflict – where the same object is both desirable and undesirable. It is found that as the goal gets nearer its desirability increases, but fear or other avoidance forces increase even more. The anxiety induced by the prospect of parachute-jumping, for example, increases rapidly as the time approaches. A small child who wants to stroke a horse finds that her fear increases as she gets closer to the horse, and she vacillates at a short distance from it. Rats who are both fed and shocked at the end of a maze stop part of the way down it. Miller (1944) presented a theoretical analysis in terms of approach and avoidance 'gradients', where the avoidance gradient is steeper and the crossing-point shows where they balance (Figure 1.1).

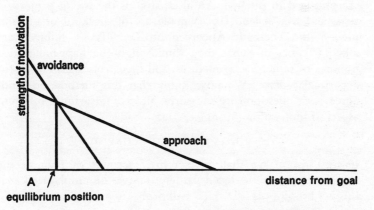

Figure 1.1   Analysis of approach–avoidance conflicts.

A further source of restraint on aggressive and egoistic drives is concern for others. Aggression is inhibited by another's signs of distress; help is stimulated by empathy with the other.

However, the main sources of restraint on selfish behaviour come from cultural learning. As well as biological evolution there is also social evolution, whereby the elements of culture which help a society to survive are retained. Some of the most important aspects of culture are the moral values and other norms of behaviour, which keep aggressive, sexual and selfish behaviour in check.

*The measurement of motivation* People vary in the energy with which they pursue the goals of sex, dominance, affiliation and so on. How can these individual differences be assessed? We need to distinguish between their normal or typical level and their state at a particular moment. Questionnaires have been constructed by Spielberger (1972) for *state anxiety* and *trait anxiety*, using rather different questions. Buss and Perry (1992) developed a questionnaire measure of aggression, which assesses four types of aggression: physical, verbal, anger and suspicious hostility. Men score high on the first factor, assertive individuals on the second.

Questionnaires suffer from the problem that they may only measure the motives that people are consciously aware of and are prepared to disclose. An alternative is the use of projection tests, and McClelland (1987) made use of the kind of pictures used in the Thematic Apperception Test (TAT). Subjects are asked to imagine what they think might be happening in a number of rather vague pictures, and their stories are scored for a particular drive. We now know that this method does not agree with questionnaire measures, and is measuring a different aspect of motivation (Spangler, 1992).

### THE ROOTS OF SOCIAL BEHAVIOUR

In this section we shall give a brief account of each of the motivational systems listed earlier. It must be emphasized that this is a provisional list which will probably have to be revised in the light of future research.

1 *Biological needs* Basic biological drives, such as the need for food, may lead to various kinds of interaction. They may result in drawing together the members of a primitive group in a co-operative task which none could accomplish alone. This also happens, in a simpler way, with animals. In primitive societies there is usually co-operation over agriculture, hunting and house-building. In modern societies work leads to satisfaction of biological needs less directly. However, bodily needs for food, drink, warmth and comfort affect our behaviour a lot of the time, and are important sources of motivation which have often been overlooked by social psychologists (Argyle, 1991).

2 *Dependency* The central goal of this drive is obtaining and keeping nurturant and supportive relationships. Several kinds of social behaviour are found in dependent individuals, including seeking help, being suggestible and compliant, especially to people in authority, being sensitive to others, and being anxious both when alone and when performing in front of others.

Dependency may be aroused in adults in situations which are new and frightening, and where others know the ropes. Dependence, or submission, is closely related to its opposite, dominance, in that some people may show both types of behaviour on different occasions. The so-called 'authoritarian personality' is submissive to people of greater power or status, and dominant to those of less.

Dependency is the first form of social motivation. Infants are physically dependent on their mother (or whoever is looking after them). There is an innate tendency to respond to pairs of eyes and to female voices; both are in range during feeding, and this is part of the rather complex process whereby an infant develops an early attachment to the mother. Bowlby (1971) proposed that both in animals and humans there are innate signals, especially crying and clinging, which elicit care-giving from parents. By twelve months, infants become, in different degrees, 'attached' to their care-givers; this relationship in weakened form is very long lasting, and it affects other relationships later, especially romantic love. Affiliative, co-operative and extraverted behaviour are also stronger in those who had early close relations with their mother. During the period from one to five years of age, children learn to bear greater physical distance from their mother and longer periods of separation. They have to be trained to be more independent, especially when younger children appear on the scene.

Dependency is stronger when the mother has been responsive and overprotective, and when there has been a close relation between mother and infant (Schaffer and Emerson, 1964). This is interpreted by some in terms of the social learning of an acquired drive. The psychoanalytic story is that dependence is derived from the oral phase, and this is given some support by the link between dependency and obesity, smoking and alcoholism (Bornstein, 1992).

3 *Affiliative motivation* Most people seek the company and approval of others, are unhappy if they are lonely or rejected, and are very distressed by isolation. In laboratory situations it is found that subjects strong in affiliation spend time establishing personal relationships with other people rather than getting on with the appointed task. In particular they are keen to interact with other people of similar age, position, etc. to themselves. It probably leads to interaction with members of the opposite sex as well, and at present we are unable to disentangle its effects from those of the sexual drive – with which it appears to be rather closely related.

Women seem to have stronger affiliative needs than men: they spend more time in the company of others, have more friends and form more intimate friendships (Dickens and Perlman, 1981).

The McClelland group developed a projective test measure of need for affiliation (n.Aff), thought of as the need to be with people, and it does correlate with spending a lot of time with others. However, a series of experiments found that n.Aff consisted mainly of avoiding conflict and criticism, and was really a fear of rejection, and that this led to unpopularity. McAdams (1988) developed a different measure, of the need for intimacy (n.Int), with different pictures, now looking at enjoyable close relationships. People who score high on this measure are warm, loving and co-operative, and not dominant or self-centred. Their actual behaviour is different too: they spend a lot of time with friends, engage in self-disclosure, are good listeners, engage in more reciprocal dialogue and are sensitive to faces (McClelland, 1987).

Psychologists think of motives in terms of what individuals want, and of social motives as responses wanted from others. This is part of the story of affiliative or intimacy motivation – people want to be liked. But it is more than this, especially for those high in n. Int, who are seeking a close relationship. Much of the behaviour associated with the affiliative drives requires co-operation; that is, it takes two (or more) to do it – as in dancing, tennis, sex and conversation. We shall see later that in certain relationships, like romantic love and close friendship, people are also very concerned about the welfare of the other person.

Infants as young as two months want to interact, and are happy to do so with their mothers over closed-circuit television, but are not at all happy just to watch an earlier clip of her behaviour (Trevarthen, 1980). It has long been believed that affiliative behaviour develops in some way out of dependency. There is quite a lot of evidence to support this theory: the Harlows' monkeys showed no later affiliative behaviour if they had been reared in isolation, and affectionless psychopaths often have a history of maternal deprivation. Co-operative and extraverted behaviour are stronger in children who experienced earlier close attachment (Sroufe, Fox and Pancake, 1983). Many studies have found a relationship between maternal warmth and children becoming friendly and socially outgoing.

Affiliative motivation can be aroused in several ways. Periods of isolation and loneliness heighten it; going to college, with loss of previous friends, may do this. It has often been observed that fear makes people seek each other's company. Schachter (1959) found that college girls who had been made anxious by the prospect of receiving electric shocks from 'Dr Zilstein' chose to wait with other subjects rather than alone; this was especially the case for those who were made most anxious, and for first-born and only children. Conducting a sociometric survey, in which people nominate their friends, arouses it, as does giving people a task for which the reward is receiving the experimenter's approval. The prospect of parties or other enjoyable social events probably has a similar effect.

Extraversion is very similar to affiliative motivation, but is usually regarded as a personality trait and measured by questionnaire. It probably includes some social competence as well as motivation, and is correlated with the choice and enjoyment of social situations – but of parties and teams rather than intimate situations (see Chapter 5). We shall see later that social skills are very important in forming relationships; affiliative motivation alone is not enough (p. 162).

4 *Dominance* This refers to a very important group of motivations, including needs for power – to control the behaviour or fate of others – and for status or recognition – to be admired and looked up to by others. Dominant people want to talk a lot, have their ideas attended to and be influential in decisions. People strong in dominance take part in a struggle for position, the winner emerging as the 'task leader', i.e. the person responsible for decisions (see Chapter 8). The same is true in groups of monkeys; dominance here is usually established by threat displays or actual fighting, and the winner receives deference from the others and most access to the females.

One approach to dominance has been as the need for power (Winter, 1973). A projection test measure was found to be aroused by films of politicians making speeches. Those high in this need are competitive, sometimes aggressive, try to dominate in small groups, are more influential but may be disliked, choose influential occupations, and like prestige possessions like credit cards and cars. Managers were found to have a combination of high power and low affiliative motivation – they were more concerned with being influential than being liked – together with strong self-control. However, this motivational pattern had some negative physiological consequences: weaker immune system and higher blood pressure. The origins of need for power lie partly in mothers being permissive over sex and aggression. The origins of the high power/low affiliation pattern lie in strong, self-controlled fathers and a younger sibling to be responsible for (McClelland, 1987).

Another approach to dominance is via assertiveness. This has usually been thought of as a set of social skills, which can be taught. It has recently been found that women are assertive in a way that is different from men. Women are more concerned with obligations to others and think it is important in assertive situations to be friendly and not to hurt people's feelings (Wilson and Gallois, 1993).

There may be innate, instinctive origins of dominant behaviour. Dominance is thought to have developed during evolution, since it has the biological function of providing leaders who can keep order in the group and repel enemies. Males are more dominant than females in every human society, and among monkeys and other mammals (Wilson, 1975). It has been shown that injecting male monkeys or other male animals with male sex hormones produces more aggression and dominance.

5 *Sex* This motivates important forms of behaviour, such as approaching members of (usually) the opposite sex in order to engage in certain kinds of social interaction and bodily contact. In the lower animals sexual motivation is instinctive; arousal is controlled by sex hormones and leads to the fulfilment of the biological purpose of reproduction. In humans sex seems to have become a pleasurable end in itself, and is controlled by the cortex rather than by sex hormones. For present purposes sexual motivation can be looked at as a social approach drive similar to the need for affiliation, but which is usually directed towards members of the opposite sex and may lead later to various forms of bodily contact, in a set order, and finally intercourse. Above all, it often leads to love and marriage.

Sexual arousal is produced by certain non-verbal cues: seeing physically attractive members of (usually) the opposite sex, being touched in certain ways and certain places, and experiencing smells such as those from perfume. In addition, erotic pictures and films are very arousing — as measured by subjective reports or penis expansion; the most arousing are films of intercourse, genital petting and oral sex (Baron and Byrne, 1991). Pornographic pictures and films often contain aggressive elements and can produce aggression as well as sexual arousal. Humans can also be aroused by a wide range of stimuli which have become associated with sex.

Sexual motivation depends partly on sex hormones. Castration reduces testosterone in male animals and results in less sexual activity. Castration of human adults has much less effect, showing that sexual motivation has been transferred to the brain. Social learning plays an important role in sexual motivation. Some individuals acquire such strong restraints and guilt feelings that they are unable to engage in it. Guilt and restraints may be acquired from parental discipline of early manifestations of sexuality, such as playing with the genitals; sexual behaviour in later life then comes to be associated with anxiety. Homosexuality (among boys) is partly a product of an environment with few girls. In the days when homosexuality was 'treated' by psychologists, it was found necessary to include training in heterosexual skills.

There are individual differences between the very inhibited, who fear and avoid sex, and those who seek it without any feeling of guilt, though the restraints are greatly weakened by alcohol. There are great variations between individuals and between cultures in attitudes towards sex – in whether, for example, premarital intercourse, extramarital intercourse, homosexuality, etc., are considered desirable or not. Surveys by Kinsey and others have shown how there are quite high rates of premarital and extramarital intercourse; these have increased greatly since World War II, during the so-called 'sexual revolution', though permissiveness has been reduced recently by fear of AIDS (Baron and Byrne, 1991). Working-class people have much higher rates for pre- and extramarital sex, and there are several possible explanations for this (Argyle, 1994). There are many mistaken beliefs about sex, which no doubt also affect behaviour, for example that masturbation makes you go blind, that blacks have bigger penises than whites, etc. (Mosher, 1979).

Among monkeys and other animals sexual behaviour tends to

be unrestrained; in civilized society it is possible only under very restricted conditions. Sex may have instinctive roots, but it is heavily influenced by cultural rules and is to a large extent 'scripted'. In every culture the accepted order of events of increasing intimacy is generally followed; there are for example rules about whether there is bodily contact while dancing (Gagnon and Simon, 1973). Even the most primitive tribes have rules controlling intercourse and marriage – the structure of society depends on it.

Sexual motivation is continually being aroused, though there are difficulties in the easy satisfaction of this need. This is partly due to external restraints: the potential partner is unwilling or others would disapprove. It is also due to internal restraints in the personality. Sexual motivation thus affects social behaviour in many situations. This is another example of an approach–avoidance conflict, in which the equilibrium consists of various forms of sexual behaviour short of intercourse, and often without physical contact at all, such as conversation and eye contact. A great deal of humour is based on sex; Freud was probably right in thinking that this provides an alternative outlet.

6 *Aggression* This is behaviour which is intended to harm, physically or verbally, people (or animals) who want to avoid such treatment. It includes not only *angry* aggression but also *instrumental* aggression – to gain another goal, such as escape or approval.

Aggression in animals is biologically useful – in defending territory and group, and in giving individuals priority over food and (for males) access to females. Aggression in animals occurs when they are frustrated, i.e. when goal-directed activity is blocked and expected rewards are not obtained.

During the course of evolution actual aggression, like biting, is partly replaced by threat signals, such as showing the teeth, especially during conflicts within the group. Humans use verbal aggression more often than physical aggression. We are more aggressive if the frustration is fairly severe, if it is perceived as arbitrary or illegitimate, and if there is no great danger of punishment or disapproval for aggressive behaviour. Animals fight when attacked (unless they run away); for humans, insults provoke more aggression than frustration. Insults and attacks are more likely to evoke an aggressive response in the presence of an audience – in order to preserve one's reputation, a form of self-presentation. Aggression is heightened by pain, heat, high levels of sexual excitement or other sources of physiological arousal. It is increased by large, but not by small, quantities of alcohol. When a person is in a bad mood he is more likely to respond aggressively to small annoyances.

Aggression is quite common in American families. Sixteen per cent of spouses hit each other at least once a year; 34 per cent of parents hit children aged fifteen to seventeen; 64 per cent of siblings hit each other, and 10 per cent hit a parent (Straus and Gelles, 1990). Boys and young men fight most, and aggression is a normal part of life in some parts of the world, like Northern Ireland. Aggression appears to be an innate response to frustration and attack in animals and men, but is not a drive since it does not occur in the absence of these stimuli and is not a need which must be satisfied. However, there are individuals who initiate aggression, for example school bullies, and aggressive male offenders in later life.

There is more than one kind of aggressive personality. Anti-social personalities, or 'psychopaths' (discussed further on pp. 242-3), are often aggressive in an instrumental way – to dominate and control others, to show how tough they are. Another kind of aggressive person is easily provoked to rage, sensitive to slights, lacking in control and reacts very emotionally; murderers are often like this (Berkowitz, 1993).

Aggressiveness is partly innate, as shown by twin studies with violent offenders. Aggressive offenders have high levels of testosterone and other substances, which may be causes of their aggression. Childhood experience is a further source, especially rejection and physical punishment by parents, together with permissiveness or approval for aggression (Olweus et al., 1986). Aggressive boys watch more violent films and TV, but which causes which? Longitudinal studies have shown that watching aggressive TV is a causal predictor of later aggressiveness (Geen, 1990). There are also more immediate effects, as with 'copy-cat' crimes and suicides, and increased violence after televised prize fights.

Men display more aggression than women, especially physical aggression. Women are more restrained here and only become aggressive when they lose emotional control. Men may use aggression more deliberately, in an instrumental way, and it is a normal part of the play of young males (Campbell, 1993).

Aggression is prevented in animals if one or other antagonist gives appeasement signals – looks away, adopts a submissive posture, etc. It has been found in experiments that human subjects will give lower electric shocks to a victim if they can see his signs of pain, because they experience the same suffering themselves, by empathy. Empathetic concern for others acts as a restraint on aggression, especially for males (Miller and Eisenberg, 1988). Aggression often results in punishment, so that for most people there is a strong avoidance component in the first place, partly internalized as part of the conscience, partly due to fear of retaliation or punishment. In the days of capital punishment there was a fall in the murder rate for about three weeks after an execution.

The conflict analysis predicts that an indirect form of aggression will occur, which may consist of verbal rather than physical attacks, displacement of aggression on to weaker people, or mere aggression in fantasy, such as watching western films or wrestling matches. Like sex, aggression is constantly aroused and restrained in social situations, and may be manifested very indirectly. The urge to aggress is also reduced by humour (for example funny cartoons) as long as it is not hostile, by apologies, and by a calm but friendly and assertive attitude (Berkowitz, 1993).

7 *Self-esteem and social anxiety* Many psychologists have postulated a need for self-esteem, i.e. a need to evaluate the self favourably. There are a number of situations in which concern with the self and the reactions of others becomes heightened. Appearing in front of audiences or TV cameras makes some individuals very anxious; social errors can produce acute embarrassment; and the sheer presence of others is arousing and motivating. All of this can be interpreted as a fear of disapproval, of

negative evaluation by others (Geen, 1991). There is a positive side to this too: some people like appearing in public or in front of TV cameras, as they are confident of positive reactions. The link with the self is that self-image and self-esteem depend a lot on the reactions of others, especially for those whose self-image is not firmly established, such as young people. We want to think well of ourselves, so we need others to think well of us.

A second type of motivation in this area which must be postulated is the need for a clear, distinct and consistent self-image. Part of this is a desire to regard oneself as a unique person, distinct from others. It will be shown later that adolescents often behave in deviant ways, or rebel against their families, simply in order to be able to see themselves as separate individuals. They may become punks, or join other socially unpopular groups, because of the distinctive identity gained thereby (see Chapter 8).

The origin of the need for self-esteem may be in the favourable evaluations made by most parents about their children. Children accept or partly accept these valuations, and seek to make later experiences and evaluations consistent with them (Secord and Backman, 1974). If the parents give negative evaluations, in later life the child may accept this view of himself and show no sign of a need for self-esteem.

There seem to be cultural differences in the extent to which self-esteem is important. In the East 'loss of face' is a much more serious matter than in the West.

8 *Altruism and concern for others* Discussion of motivation can sound as if humans and animals are trying to satisfy their own, 'selfish' needs; but we shall see that affiliative motivation seems to include concern for the welfare of other people, in romantic love and close friendships. Animals engage in a great deal of help – for their young, giving warning calls, helping at the nest, and in other ways. They particularly help their close kin – and so do we. Sociobiologists think this is because we want our genes to survive and so look after our immediate relations, who share a proportion of those genes – 50 per cent for children, brothers

and sisters, 25 per cent for grandchildren, etc. A tendency towards generalized reciprocal altruism will also lead to survival, since those who exhibit this will benefit when they in turn are in need (Dawkins, 1976a). Humans help their relatives; they also do voluntary work, give money to charities, help in accidents and other emergencies – though they do more for family, friends and members of their own group.

Part of the motivation for help is via empathy – i.e. sharing another's feelings, for example of distress, or understanding how they see things. Batson (1991) carried out experiments in which subjects could offer to take the place of another supposed subject, 'Elaine', who had received the first two of a number of electric shocks. More subjects offered to do so if they were told that Elaine came from the same town or college as themselves. This and other experiments show that empathetic concern is different from personal distress; the latter could be relieved simply by leaving the situation.

When empathy has been aroused there are other decisions to be made before help occurs. In one experiment it was arranged for a stooge to collapse on the New York underground. Strangers came forward to help more rapidly if (a) the stooge was white rather than black, (b) he was not drunk, and (c) there were not many other people present who might help (Piliavin et al., 1969). Other studies show that helping behaviour is more likely to occur if another person has just been seen giving help in a similar situation.

The pattern of help – who is helped and how much – varies between cultures and evidently depends on cultural norms. As well as biological evolution there is also 'social evolution', and the contents of moral norms are always developing. There is increasing concern in our society with care for animals, the environment and the Third World, for example. Moral rules include prescriptions about help and concern for others, restraining aggression, and selfish behaviour. They are partly due to moral leaders, like Moses and his Ten Commandments, and partly to a kind of group problem-solving. Once such norms are established they are taught to children and enforced by moral pressure, and sometimes by law. They include the rules of reciprocity (repay gifts and favours), responsibility (look after those who depend on you) and equity, or fairness.

Helping others is rewarding to the helper: it enhances positive moods and relieves depression, as Cialdini, Kenrick and Bauman (1982) have shown. So perhaps altruism is like a kind of drive after all. Curiously, people in a good mood also help a lot, though it is not known why. Children, at an early age, often respond helpfully to another's distress, and by the age of three engage in a lot of co-operative play. They become more helpful if their parents provide a good example, exhort and explain the need for help, and reinforce any helping.

9 *Achievement motivation and related drives* Need for achievement (n.Ach) is the drive to seek success, by attaining a high level of performance, at work, sport or in other spheres. It can be measured by the TAT method, and this predicts success at tasks which are intrinsically challenging, and spontaneously generated achievement efforts; it can result in high incomes and promotion. It predicts success at a variety of professional jobs. Questionnaire measures have a rather weak correlation with the TAT measure and appear to measure motivation to gain social rewards, like IQ scores and exam results (Spangler, 1992). Achievement motivation is like a drive in that it can be aroused, either by task demands (TAT measure) or hope of social recognition (questionnaire measure). It is unlike a drive in that it doesn't seem to satiate: the high-jumper who jumps as high as he hoped to simply revises his target upwards, and the same principle applies to other fields. Cassidy and Lynn (1991), in a big study in Northern Ireland, found that a questionnaire measure was a good predictor of upward social mobility between the ages of sixteen and twenty-three.

Achievement motivation has a lot in common with other measures of intrinsic work motivation, like the Protestant Work Ethic. Middle-class people have this kind of motivation; they want to work for its own sake and to achieve something, not just for the economic rewards (Argyle, 1994). Achievement motivation is higher in first-born children, those who have been encouraged to be independent and children with achieving parents. Weiner (1974) has produced evidence that high achievers differ in attributing failure to lack of effort rather than lack of ability – so that they try harder next time.

Achievement motivation in women is different in certain ways. 'Fear of success' is found in women likely to deviate from approved forms of female accomplishment; but men doing well at nursing, for instance, can have a similar problem. Women often need social approval, and this may prevent them taking a stand and risking unpopularity, which is necessary for some kinds of achievement.

There are also a number of acquired needs which affect social behaviour: for money, and needs related to interests, values, work or career.

In particular social situations, certain drives are likely to be aroused and satisfied. The immediate goals and plans which are formed are a complex product of a person's needs and the nature of the situation. Thus a dinner party may become the occasion primarily for sexual activity, affiliation, self-esteem, social contacts related to work or other interests, and so on.

Some of the social situations with which we shall be concerned later can be regarded as exercises of professional social skill – for example interviewing, teaching or selling. Here the performer of the skill is trying to affect the behaviour of others, not primarily because of his social needs but for professional reasons. He wants the others to learn or buy, just as a person strong in affiliation wants others to respond in a warm and friendly manner. Of course the social-skill performer has other motivations – for achievement, money, etc. – which make him keen to do well at his job, but the *immediate* goals for him are those of getting the client to respond in the specific ways required by the situation. The social-skill performer will also in most cases be affected by social drives, and the client may be primarily affected by these.

## FURTHER READING

Argyle, M., *Cooperation: The Basis of Sociability*, Routledge, London, 1991.

Baron, R. A., and Byrne, D., *Social Psychology: Understanding Human Interaction*, 6th edn, Allyn and Bacon, Boston, 1991.

McClelland, D. C., *Human Motivation*, Cambridge University Press, 1987.

Weiner, B., *Human Motivation*, 2nd edn, Holt, Rinehart and Winston, New York, 1989.

## CHAPTER 2

# FACE, GAZE AND OTHER
# NON-VERBAL COMMUNICATION

In Chapter I the goals which people seek in social interaction were discussed and it was argued that these goals are satisfied by certain behaviour on the part of others. In order to get these responses people make use of a variety of verbal and non-verbal elements of behaviour. In conversation, for example, there are alternating utterances, together with continuous facial expressions, gestures, shifts of gaze and other non-verbal acts on the part of both speaker and listener. We shall start with the non-verbal elements, which communicate attitudes and emotions as well as supplementing the verbal interchange in various ways.

The reader may feel that he is in the position of Molière's Monsieur Jourdain, who discovered that he had been speaking prose all those years. However, it is necessary to categorize and label the whole range of social acts, of different types and degrees of complexity, in order to move towards a scientific analysis of social behaviour.

NVC (as it is usually called) is the only means of communication amongst animals. Similar signals are used by man, and the evolutionary origins of some of them have been traced. Showing the teeth by animals in anger, for instance, is derived from the act of attacking, but it is now used when there is no intention of actually biting. This is an example of a non-verbal signal having meaning by being similar to or part of another act. Van Hooff (1972) has suggested the origins of human smiling and laughter: the lower primates have an expression known as the 'bared-teeth scream face', used in fear and submission, which has gradually evolved into our smile. Young primates also use a 'play-gnaw' accompanied by a kind of barking, which has become the human laugh.

All social signals are encoded and decoded by a sender and a receiver.

Often the sender is unaware of his or her own NVC, though it is plainly visible to the decoder. Sometimes neither is aware of it; an example is dilation of the pupils of the eyes in sexual attraction, which affects the receiver though he doesn't know why he likes the sender. Social skills training or reading this book will increase sensitivity to the NVC of others and control over the NVC signals which are emitted.

Research on how emotions, for example, are encoded can be done by showing subjects films which are happy, frightening, depressing, etc. Research on decoding can be done by showing specially prepared films or playing tapes, to see how subjects interpret them.

The examples above refer to the use of NVC to send emotions or attitudes to other people. NVC is also used to support and accompany conversation in quite intricate ways, and it plays an important role in greetings and other rituals, and is the main channel for self-presentation.

There are a number of different channels, and we will start with the face.

DIFFERENT NV CHANNELS

1 *Facial expression* The face is an important communication area, and can indicate emotional reactions, and attitudes to other people, as well as moment-to-moment commentaries on conversation. People smile and produce other expressions because they have facial muscles, such as the *zygomatic*, which pulls the corners of the mouth up in a smile, and the *corrigator*, which pulls the eyebrows together in a frown. The facial muscles are activated by the facial nerve. Sometimes people smile because they feel happy or like someone, but they can also smile when in

quite different moods, when it may be advantageous to do so. The facial nerve is activated by areas in the mid-brain producing genuine emotional expressions, and it is also activated by the motor cortex, which can produce socially correct or other bogus expressions; the upshot may reflect a battle between the two. The origins of these processes are entirely different: the mid-brain system has its roots in evolution; the influences from the motor cortex system derive from socialization in the culture, and cultural history. The evolution of facial expressions can be clearly seen in apes and monkeys, who communicate a great deal in this way. Izard (1975) cut the facial muscles of some infant monkeys and their mothers and found that the pairs failed to develop any relationship with each other.

One of the main functions of facial expression is to communicate emotional states, and attitudes such as liking and hostility. It must be admitted that the origins of smiling are rather obscure, but they may lie in the primate 'play face', or the 'bared teeth scream face' used in submission. Ekman and others (1972) have found that there are six main facial expressions, corresponding to the following emotions:

happiness;
surprise;
fear;
sadness;
anger;
disgust or contempt.

These six emotions have an innate, physiological basis: they are found in all cultures, correspond to distinctive patterns of physiological arousal and are found in young children, while similar expressions are found in non-human primates.

The six emotions can be discriminated quite well, though similar ones can be confused, such as anger and fear, or surprise and happiness. In addition, unlike monkeys, we often conceal our true feelings; it is not always easy to decode a smiling face, for example. These facial expressions seem to be much the same in all cultures, though Ekman has shown that there are 'display rules' which specify when an emotion may be shown – whether to cry at funerals or to show pleasure when you have won.

Ekman and Friesen (1969) showed an unpleasant film, of a sinus operation. Both American and Japanese subjects displayed negative facial expressions, including ones of disgust, while watching the film, but at a subsequent interview the Japanese had happy faces while the Americans did not. Shimoda, Argyle and Ricci Bicci (1978) found that Japanese could decode British and Italian facial expressions *better* than Japanese ones (Table 2.1), probably because Japanese are not supposed to display negative emotions like anger and sadness. They were probably helped by having seen Western films. The explanation for Japanese restraint of negative facial expressions is that the samurai taught that the superior person showed no facial expression (their equivalent of the stiff upper lip) and this was later modified to inhibiting negative expressions.

| | Performers | | |
| Judges | English | Italian | Japanese |
| --- | --- | --- | --- |
| English | 63 | 58 | 38 |
| Italian | 53 | 62 | 28 |
| Japanese | 57 | 58 | 45 |

Table 2.1    Cross-cultural recognition of emotions (percentages correct Shimoda, Argyle and Ricci Bicci, 1978).

A number of facial expressions do not really arise from emotions but indicate cognitive reactions. The face gives a fast-moving display of reactions to what others have said or done and a running commentary on what the owner of the face is saying. The eyebrows are very expressive in this way:

fully raised    – disbelief;
half raised     – surprise;
normal          – no comment;
half lowered    – puzzled;
fully lowered   – angry.

The area around the mouth adds to the running commentary by varying between being turned up (pleasure) and turned down (displeasure). These facial signals lead to reactions from others;

for example, looking puzzled may lead to clarification, and a smile acts as a reinforcement, encouraging the kind of act which led to it.

We are fairly aware of our facial expressions and can control them. However, there may be 'leakage' of the true emotion to less well controlled parts of the body. A nervous person may control his face but perspire, clench his hands tensely together or have a shaky voice.

Facial expressions are perhaps social signals rather than direct expressions of emotion. Kraut and Johnston (1979) found that people at a bowling-alley did not smile or frown at the skittles when they hit or missed them, but smiled or frowned when they turned to face their friends (see Table 2.2).

|              | Hit | Missed |
|--------------|-----|--------|
| at people    | 42  | 28     |
| at skittles  | 4   | 3      |

Table 2.2   Smiling at the bowling-alley (%) (Kraut and Johnson, 1979).

Furthermore, adopting a facial expression may affect the emotion experienced (see p. 98). On the other hand, people also make facial expressions which reflect their emotions while watching films alone. Fridlund (1991), however, has argued that solitary emotions are addressed to an imaginary audience; he found that facial expressions were stronger in subjects who believed that someone in the next room was watching the same TV film.

The final verdict is that facial expressions are partly deliberate social signals, but that they also reflect true emotional states.

2 *Gaze* Gaze is of central importance in human social behaviour. It acts as a non-verbal signal, showing, for example, the direction of the gazer's attention; at the same time it opens a channel, so that another person's non-verbal signals, and particularly their facial expression, can be received. Gaze, then, is both a signal for the person looked at and a channel for the person doing the

looking. It is linked with the social skill model, since this channel is the main one for receiving feedback. Consequently the *timing* of gaze, in relation to speech, for example, is important.

During conversation and other kinds of interaction individuals look at each other, mainly in the region of the eyes, intermittently and for short periods; this will be referred to as 'gaze' or 'looking at the other'. For some of the time two people are doing this simultaneously; this will be called 'mutual gaze' or 'eye contact' (EC).

Direction of gaze is recorded by observers, watching directly or working from videotapes, who press buttons when one interactor is judged to be gazing at another (Figure 2.1).

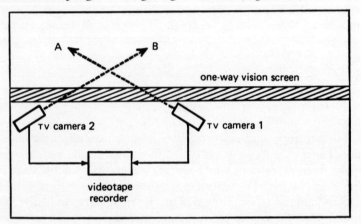

Figure 2.1.   Laboratory arrangements for studying gaze.

Several different aspects of gaze can be recorded, and typical figures from one of our experiments are given below.

| | |
|---|---|
| Total individual gaze | 61% |
| Looking while listening | 75% |
| Looking while talking | 41% |
| Average length of glances | 2.95 secs |
| Mutual gaze | 31% |
| Average length of mutual glances | 1.18 secs |

(From Argyle and Ingham, 1972.)

When two people are talking, they look at each other between 25 per cent and 75 per cent of the time (61 per cent in the experiment above), though we have seen the full range from 0 to 100 per cent; I shall discuss these individual differences later. They look nearly twice as much while listening as while talking, except interactors of high power or status, who are found to look as much while talking as when listening (p. 31). Individual glances can be anything up to 7 seconds or so (average 2.95 seconds in the above experiment), and mutual glances are rather shorter.

Interactors can tell with some accuracy when they are being looked at, as can observers of the interaction. On the other hand Von Cranach and Ellgring (1973) have found that interactors cannot tell with much accuracy which part of their face is being looked at. What is being recorded as gaze is really gaze directed to the face; studies with eye-movement recorders show that people scan each other's faces with repeated cycles of fixation, each fixation being about a third of a second long, though they fixate on the eyes more than anywhere else.

In addition to the amount and timing of gaze, the eyes are expressive in other ways:

pupil dilation (from 2–8 mm in diameter);
blink rate (typically every 3–10 sec);
direction of breaking gaze, to the left or right;
opening of eyes, wide-open to lowered lids;
facial expression in area of eyes, described as 'looking daggers', 'making eyes', etc.

Gaze is used as a social signal very early in life: mutual gaze with the mother first occurs at the age of three or four weeks. Visual interaction between mother and infant plays an important part in forming the bond between them: by six months infants are upset when EC is broken, by eight months it plays an important part in games with the mother.

Gaze is an important signal for liking and disliking; we look more at people we like. Exline and Winters (1965) arranged for subjects to talk to two confederates and then to state their preference for one or the other; in subsequent interaction they looked much more at the one they preferred. Rubin (1973) found that couples who were in love (as measured by his questionnaire) spent a higher proportion of time in mutual gaze. Of course liking or loving are communicated by a combination of cues; as well as looking there is smiling, a friendly tone of voice and the contents of speech.

Although gaze and EC are pleasant, especially with those we like, EC is unpleasant and embarrassing if there is too much of it and if mutual glances are too long. This may be because unpleasantly high levels of physiological arousal are generated, or it may be because of the fact that there are also avoidance components connected with EC. One of these is that mutual gaze is distracting and adds to the cognitive load. If subjects are asked to look continuously there are more speech disturbances of various kinds (Beattie, 1981). It is more comfortable watching others from behind a one-way vision screen than watching others who can look back.

If there are forces both to engage in EC and to avoid it, there will be a state of conflict of the kind described earlier (p. 7). It follows that there is an equilibrium level of looking for each person and of EC for any two people, and that when the approach forces are relatively strong there will be more EC. We will now consider some implications of this equilibrium when the positive forces for EC are mainly affiliative or sexual, as opposed to dominant or aggressive.

We suggest that intimacy is a function of the following:

physical proximity;
eye contact;
facial expression (smiling);
topic of conversation (how personal);
tone of voice (warm);
etc.

If we suppose that there is an overall equilibrium for intimacy, it follows that when one of these component elements is disturbed there will be some complementary change among the others to restore the equilibrium. Several examples of this have been observed.

Argyle and Dean (1965) tested the hypothesis that greater proximity would result in less EC. Subjects took part in three three-minute discussions with stooges trained to stare, at distances of two, six and ten feet. The amount of EC was recorded by observers in the usual way (Figure 2.2). In later experiments it was found that the same results were obtained with pairs of genuine subjects. The effect is greatest for male–female pairs; the change is mainly in looking while listening, and changes of EC are due to amount of individual gaze, not changes in coordination.

The gaze-distance effect has been widely confirmed, as have a number of other derivations from the affiliative balance theory (Patterson, 1973). There is less gaze at the points where a person is smiling and when intimate topics are discussed.

What is the meaning of gaze to the person looked at? If A becomes aware that B is looking at him, the main message received is that he or she is the object of B's attention, that B is interested in him and willing to be involved. If they are not already interacting, gaze indicates that something is about to start. The nature of the action which is likely to occur varies with the situation, for example boy–girl, chairman–committee member, diner–waiter. In addition, when B looks, A feels observed, that he is the object of another's attention. There are those who find this a disturbing experience, and some mental patients feel that they are being transformed into objects, observed as if they were insects, and, for some psychotics, turned into stone. We shall discuss this experience further in Chapter 9.

When there is mutual gaze, this is experienced as a special kind of intimacy and union, in which each is attending to and receptive to the other. Mutual gaze produces an increased level of physiological arousal, such as higher heart rate.

If A loves B, his or her pupils will dilate, and B will decode the signal correctly, though without awareness. In Italy girls used to enlarge their pupils with drops of belladonna. The eyes are used a lot in courtship, and girls both make up their eyes and enlarge their eye display by dark glasses.

If two people of different power or status meet, the low-power person looks at the other much more as he listens than as

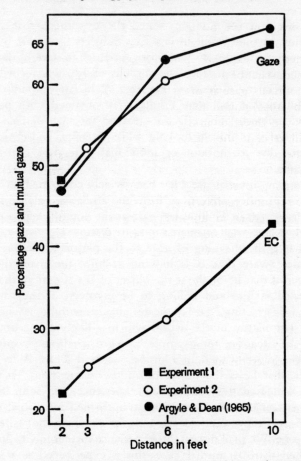

Figure 2.2   The effects of distance on gaze and mutual gaze (from Argyle and Ingham, 1972).

he talks, while there is no such difference for the high–power individual, who looks as much whether talking or listening. There is no difference in gaze for low-power and medium-power individuals, suggesting that for humans there is no submission display. Those with high and low needs to control others behave in a corresponding way (Ellyson, Dovidío and Fehr, 1981). This may reflect the 'attention structure', whereby monkeys keep an eye on their leaders. Dislike may result in the 'cutting' of one person by another, or use of the 'hate stare', directed, for example, by some blacks towards whites in the southern states of the USA.

In animals gaze is often used as a threat signal. Exline and Yellin (1969) found that a monkey (in a strong cage) would attack or threaten an experimenter who stared at him, but would relax if the experimenter averted gaze – which is an appeasement signal. A number of experiments show that gaze can act as a threat signal for humans too. Ellsworth (1975) found that staring confederates on motorcycles caused motorists to move off more rapidly from stop lights; other studies found that people stared at in libraries either left or built barricades of books. Marsh, in studies of football hooligans, found that a single glance at a member of the opposing group can be an occasion for violence, with cries of 'He looked at me!' (Marsh, Harré and Rosser, 1978). Kurtz (1975) found that if the occupant of a work table greeted newcomers with a long gaze, this was interpreted as a hostile stare and prevented the newcomer using the table; i.e. it was successful in defending the territory. In contrast Ellsworth found that a mere glance from a person in need increased the likelihood of help being given.

3 *Voice* The voice communicates a lot in addition to words. Animals and small children communicate their emotions by cries, shrieks, grunts and barks, but we do it by the way words are spoken. Scherer (1981) and others have studied the voices produced by people in different emotional states. A depressed person for example speaks slowly, at a low and falling pitch. Someone who is anxious speaks fast but unevenly, in a raised pitch and a breathy voice, and makes a lot of speech errors. Voices also vary in 'speech spectrum'; for example angry voices are discordant, happy voices have purer tones, and there are other variations which can be described as 'nasal', 'robust', 'tense', etc. These paralinguistic aspects of speech convey information about emotions, attitudes, personality and social origins.

The voice is 'leakier' than the face; that is, true emotions which are being concealed tend to show through, probably because we look in mirrors more than we listen to tape recordings of our voices. There is an interesting gender difference here: women are more 'polite' decoders, i.e. they attend relatively more to faces than men do, and therefore receive the messages they are intended to receive. The explanation is probably that in the female subculture women trust each other more than men; in the male subculture men are more competitive, deceptive and suspicious (Rosenthal and DePaulo, 1979).

Voices give impressions of personality which are partly correct. Extraverts for example speak louder, faster, at a higher pitch, with fewer pauses. This general style is seen as assertive and competent, and is found to be persuasive. Type A personalities, who are aggressively ambitious and prone to heart attacks, are partly identified by their loud, fast and explosive speech style.

People speak in different accents, which are related to and convey information about their geographical origins and social class. British accents are perceived along a single dimension of general prestige, with 'received pronunciation' at the top, Birmingham and Cockney accents at the bottom (Giles and Powesland, 1975). Experiments by Lambert in Canada and Giles in Britain show that if the same person records a passage in different accents he is rated by different judges as possessing the stereotyped properties of the cultural or social groups in question. If subjects are asked to read lists of words, they speak more carefully and use an accent corresponding to a higher social class – as found by Labov in New York; in Britain they are less likely to drop 'h's, for example (see p. 74).

When people from different classes meet, if they like each other or want to get on, they 'accommodate', i.e. move towards each other's speech style. Thakerar, Giles and Cheshire (1982) found this in conversations between senior and junior nurses (p.69).

4 *Gestures* While a person speaks he moves his hands, body and head continuously; these movements are closely coordinated with speech and form part of the total communication. He may:

1 display the structure of the utterance by enumerating elements or showing how they are grouped;
2 point to people or objects;
3 provide emphasis;
4 give illustrations of shapes, sizes or movements, particularly when these are difficult to describe in words.

These 'illustrators' are iconic, i.e. resemble their referents, and can convey useful information. Graham and Argyle (1975) found that shapes could be conveyed much better, in one minute of speech, if hand movements were allowed. The effect was greater for those shapes for which there were no obvious words, and more information was conveyed in gestures by Italian subjects than by British ones. There is also evidence that gestures are part of the act of speaking and serve to help the speaker (p. 50).

A quite different kind of gesture is used independently of speech, and these have arbitrary, conventional meanings, like our hitchhike sign, nodding and shaking the head, clapping, beckoning, various rude signs, religious signs and so on. These do not resemble their objects as closely as illustrative gestures do, and they have complex histories in the local culture, for example Churchill's 'V for victory' sign Italy is particularly rich in them, and here Desmond Morris and colleagues (1979) have studied a number, such as the hand purse, the cheek screw and the chin flick, which are only meaningful in certain Mediterranean countries. The signs for 'yes' and 'no' are interesting. In southern Italy (i.e. that part of the country south of a line running east–west to a point somewhere between Rome and Naples) people toss their heads back to indicate 'no', as in Greece, instead of shaking them. Some gestures are extremely rude and can result in the gesturer being attacked, and even killed, in parts of the eastern Mediterranean. However, our own culture has quite a large emblem vocabulary too: Johnson, Ekman and Friesen (1975) found seventy-six which were widely used and understood in the USA.

Head nods are a rather special kind of gesture and have two distinctive roles. They act as 'reinforcers', i.e. they reward and encourage what has gone before, and can be used to make another person talk more, for example. Head nods can also play an important role in controlling the synchronizing of speech: in Britain a nod gives the other permission to carry on talking, whereas a rapid succession of nods indicates that the nodder wants to speak himself.

Gestures also reflect emotional states. When a person is emotionally aroused he produces diffuse, apparently pointless, bodily movements. People often touch themselves during certain emotions: fist-clenching (aggression), face-touching (anxiety), scratching (self-blame), forehead-wiping (tiredness), etc. These 'autistic' gestures are not normally used to communicate, since they are also used in private, and appear to express attitudes to the self, such as shame and self-comforting.

When speech is impossible, gesture languages develop. This happens in noisy factories, the army, racecourses and underwater swimming. Some of these languages are complex and enable elaborate messages to be sent, as in deaf languages and the sign language used by some Australian aborigines. Some examples are given in Figure 2.3.

5 *Posture* Attitudes to others are indicated, in animals and humans, by posture. A person who is trying to assert himself stands erect, with chest out, squaring his shoulders, and perhaps with hands on hips. A person in an established position of power or status, however, adopts a very relaxed posture, for example leaning back in his seat or putting his feet on the table. Positive attitudes to others are expressed by leaning towards them (together with smiling, looking, etc). If two people are getting on well with each other they often adopt similar, mirror-image postures.

Posture does not show emotions very clearly, though Bull (1987) found that boredom and interest were clearly shown. Perhaps the main dimension of meaning is tense to relaxed. Depressives have a particularly drooping posture.

One way of studying posture is with stick figures. Sarbin and Hardyk (1953) found by this method a number of postures which had clear meanings (Figure 2.4).

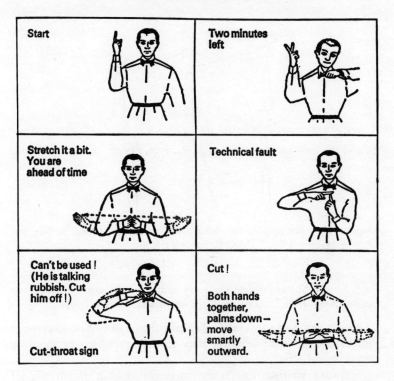

Figure 2.3   Non-verbal signals used in broadcasting (from Brun, 1969).

People also have general styles of expressive behaviour, as shown in the way they walk, stand, sit and so on. This may reflect past or present roles – as in the case of a person who is or has been a soldier; it also reflects a person's self-image, self-confidence and emotional state. It is very dependent on cultural fashions:

In a street market I watched a working-class mum and her daughter. The mother waddled as if her feet were playing her up. Outside a Knightsbridge hotel I watched an upper-class mum and her daughter come out from a wedding reception and walk towards Hyde Park Corner, the mother on very thin legs slightly bowed as though she had

Figure 2.4   Some postures with clear meanings (from Sarbin and Hardyk, 1953).

wet herself. She controlled her body as if it might snap if moved too impulsively. Both daughters walked identically. [Melly, 1965]

This last example shows the effect of cultural norms on expressive behaviour; style of walking may give information in this case about social class.

Popular writing on 'body language' makes much use of psychoanalysts' observations on the sexual significance of their patients concealing or protecting their breasts, crossing and un-crossing their legs, and so on. This makes entertaining reading, but unfortunately it has little scientific basis. A more likely possibility is that posture is used as part of more intentional self-presentation – a monk's humble manner, a soldier's upright posture, an intellectual's eccentricity, for example.

6 *Touch, bodily contact* This is a very powerful social signal, because of its links with both sex and aggression. Touch plays a central role in sexual behaviour, and during the growth of sexual relationships much use is made of touching hand and waist, and kissing (Guerrero and Anderson, 1991).

There are many ways of touching people, but only a few are used in any one culture – in ours, for example, shaking hands,

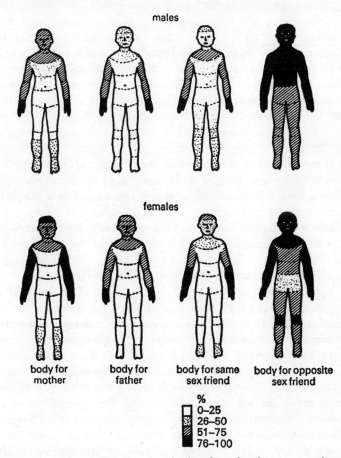

males

females

body for
mother

body for
father

body for same
sex friend

body for opposite
sex friend

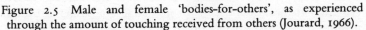

%
0–25
26–50
51–75
76–100

Figure 2.5 Male and female 'bodies-for-others', as experienced through the amount of touching received from others (Jourard, 1966).

patting on the back, kissing, etc. Jourard (1966) made a survey of who has been touched by whom and where, and his results for American students are shown in Figure 2.5. It can be seen that there are great differences in who is touched by whom, and on which parts of their anatomy.

Children are touched a lot, while friends touch each other in a restrained way. Touch is used in most greetings – hand-shaking, kissing and embracing – though in India and Japan non-touching greetings are used. It plays an important part in many ceremonies – weddings, graduations, etc. – and probably helps to bring about the changes that such rituals produce. The general meaning of touch is a combination of warmth and assertiveness, so there is a certain ambiguity about it. While women generally like being touched by men, they dislike it if they think that dominance rather than warmth is being communicated (Henley, 1977).

Touch often has quite a strong positive effect. For example, if people are asked to sign a petition, give an interview, give change for a telephone call or return money left in a telephone box, touching increases the percentage who will comply (e.g. Willis and Hamm, 1980). If librarians touch borrowers when handing over their books, the borrowers like the librarians and the library more (Fisher, Rytting and Heslin, 1975). In general, touch leads to liking and often to social influence.

Touch is governed by strict rules about who may be touched, on which parts of their body, in what way and on which occasions. Bodily contact is encouraged between people in certain relationships, discouraged in others. Argyle and Henderson (1985) found a number of rules for different relationships. Touching was prescribed for certain close relationships – spouses, dating couples, close family and in-laws – but was not permitted (in general) for less close relationships, for example at work, between neighbours or in professional relationships. Common observation suggests that there are a number of situations in which bodily contact is more acceptable: sport, dancing, games, crowds, medical and other professional attention, encounter groups, greeting and partings. In all of these situations different rules apply; a specialized kind of touch is used, with no implication of great intimacy. Shaking hands in greeting does not have the same significance as holding hands by courting couples; nor does embracing of football players who have scored goals.

Anthropologists distinguish between contact cultures (such as North Africa) and non-contact cultures (such as Europe, India, North America). In Britain we use touch very little, but there has been some interest in 'encounter groups' in the USA and

Britain. The greater use of bodily contact in these sessions is found to be exciting and disturbing – but it must be remembered that those concerned have been brought up in cultures in which there are strong restraints against bodily contact, and they will have internalized these restraints.

7 *Spatial behaviour* Encounters are usually started by people moving sufficiently close and into the right orientation to see and hear one another (and are ended by moving away again). Closer distances are adopted for more intimate conversations; at the closest distances, different sensory modes are used – touch and smell come into operation, and vision becomes less important (Hall, 1966). We move closer to people whom we like, and proximity is an important cue for liking. Argyle and Dean (1965) proposed that proximity is the outcome of a balance between approach and avoidance forces, so people will seek just the right degree of proximity with a particular individual, and may lean forwards or back to attain it.

Orientation also signals interpersonal attitudes. If person A is sitting at a table, as shown in Figure 2.6, B can sit in several different places. If he is told that the situation is co-operative he will probably sit at $B_1$; if he is told he is to compete, negotiate, sell something or interview A, he will sit at $B_2$; if he is told to have a discussion or conversation he usually chooses $B_3$ (Sommer, 1965). This suggests (a) that one can become more sensitive to the cues emitted, often unintentionally, by others; and (b) that one can control non-verbal as well as verbal signals.

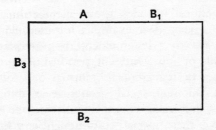

Figure 2.6   Orientation in different relationships.

Dominance, however, is signalled neither by proximity nor orientation, but by the symbolic use of space – at the front of a lecture room or on the rostrum, for example.

Manipulating the physical setting itself is another form of spatial behaviour – placing a desk to dominate the room or arranging seats for intimate conversation. Rooms and buildings have more complex spatial properties, as in the different areas of churches, lawcourts and many places of work, where each area conveys status, a particular role and a relation to those in other areas. The closeness between two people, or their relative status, can be decided by the architects or furniture.

Individuals have 'personal space', and feel uncomfortable when this area is invaded. Schizophrenics and violent offenders have very large personal spaces, especially behind them. On the other hand, people seem to forget about their personal space when in crowded tube trains or lifts, though they usually don't look at or speak to the other people there.

Another kind of space is 'personal territory', like a bedroom or a study, which a person feels belongs to him, which contains items he wants to use, and which he wants to control access to.

There are considerable cultural differences in spatial behaviour. In some cultures people like to sit or stand nearer and more directly facing than in other cultures, and this can cause obvious problems in inter-cultural contacts. A European or Asian may back away, turning, to establish the preferred angle and distance, but be pursued in a spiral by an Arab or Latin American.

8 *Appearance* Clothes are not just for keeping warm; they also send information about the wearer – his or her job, status, personality, political attitudes, group membership, even mood. Uniforms are a very clear example, for example in a hospital or lawcourt, but to a lesser extent in most places of work, indicating rank or job. Different personalities prefer different clothes – more or less colourful, formal or sexually inviting, for example. Different social groups wear different clothes; hippies, artists, politicians, country gentlemen and football hooligans all have their special costumes. We discuss later the theory that clothes are worn for 'self-presentation', but conclude

that sheer conformity to the norms of groups is also important (p. 215).

Different clothes are worn for different situations. Tse'elon (1989), working at Oxford, found that women dressed for about six different classes of situations: work, informal social, formal social, etc. The *same* clothes worn on different occasions can have quite different meanings and may be totally inappropriate. There are also specialized clothes for many kinds of leisure – tennis, skiing, Scottish dancing, etc., even walking.

Clothes, hair and other aspects of appearance differ from other non-verbal signals in that there are changes in fashion. The explanation is probably that élite fashions are copied by those of lower social status, so the higher-status groups have to adopt newer fashions to show that they are different. This doctrine was confirmed in an American survey by Hurlock (1929), in which 40 per cent of women and 20 per cent of men admitted that they would follow a fashion in order to appear equal to those of higher status, and about 50 per cent said they changed their styles when their social inferiors adopted them. This gives some support to the 'trickle-down' theory of fashion – in 1928. The fashion scene has now changed a lot. The clothing industry reproduces new styles at all levels simultaneously, so that fashion trickles mainly horizontally, and even upwards, such as when the styles of rebellious and radical youth are taken up.

Clothes can create very clear impressions, for example of social class, as Sissons (1971) found in an experiment at Paddington Station, in which an actor dressed up either as upper-middle or working class and asked unsuspecting subjects the way. We give examples later of the greater social influence of individuals in various roles when they are more respectably dressed.

Hair is another important aspect of appearance. In many times and places long hair has been worn by male outcasts, intellectuals, drop-outs and ascetics; having it cut represents re-entering society or living under a disciplined regime, as monks and soldiers do. On the other hand, some rebellious groups wear very short hair (skinheads, for example), and long hair for males has sometimes been socially acceptable. Perhaps hair has no constant meaning at all but is simply an important area for expressing opposition to prevailing norms.

Physical attractiveness (p.a.) has a number of important effects on others and will be discussed under 'person perception' in Chapter 5. However, p.a. is to a large extent under our own control, and so can be regarded as a kind on NVC. It has been said, 'If a girl wants to be a well-stacked, blue-eyed blonde, then she can be, tomorrow.' An easier way of enhancing p.a. is simply to smile, as a recent experiment showed (Reis et al., 1990). It is also possible to get rid of various 'stigmas', like bad teeth, and obesity.

Physical appearance is a most important cue in courtship, as will be shown later in this chapter (p. 49). It is also one of the domains for 'self-presentation' in general, as will be shown in Chapter 8.

### THE DIFFERENT FUNCTIONS OF NVC

1 *Expressing emotions* We have seen that the face has evolved as a special communication area, which can convey at least six emotions. These expressions are shown more clearly in the presence of other people and are to some extent deliberate communications, but they also reflect inner physiological states. The expressions shown are partly controlled by 'display rules'. Similar considerations apply to tones of voice; the barks and shrieks of animals have been replaced by pitch, loudness, etc., while speaking. A third area is bodily movement, including gestures and postures.

Research on decoding emotional expressions has compared the amount of information obtained through these three channels, by showing subjects face or body only, or playing recordings of the voices of target persons filmed while in different emotional states. Rosenthal and DePaulo (1979) obtained the following accuracy scores:

| | |
|---|---|
| Facial expression | 3.88 |
| Body | 2.82 |
| Tone of voice | 1.82 |

(ratios to standard deviations)

In this and similar studies, facial expression was found to communicate most information, body next and tone of voice least. If verbal contents are compared they convey even less information about emotions. The success rate for judging facial expressions is about 60 per cent, and for the other channels less; it is better for posed than for spontaneous expressions, and better for longer exposure of the stimuli. The voice, however, is a leakier channel, showing emotions that are being concealed, and men attend to it more than women (pp. 33–4). A number of studies have also found that subjects who see videotapes of body only can make more accurate judgements of negative emotions than those who see face only (Ekman and Friesen, 1969). Some emotions are conveyed better by particular channels: the face shows happiness best, followed by anger; the voice conveys sadness and fear best; the body shows tense and relaxed best.

There is a lot of evidence for 'emotional contagion', that is, that people often catch each other's emotions, by some primitive mechanism. They mimic the other's emotional expression, copying their facial, bodily or vocal behaviour, and as a result share their emotion, via facial feedback for example. There is evidence of a fairly high correlation between the facial expressions of two interactors, and this could result in them having the same emotional state via the process of facial feedback (Capella, 1992). This process is very fast, and may be conscious or unconscious. It is most likely to happen from infants to mothers, in couples in love, for women, and for psychotherapists from patients (Hatfield, Capiocco and Rapson, 1992).

To tell what emotion someone is in, we also make use of information other than NVC. We take account of the contents of speech and also of the nature of the situation. We use our experience to disentangle any contradictions here; for example we know that people don't usually pretend to be miserable when they aren't, though they often pretend to be happy.

We have seen that true emotions are often concealed, overlaid with some other expression. How far can deception be seen through? People correctly use certain cues to deception, such as hesitant speech and raised pitch (Zuckerman et al., 1981). False smiles are different from real ones: they have a more sudden onset, and eyes and cheeks are less involved. There may be other facial leakage, such as blushing and asymmetrical expressions, and of course leakage in voice and body.

2 *Indicating interpersonal attitudes* Animals conduct their entire social life by means of NVC; they communicate with other animals, find mates, rear their young, establish dominance hierarchies and co-operate in groups, by means of facial expression, postures, gestures, grunting and barking noises, etc. It looks as if much the same is true of humans.

One of the most important attitudes to others is friendly–hostile and this is sent quite clearly. The main signals for liking are higher levels of (1) smiling, (2) gaze, (3) proximity and (4) touch; (5) posture with arms open, not on hips or folded; and (6) voice with higher pitch, upward pitch contour, purer tone. Display rules somewhat confuse the situation, since we are socialized not to send hostile signals; the result is that people know who likes them but are less well informed about who dislikes them. And at pleasant social occasions, like parties, there is a generally agreed rule that lots of positive signals should be sent (Argyle, Graham, Campbell and White, 1979). Sending these positive social signals is an important social skill, and one lacking in the lonely and socially incompetent.

Again, NV signals are more effective than verbal ones. An experiment was carried out (Argyle, Salter, Nicholson, Williams and Burgess, 1970) in which superior, equal and inferior verbal messages were delivered in superior, equal and inferior non-verbal styles, nine combinations in all, by speakers recorded on videotapes. Two of the verbal messages were as follows:

1 It is probably quite a good thing for you subjects to come along to help in these experiments because it gives you a small glimpse of what psychological research is about. In fact the whole process is far more complex than you would be able to appreciate without a considerable training in research methods, paralinguistics, kinesic analysis, and so on.

2 These experiments must seem rather silly to you and I'm afraid they are not really concerned with anything very interesting or important. We'd be very glad if you could spare us a few moments afterwards to tell us how we could improve the experiment. We feel that we are

not making a very good job of it, and feel rather guilty about wasting the time of busy people like yourselves.

Some of the results were as shown in Figure 2.7. It can be seen that the non-verbal style had more effect than the verbal contents, in fact about five times as much; when the verbal and non-verbal messages were in conflict, the verbal contents were virtually disregarded. Much the same results were obtained in another experiment on the friendly–hostile dimension.

A number of further investigators, though not all, have obtained similar results. Within NV signals, visual cues are stronger than vocal. Bugenthal, Kaswan and Love (1970) found that children reacted negatively to criticisms made with a smile and to negative messages whether verbal or non-verbal, especially from women. It should be emphasized that NV messages are only dominant for conveying emotions or attitudes; the verbal component is much more important for most other kinds of information (Friedman, Prince, Riggio and DiMatteo, 1980).

The explanation of these results is probably that there is an innate biological basis to these NV signals, which evoke an

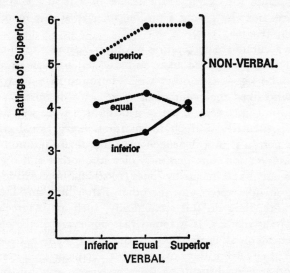

Figure 2.7   Effects of verbal and non-verbal cues (Argyle *et al.*, 1970).

immediate and powerful emotional response – as in animals. In human social behaviour it looks as if the NV channel is used for negotiating interpersonal attitudes, while the verbal channel is used primarily for conveying information.

A second important interpersonal attitude is dominant–submissive. Dominance is communicated by (1) a non-smiling, frowning face; (2) posture – full height, expanded chest, hands on hips; (3) gestures – pointing at the other or his property; (4) touching but not being touched back; (5) gaze – looking while talking; (6) voice – loud, low pitch, slow, interrupting, a lot of talk. These signals work extremely fast: Rosa and Mazur (1979) found that informal status in small groups could be predicted from length of initial glances during the first seconds of meeting. The foreman of a jury often elects himself by sitting in the right seat and in the right posture. NVC in an established hierarchy is a little different: the dominant person may sit rather than stand, and in a relaxed way. Dominance or assertiveness signals are an important social skill, essential for the effective performance of many professional and leadership rules, such as teaching or committee chairmanship; for example, the leader of a triad controls who will speak next by giving a prolonged gaze at one member of the group (Kalma, 1992).

How accurate are perceptions of others' attitudes to ourselves? Tagiuri (1958) surveyed likes and dislikes in sixty groups of people who knew each other well. He found that most people knew who liked them but made quite a lot of mistakes about who did not like them: 9 per cent of dislikes were seen as likes.

It is particularly difficult to interpret interpersonal attitudes when a person is in a dependent or subordinate position. In an act of ingratiation, one person is nice to another and then asks for a favour. Experiments by Jones (1964) and others have found that ingratiators agree with the other, flatter him, and look and smile more; they do this strategically, such as disagreeing on unimportant matters. It is found that observers of these events interpret them as ingratiating if the actor is in a dependent position. In real life the boss or other recipient of ingratiation may find it very difficult to tell whether his subordinates like and admire him or not.

Sexual attraction is a third important interpersonal attitude. It is like 'friendly' but with some extra NV signals. Buss (1988) studied the courtship strategies which were most used by young Americans. For both sexes, being well groomed and washed (especially hair), keeping fit, looking healthy, wearing attractive, stylish clothes, smiling often and giving encouraging glances were used a great deal and were believed to be effective. For women, wearing make-up, increasing bodily exposure, wearing sexy clothes and flirting were said to work, and they altered their appearance more than men. Men touched more, boasted about their financial resources and prospects, and displayed their strength and athleticism. In a later study of thirty-seven cultures, Buss (1989) found that women looked for a mate who was rich and ambitious, while men looked for girls who were young and attractive (and, in twenty-three cultures, chaste). Successful courtship requires the skilled use of these cues. However, their use is governed by situational rules, for example, some of them can be used more freely at parties than at work, in the dark more than in the light, and most follow a sequence of gradually increasing intimacy.

3 *Supporting verbal communication* While two (or more) people are talking they are emitting constant streams of NV signals, which are closely integrated with the words spoken. We will start with those of the person speaking.

*The speaker* uses pitch, stress and timing to modify the meaning of words. These NV signals are closely linked to speech and should perhaps be regarded as part of it. Timing is used to indicate punctuation, and short pauses (under $\frac{1}{5}$ sec.) to give emphasis. The pattern of pitch indicates whether a question is being asked and also 'frames' an utterance, to show, for instance, whether 'Where do you think you're going?' is a friendly inquiry or a prohibition. Variations in stress also indicate which it is, an emphasis on 'you're' in this case suggesting prohibition. Variations in loudness place stress on particular words or phrases – for example, on 'where' or 'you' in the question above. It can make clear which possible meaning an otherwise ambiguous sentence has, as in 'They are hunting *dogs*.' These 'prosodic' signals send a message about the message.

The speaker accompanies utterances with gestures that illustrate them, either delivered at the same time or started in the pause before a phrase starts. The related gestures do not cross phrase boundaries, and it is now believed that words and gestures are a joint production, from the same inner speech (McNeil, 1985). In addition to providing illustrations, gestures may point out objects, and can mark or enumerate different points being made.

It is found that glances are synchronized with speech in a special way. Kendon (1967) found that long glances were made, starting just before the end of an utterance, as shown in Figure 2.8, while the other person started to look away at this point. The main reason why people look at the end of their utterances is that they need feedback on the other's response. This may be of various kinds. A wants to know whether B is still attending; his direction of gaze shows if he is asleep or looking at someone else. A also wants to know how his last message was received – whether B understood, agreed, thought it was funny. At pauses in the middle of long speeches A will look for continued permission to carry on speaking, and B will nod or grunt if he is agreeable to this.

However, gaze is only a minor full-stop signal for synchronizing purposes; verbal and vocal cues are more important. The social skill model, which will be presented in Chapter 11, uses the similarities between social behaviour and motor skills, like driving a car; in both cases feedback is needed to take corrective action, and it is obtained by looking in the right place at the right time.

*The listener* also sends a lot of NV signals, providing 'back-channel' or feedback information to the speaker. In addition to such specific feedback there is also more general 'listening behaviour'. For an encounter to be sustained, those involved must provide intermittent evidence that they are still attending to the others. They should not fall asleep, look out of the window or read the paper; they should be at the right distance, in the right orientation, look up frequently, nod their heads, adopt an alert,

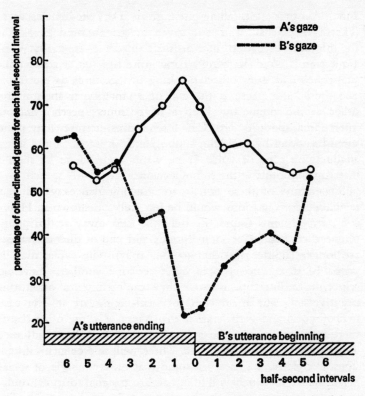

Figure 2.8  Direction of gaze at the beginning and end of long utterances (Kendon, 1967).

congruent posture, and react to the speaker's bodily movements.

Listeners use a lot of facial expression, especially for pleased–displeased and for reactions like puzzled and surprised. Head nods show agreement, while head shakes are rare. Vocalizations like 'uh-huh', 'really?', etc., provide feedback and are not intended to interrupt. Posture indicates interest or boredom.

When two (or more) people are conversing they usually manage the turn-taking with a high degree of synchrony, i.e. there are few interruptions or pauses. How is this achieved? The 'terminal gaze' used at the ends of utterances to collect feedback is one cue; if this is not given a delay in reply is likely (Kendon,

1967). Another cue is falling pitch, given at the ends of utterances (except questions); it is not given at grammatical breaks in the middle. The pattern of words is a third cue, especially when a question is asked. Keeping a hand in mid-gesture is a powerful suppressor and stops others breaking in. So, to keep the floor, one should not pause at the end of a sentence or look at the other at this point, but keep a hand in mid-gesture and, if interrupted, speak louder! If the listener doesn't want to speak he should respond by nodding, smiling and saying 'Uh-huh' in an encouraging tone of voice. If he wants to break in he should interrupt smoothly at the end of a clause.

Since some of these signals are visual it was expected that telephone conversations would be less well synchronized. However, experiments found precisely the opposite: over the telephone there are fewer interruptions and pauses, and utterances are longer (Rutter and Stephenson, 1977). The explanation is probably that, since people can't see one another, they are reluctant to interrupt because they can't smile to offset this negative act. The main cues for turn-taking are in any case mainly vocal and verbal rather than visual. On the other hand, there is more 'listening behaviour' over the telephone – 'I see', 'How amazing', 'Uh-huh', etc. These replace feedback expressions. People have to learn a somewhat different style of social performance in which visible signals are transferred to the auditory channel.

Conveying information and solving problems can be done just as well over the telephone, provided visual materials like maps or charts are not needed. However, vision does make an important difference in certain kinds of interaction. People get to like and trust each other more, and co-operate more readily, if they can see one another. If bargaining is done over the telephone, the person with the better case wins; when two people can see each other, they become concerned about being approved of by each other and sustaining the relationship, with the result that the person with the weaker case sometimes wins (Short, Williams and Christie, 1976).

It has been concluded by some investigators, from fine analysis of films of interactors, that bodily movements are finely co-ordinated at fractions of a second in a 'gestural dance' (Kendon, 1977). A careful statistical study by McDowall (1978), however, failed to find such synchronizing at one eighth of a second. Gestural dance is, however, found at the level of utterances and the main divisions of utterances: head nods, shifts of glance and the beginning and ending of gestures are certainly co-ordinated at this time-scale (Rosenfeld, 1981).

4 *Greetings and other rituals* NV signals come in combinations; a smile is commonly combined with a gaze and a friendly tone of voice, for example. They also occur in sequences of interaction between two or more people. Most social behaviour consists of verbal as well as non-verbal signals, and we have seen how NVC operates in conversation. When there is little speech we can look at the NV sequences separately. For example, the following sequence has been found in greetings, by Kendon and Ferber (1973) and others:

1 Person A waves, smiles, looks and says something like 'Hi'. B probably responds, and there is a brief mutual gaze.
2 A moves nearer to B, looks away, grooms himself, frees his right hand.
3 A and B shake hands or make other bodily contact; second smile; second mutual gaze; second verbal greeting.
4 A and B stand at an angle and conversation begins.

When a third person approaches two others, if they are willing to talk to him, they open up to give him the third side of a triangle to make what Kendon calls a 'facing formation'. The three move about but maintain an equilibrium level of distance and orientation to each other. When one leaves he starts by a move away, revealing his intentions; this is followed by a move *in* and then by his departure (Kendon, 1977).

Rituals and ceremonies are repeated patterns of behaviour which have no instrumental function but which have certain social consequences. They include 'rites of passage' like weddings and graduations, and greetings and farewells, where a change of status or relationship is brought about. Some ceremonies appear to have the function of confirming social relationships, like drill parades; others are intended to heal, though by symbolic rather than medical methods, while others express religious beliefs and hopes. In these events 'ritual work' is accomplished, i.e. a change of state or relationship is brought about by the ritual. The French anthropologist Van Gennep (1908) maintained that rituals all have three main phases – separation, transition, incorporation – which fit rites of passage quite well. Greetings, on the other hand, could be said to have a different structure – of moving towards and away from a climax.

Exactly how the ritual work is done is not known, but it is clear that NVC plays an important part in it. Some NV signals here work by similarity or analogy: wine stands for blood; in some primitive rites to cure barrenness, red paint represents menstrual blood. Other signals have meaning through arbitrary associations, as in the case of flags, totem animals or other objects representing social groups. Rituals are usually conducted by a priest or other official; at the height of the ceremony he usually looks at and touches those who are being processed, which probably heightens the social impact of his work. The elements used may symbolize the state of affairs being brought about – putting on a chain of office, or the red paint which stands for menstrual blood, for example.

## CONCLUSIONS

It is interesting that humans make so much use of NVC. Animals use it because it is the only means of communication they have, but why do we? There are several reasons:

1 NV signals are more powerful for communicating emotions and interpersonal attitudes; they put the recipient in a state of immediate biological readiness, to deal with aggression, love or whatever. The power of ritual to change relationships is probably due to the NV components.

2 Some messages are more easily conveyed by gesture than by words – shapes, for example – especially if we don't know the language well enough to describe things.

3 The verbal channel is often full, and it is useful to use another channel for feedback and synchronizing signals.

4 It would be disturbing to focus attention on some messages by putting them into words – such as certain aspects of self-presentation, or partly negative attitudes to others.

### FURTHER READING

Argyle, M., *Bodily Communication*, 2nd edn, Methuen, London, 1988.
Argyle, M., and Cook, M., *Gaze and Mutual Gaze*, Cambridge University Press, 1976.
Ekman, P., *Emotion in the Human Face*, Cambridge University Press, 1982.
Feyereisen, P., and De Lannoy, J.-D., *Gestures and Speech*, Cambridge University Press, 1991.

## CHAPTER 3

# VERBAL COMMUNICATION AND CONVERSATION

Speech is the most complex, subtle and characteristically human means of communication. Most animal noises simply communicate emotional states. Human speech is different in that it is learnt, can convey information about external events, and has a grammatical structure and sentences that can convey complex meanings.

Linguists sometimes present language as printed words on paper. This is a mistake: the real unit is the utterance by one individual to one or more others, in a situation, in a conversational sequence, where he or she is trying to influence the other. Utterances are units of social behaviour, but they are very special units, since they use words and grammar, and convey meanings. Conversations similarly are special sequences of behaviour, with a complex structure, and they require special skills to be performed properly.

Austin (1962) drew attention to utterances such as promising, ordering, apologizing, judging guilty, declaring garden parties open and making bets, which he called 'performative utterances'; they are neither true nor false, but they affect what is going to happen. He went on to argue that all utterances do things in this way, and can be looked at as items of social behaviour which are intended to influence the hearer in some way. They are all 'speech acts'.

*Different kinds of utterance* There are several different kinds of verbal utterance:

*Orders and instructions* These are used to influence the behaviour of others; they can be gently persuasive or authoritarian.

*Questions* These are intended to elicit verbal information; they can be open-ended or closed, personal or impersonal.

*Information* This may be given in response to a question, or as part of a lecture, or during a problem-solving discussion.

These are the most basic kinds of utterance, but there are several others:

*Informal speech* This consists of casual chat, jokes and gossip, and is directed more towards strengthening and enjoying social relationships than conveying any particular information.

*Expression of emotions and interpersonal attitudes* This provides a special kind of information; however, this information is usually conveyed – and is conveyed more effectively – non-verbally.

*Performative utterances* These are speech acts where the utterance performs something, for example voting, judging, naming.

*Social routines* These include standard sequences like thanking, apologizing, greeting, etc.

*Latent messages* In these the more important meaning is made subordinate, e.g. 'As I was saying to the Prime Minister . . .'

A central feature of language is *syntax*, that is, the rules for combining verbs, nouns, etc., into sentences. Sometimes we can communicate without much syntax, for example when ordering 'two pints of beer'. In order to convey information a sequence of different kinds of word is needed – 'I[pronoun] ate[verb] the apple[noun].' The same applies to questions, orders and the other kinds of utterance listed above. In fact the structure of most sentences is much more complex than this, with subordinate clauses and other elaborations.

The *skilled use of language* requires more than knowledge of grammar. Polite and persuasive utterances are quite tricky. For example, to get someone to post a letter, 'If you're passing the letter-box, would you mind posting this?' might do the job, while 'Post this letter' might not. Orders may be disguised as suggestions, or even questions.

There is an important non-verbal component in skilled utterances. The amount of warmth, directiveness or questioning is shown by the tone of voice and pitch pattern.

## SHARED VOCABULARY

Language is possible only if there is a *shared vocabulary*. In order to talk about a particular topic, two people need to have common words for this area of activity or interest. The vocabulary may be quite small, as when serving tea or coffee, or very large, as for those working in botanical gardens or medicine. There are different technical vocabularies for cooking, sewing, cricket and many other activities. Criminals use special 'argots', or anti-languages, with alternative words from those used in straight society, such as for prostitutes and policemen. This is partly to prevent others understanding, partly a technical vocabulary and partly to maintain an alternative view of society (Halliday, 1978).

Conversationalists often need to refer to particular persons or objects; how do they do this? It depends on common ground, on being able to identify which person, dog, house or whatever is being referred to. Krauss and Weinheimer (1964) gave pairs of subjects a number of shapes to discuss in a communication task; the shapes most often referred to were gradually given shortened names, roughly describing their shapes. Many utterances add new information to old, like 'the coffee machine has conked out again'. This shared ground is cumulative; it builds up during the course of a conversation, as in a tutorial or a school lesson. Between people who know each other well or who belong to the same group or community, or who work together, there is extensive common ground (Clark, 1985).

Inter-subjectivity is most important in verbal communication – 'encoding involves anticipatory decoding' (Rommetveit, 1974) – and the lack of it is a major source of social incompetence. Many mental patients fail in this way. Blakar (1985) found that pairs of schizophrenics couldn't cope with a problem-solving task about finding a route on a map; they never discovered that they had been given different maps.

## CONVERSATION

Most social behaviour involves conversation. There are several different kinds, including professional encounters where the interviewer or teacher directs it, more symmetrical discussions, rambling social chat, and sequences like church services which have been scripted beforehand.

There are rules for putting words together in sentences in the right order. Are there similar rules for putting utterances, smiles or other units of social behaviour in the right order? Is there a 'social grammar'? There could be rules which people know about; for example, at an auction sale they should take turns to bid, and should bid more than the last person, not less. Or there could be more obscure rules, like those of grammar, which most people follow though they don't know what the rules are.

Clarke (1975) found that people do have an implicit knowledge of rules of sequence. He recorded and transcribed actual conversations, which were informal and apparently rambling; individual utterances were typed on cards and shuffled into random order; another group of subjects could put them back into more or less the right order – showing that we have some knowledge of the rules of sequence, even though we cannot state them very readily. Try putting the following sequence in the right order:

A: No, bloody awful.
A: Well, what's been happening at home?
B: Did you have a good day at the office, dear?
B: Nothing much.
A: Hello.

In another study he found that 'nested' sequences are quite acceptable. For example:

A: Would you like a drink?
B: What have you got?
A: Sherry – or gin and tonic.
B: I'd like some sherry please.

On the other hand Clarke has found that people don't seem to plan very far ahead, though they may be aiming for a particular goal, like getting another to agree to something or ending a class at a certain time.

What are the rules of sequence for verbal utterances? They probably include the following:

1 An utterance by A should be responded to by B or C, without too much delay and without interruption.

2 B's response should be on the same subject, unless some explanation is given.

3 B should keep to the same type of conversation e.g. interview, polite conversation, psychotherapy; or he should negotiate a change of episode.

4 People should not suddenly arrive or leave, or start a new activity, without appropriate greeting or farewell rituals.

If rule 3 was broken there would be conversations like:

A: Shall we deal with item 7 on the agenda now?
B: Have you heard the one about the Japanese rabbi?
C: The trouble is I get these terrible impulses to rape my sister.

Each of these belongs to a different social context.


*Two-step sequences* These are the simplest sequences. We can find the probability of one kind of act leading to another, in a so-called Markov chain; the basic layout is shown in Table 3.1. This shows that when A produces social act type 1, it is followed in 15 per cent of cases by B using type 1; on 75 per cent of

|  |  | next act by B | | |
|---|---|---|---|---|
|  |  | 1 | 2 | 3 |
| last act by A | 1 | 15 | 75 | 10 |
|  | 2 | 20 | 15 | 65 |
|  | 3 | 70 | 15 | 15 |

Table 3.1   Example of reactive Markov chain, with three categories.

occasions he responds with type 2; and on 10 per cent of occasions with type 3. This is a 'reactive' sequence, showing how an act by one person leads to an act by another. It is also necessary to consider 'proactive' sequences, where an act by A leads to another act by A; for example, a teacher comments on an answer by a child and then asks another question.

Some of these two-step sequences are more than probabilities. The question–answer sequence is a basic building-block of conversation. The second utterance is closely related to the first, and its meaning is incomplete without knowing about the previous utterance. For example, 'about 90 miles' conveys no information at all unless we know that it is a reply to some question. The first utterance of the pair has some compelling power to 'project' a relevant response. Often a question leads to a straightforward and relevant answer, but this is not the only possibility. The reply may be another question, which often results in an insertion routine, as in

A: Are you coming tonight?
[B: Can I bring a guest?
[A: Sure.
B: I'll be there.

A question may be open or closed. An open-ended question usually results in a fairly long answer, especially if non-verbal encouragement is also given.

There are other kinds of 'adjacency pairs', including request–comply (or –refuse), summon–answer, offer–accept (or –decline), thanks–acknowledge, greetings and partings, reciprocation of self-disclosure and reciprocation of friendly (or hostile) remarks.

Another approach to the rules governing conversation is due to Grice (1975), who proposed his 'co-operative principle': make your conversational contribution such as is required, at the stage at which it occurs, by the accepted purpose or direction of the talk exchange in which you are engaged. He adds a number of more specific maxims: provide no more or less information than is needed, be relevant, tell the truth and be clear. There is experimental evidence that people follow these rules to some extent. For example they do not tell others what it is known that they know already; obviously untruthful remarks ('what a nice day', when it isn't) are treated as ironic. However, they also break these rules quite a lot; for example, adolescents, as well as politicians, often fail to provide as much information as is needed, as here:

Parent:        Where have you been?
Adolescent: Out.
Parent:        What did you do?
Adolescent: Nothing.

We shall discuss 'politeness' below; often Grice's rules are broken in the interest of politeness, as when wrapping up refusals or criticisms in an indirect, long-winded set of words.

*Longer sequences* Conversationalists take account of more than just the last utterance; there is a sense in which they are influenced by *all* the previous utterances. However, Clarke (1983) found that the last three utterances are the most important. We can take the structure of some kinds of conversation up to four steps by using the social skill model, described later, which emphasizes the continuous response to feedback by those engaged in social interaction. The social skill model generates a characteristic kind of four-step sequence:

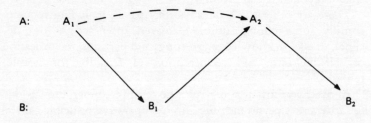

This is a case of asymmetrical interaction with A in charge. A's first move, $A_1$, produces an unsatisfactory result, $B_1$, so A modifies his behaviour to $A_2$, which produces the desired $B_2$. Note the link $A_1$–$A_2$, representing the persistence of A's goal-directed behaviour. This can be seen in the research interview:

Interviewer₁: asks question
Respondent₁: gives inadequate answer, or does not understand question
Interviewer₂: clarifies and repeats question
Respondent₂: gives adequate answer

or

Interviewer₁: asks question
Respondent₁: refuses to answer
Interviewer₂: explains purpose and importance of survey; repeats question
Respondent₂: gives adequate answer

The model can be extended to cases where both interactors are pursuing goals simultaneously, as in the following example, from a selection interview:

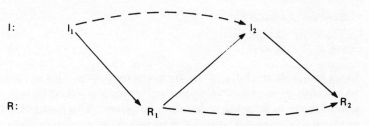

Interviewer₁: How well did you do at physics at school?
Respondent₁: Not very well, I was better at chemistry.
Interviewer₂: 'What were your A-level results?
Respondent₂: I got a C in physics, and an A in chemistry.
Interviewer₃: That's very good.

There are two four-step sequences here: I₁, R₁, I₂, R₂, and R₁, I₂, R₂, I₃. There is persistence and continuity between R₁ and R₂, as well as I₁ and I₂. Although I has the initiative, R can also pursue his goals.

Another set of sequences are the 'social routines' described by Goffman (1971). An example is the 'remedial sequence' – the behaviour which takes place when someone has committed a social error of some kind:

    1  A commits error (e.g. steps on B's toe);
    2  A apologizes, gives excuse or explanation ('I'm frightfully sorry, I didn't see your foot');
    3  B accepts this ('It's OK, no damage done');
    4  A thanks B ('It's very good of you to be so nice about it');
    5  B minimizes what A has done ('Think nothing of it').

Other such routines are those of greeting, opening conversations with strangers, introductions, thanking and parting.

*Repeated cycles* Sometimes the two-step links form repeated cycles. In an interview there is a very simple cycle:

    Interviewer:  asks question
    Respondent:  answers

Teachers often use the cycle:

    Teacher:  lectures
    Teacher:  asks question
    Pupil:     answers

More elaborate teaching cycles are given on p. 273. This includes an example of a 'proactive' sequence, where the teacher makes a second move in response to her own last move. This is important in many situations; for example it is important when replying to a question on a social occasion (see p. 71).

    The existence of a repeated cycle can be established by Markov analysis of the frequency of different kinds of response to each kind of utterance. Sometimes husbands and wives have a repeated cycle, always ending in a row in the same way. Sometimes *cycles* follow each other in a regular manner, as when a teacher starts with one style of instruction and then shifts to another. There can even be a cycle of cycles (Dawkins, 1976b).

We have confined discussion so far to sequences of verbal utterances. Similar principles apply to social acts consisting of non-verbal as well as verbal components, or of non-verbal elements alone. Bidding at an auction sale, for example, can be done verbally or non-verbally. Here the rules say what is allowed, not what most often happens. A three-step rule is needed, to prevent a customer bidding again after the auctioneer has stated last bid. Most situations have special rules of sequences – auction sales, psychoanalysis, at the pub and so on.

To study a game or a social situation we need to find the rules. But rules are only part of the story – there is also play within the rules. To predict the course of events in a game we need to know how hard each person is trying to win (plans), and also the skills and strategies used by each player. There is co-operation over keeping to the rules, even in boxing and management–union bargaining, and there is often competition within the rules, whereby each person is pursuing his particular goals (Collett, 1977).

How does an episode start? Sometimes it is part of a familiar sequence of events, which may be written down somewhere – like committee agendas and church services. Sometimes there is a person in charge who can decide on the next episode; a teacher, for example, can introduce the next part of a lesson by saying, 'Now we are going to start on fractions.' Sometimes an episode change can be made non-verbally, as when a hostess rises from the table or an interviewer gathers his papers together, puts his spectacles on and starts to look businesslike. In less formal situations anyone can try to introduce a new episode, but it has to be negotiated and agreed to by the others. Someone might start serious discussion of politics at a party but the others reject this and go back to gossip or talk about golf.

*Episode sequence* Most social encounters consist of a number of distinct episodes, which may have to come in a particular order. For example the doctor–patient interview is said to have six phases, while negotiations have three.

We have found that encounters usually have five main episodes or phases:

1 greeting;
2 establish relationship;
3 central task;
4 re-establish relationship;
5 parting.

The task in turn may consist of several sub-tasks; for example a doctor has to conduct a verbal or physical examination, make a diagnosis and carry out or prescribe treatment (p. 262). Often, as in this case, the sub-tasks have to come in a certain order. At primarily social events the 'task' seems to consist of eating or drinking accompanied by the exchange of information.

A successful interactor, then, needs to be able to use the repertoire of social moves for whatever situation he is in. Take a teacher, for example: he needs to be able to ask higher-order questions; he needs to know what leads to what, in order to control the others' behaviour, and how to set in motion various cycles of events; he should behave in accordance with the appropriate contingencies – if he is the main performer in an asymmetrical encounter he should be responsible for the direction of behaviour; and he should follow the rules.

## POLITENESS

This is not just about taking your hat off to ladies and passing the sandwiches nicely but is an essential part of conversational skill. We can define politeness as 'forms of behaviour which are as far as possible agreeable and rewarding to others'. A number of basic principles have been proposed:

1 *Being friendly* Making an encounter enjoyable – warm acceptance of the other person – is perhaps the key to politeness, from which the rest follows. This is partly done by words, but even more by the non-verbal style in which utterances are delivered.

2 *Care of other's self-esteem* Interactors should work hard to avoid damaging the 'face', or self-esteem, of the other. Praise or reference to success of other should be maximized, those of self modestly minimized.

3 *Avoid constraining the other* Indirect requests are more polite since they give the other more freedom of choice; 'Would you mind answering the phone?' is more polite than 'Answer the phone'. It is possible to place utterances on a scale of indirectness from 'mitigation' to 'aggravation'. Mitigation is where orders or

requests are given as questions, hints or suggestions, with reasons; aggravation is the opposite – 'Answer the bloody phone, for Pete's sake'.

4 *How to say 'no' or disagree* In Japan it is very impolite to say 'no' and questions are avoided for which this might be the answer. For us too it is more polite to emphasize points of agreement and minimize disagreement, as in 'Yes, but . . .' Disagreements should be wrapped up in utterances which contain agreements or other positive components, including positive non-verbal elements (Leech, 1983).

5 *Avoid rule-breaking* There are many kinds of behaviour which are commonly regarded as impolite, because they break normal rules of behaviour. Examples are interrupting, breaking into queues, talking too much, or telling unsuitable jokes.

Politeness does more than keep other people happy: it is likely to produce the desired results. A child who has learned to say 'Please could I have one of those nice sweets' is more likely to get one than the child who can't do better than 'Gimme sweetie'. Linde (1988) found that in aircrews with good safety records there was a higher level of mitigation; it keeps up social relationships and does not challenge the captain's authority. There was more mitigation when addressing superiors. But in accidents and emergencies, real and simulated, there was less mitigation; and it can lead to disaster in such circumstances, because messages delivered with mitigation are much less likely to be acted on. An emergency is not the time for 'Excuse me, captain, I'm awfully sorry to bother you while you're having coffee, but I think the port wing may be on fire.'

Politeness rules vary with the situation in other ways. We asked students to rate the importance of twenty rules for each of eight common situations; clusters of rules were found which applied to the same situations (see Fig. 5.2, p. 108). The first cluster of rules ('Should not embarrass others' etc.) was thought to apply to all situations, the other clusters to particular groups of situations. The bottom cluster ('Should avoid disagreements' etc.) applied to parties and similar pleasant social occasions, the other clusters to various formal and work situations.

There are well-known cultural differences in politeness. In Japan, and the East in general, 'face' is very important. We mentioned the difficulty of saying 'no', which is sometimes avoided by changing the subject. In Australia, when you disagree with what someone says, it is normal to say so, but in Indonesia people will remain silent. There are many cultural variations in social rules, and these will be discussed further in Chapter 7.

A special domain of politeness concerns mode of address. In many languages there is a choice of personal pronouns, like the French *tu* and *vous*. In addition people can be addressed as 'George' or 'Mr Smith'. This is partly a matter of intimacy, but also of status – subordinates are addressed by their first name, but this may not be reciprocated – so the use of first names can be rather ambiguous. It also depends on the situation: title and last name (Mr Smith) are used more in formal situations, such as in front of the customers in a shop, but much less at informal meetings, as in the canteen (Staples and Robinson, 1974). Committees, courtrooms, Parliament and other public arenas emphasize status differences, and here too the *vous* form and titles are normally used. Customs vary between organizations and cultures, Americans and Australians being very quick to move to first names, for example.

### ACCOMMODATION

There are great variations in the way people speak – in terms of language, accent, speed, loudness, etc. When two people meet they often converge, or accommodate to each other, to speak in a similar way. They do so partly because they want to be accepted by the other, partly in order to be understood better, and partly, perhaps, as the result of imitation and the demands of synchrony.

Several studies have shown accommodation of accent between speakers of different social status. In a simple but elegant study Coupland (1984) studied the number of 'h's sounded by a young woman working in a travel agency as she spoke to different clients. This varied from 3.7 per cent to 29.3 per cent, and correlated highly with the percentage of 'h's sounded by the client. Thakerar, Giles and Cheshire (1982) found that senior nurses spoke considerably faster and with a more educated accent than more junior, less well qualified nurses; when engaged in a co-operative task, however, where their status differences were relevant, nurses of different status shifted in both speed and accent, in the direction of the other's speech style.

Other experiments have shown that accommodation is successful in producing favourable attitudes on the part of others. Giles and Smith (1979) prepared eight tapes of a Canadian addressing an English audience, with combinations of accommodation or lack of it in three dimensions – pronunciation, speech rate and message content. Accommodation on speech rate and contents made the speaker more attractive to his audience, but shifting accent as well went too far, perhaps being seen as a caricature; there is an optimal degree of convergence.

Sometimes there is no convergence. Giles and Powesland (1975) give the example of 'a tough, masculine, rugby-football-playing young man seeking the favour of an exceptionally feminine and coy young lady. One might suppose that he would not advance his courtship by modelling his manner on hers but would be wiser to maintain or even exaggerate his own virile and masterful style of speech and behaviour' (p. 167). In rare cases there is *divergence*, when people do not want to get too close to the other, when preserving identity is more important than acceptance. For example, several experiments have found that Welsh subjects strengthened their Welsh accent when annoyed by rude remarks about their language by English-speakers (Giles and Coupland, 1991).

### VERBAL SKILLS IN THREE KINDS OF CONVERSATION

1 *Making friends* One of the most common areas of social difficulty is in making friends, getting to know people. Lonely and socially isolated individuals are often very bad conversationalists; they simply can't sustain a conversation unless others do all the work to make up for them.

We showed in the last chapter that non-verbal signals play an important part in the expression of liking for another person, and that their use is much more effective than saying 'I like you'. However, there are more subtle forms of words which can be effective in expressing such feelings. These are:

1 *Paying compliments* This is one of the main forms of verbal rewardingness, and often includes, in English, the word 'nice'. This overlaps with the politeness rule about maximizing praise of the other.

2 *Pleasure talk* Talking about pleasant events, keeping to cheerful topics of conversation. This kind of conversation has been found to enhance feelings of joy and reduce depression.

3 *Agreeing* The purpose of these conversations is not to solve problems but to further the relationship, so if possible one should agree with what has been said.

4 *Use of names* The other is addressed by name, preferably first name. The word 'we' is used to signal shared activities and feelings, group membership, co-operation.

5 *Being helpful* It is very rewarding to provide or offer help, in the form of information, sympathy or practical assistance.

6 *Humour* This makes social encounters more enjoyable and signals a positive attitude to others. Humour breaks down social barriers, reduces tensions, increases joy and produces shared feelings and attitudes, for example towards the object of humour.

There are several other verbal moves which are important in developing the relationship further:

1 *Searching for similarity* Finding out things shared with the other, especially interests, opinions and friends. Friendship depends on common interests and is supported by a shared social network. Kellerman and Lim (1990) found that American students go through a standard set of topics in much the same order, gradually moving from education and home town to interests, sports and family.

2 *Personal questions* These should not be so intimate as to break the politeness rule, but are important since they lead to

3 *Self-disclosure* This indicates trust and is essential for closer levels of friendship. It proceeds gradually and should be reciprocated. One of the key mistakes of people who say they are

lonely is keeping to sport, politics or other impersonal, low-disclosure topics (Ellis and Beattie, 1986).

It is in conversations like these, on informal social occasions, that 'bad conversationalists' get into trouble. There are several kinds of failure:

1 They may speak very little, never initiate any new topics and reply to questions with short answers.

> Q. Where do you come from?
> A. Didcot.
>     (*long silence*)

A more skilled move here would be to make a double or 'proactive' response; for example:

> Q. Where do you come from?
> A. Didcot. There's a very interesting railway museum there; have you seen it?

In addition to keeping the conversation going this seeks shared experience and interests.

2 Egocentricity. Having no interest in other people, their ideas or concerns, soon drives them away. This is common in mental patients (see Chapter 9).

3 Breaking rules, such as Grice's relevance rule or the rules of politeness, often results in loss of self-esteem for someone else.

4 Another kind of failure is simply not having very much of interest to talk about. One solution is to draw other people out and take an interest in *them*.

These conversational failures add up to low levels of rewardingness, also a common feature of mental patients.

2 *Conversations in professional settings* Most work and professional encounters are totally different from those just discussed. The participants are not primarily trying to make friends but have the goal of conducting some work transaction, while the situation is defined and constrained by clear rules and conventions. The

conversation depends on the nature of the situation in several ways:

1 *Goals* The goals of teaching students, selling to clients and judging candidates at a selection interview are obviously quite different. The conversation is designed to realize these goals.

2 *Repertoire of utterances* Only certain kinds of utterance are allowed, for example in psychoanalysis, management–union bargaining or a visit to the Post Office; to mix them up would produce total consternation.

3 *Sequences of utterances* There are special sequences over and above question–answer or other adjacency pairs in many professional encounters. We saw earlier one of the common sequences in teaching (p. 64) and shall look at others in Chapter 10. We shall also see that doctor–patient encounters go through a set sequence of episodes, as do selection interviews and selling.

4 *Roles and rules* If you agree to take part in a radio or TV interview, you accept the role of interviewee and are expected to answer questions relevantly, and to allow the interviewer to control the interview. Politicians often break the rules of these interviews by giving irrelevant answers or by talking too much. Sometimes the interviewee rebels and asks questions back, refuses to answer or leaves the studio, but this constitutes a news event in itself (Greatbatch, 1988); more often he evades the issue.

If you accept an invitation to a job interview you will find that the interviewer will ask the questions, not the interviewee, and that intimate or personal questions may be asked, though only if they are strictly relevant to the job.

In certain situations the conversational procedures are unfamiliar and newcomers have to learn what they are, for example in management–union bargaining, lawcourts, Parliament, psychoanalysis or encounter groups. Even regular committees have rules which may baffle newcomers, e.g. 'vote on an amendment before voting on the main motion'. Training may be needed for some professional settings (Argyle, Furnham and Graham, 1981).

3 *Conversation during ongoing social action* Talk plays a central role during ongoing encounters in everyday life – professional,

domestic and social – and in the conduct of relationships. The vocabulary, and the kinds of utterance used, varies greatly with the nature of the setting. There may be a technical vocabulary, as in *sewing*:

Stitch armhole facing back to armhole facing front at shoulders and sides.
Pin facing to armhole edge, RIGHT SIDES TOGETHER, matching notches and seams. Stitch.
GRADE seam allowances. Clip curves.
Turn facing to INSIDE. Press.
Top stitch $\frac{3}{8}$ "(1 cm) from armhole edge. [Gregory and Carroll, 1978]

The kinds of utterance used by aircrew, football players, criminals and many others are highly specialized.

The utterances which are acceptable and effective are partly described by the principles given already. A further principle is 'social intelligence' – what to say on complex or difficult social occasions. Consider some of the situations which children and adolescents find difficult. McPhail (1967) located thirty such situations, for example 'You go into a coffee bar and find that you can't pay because you haven't brought any money.' He found that the solutions offered changed greatly with age (Fig. 11.2, p. 292). Dodge showed how children and adolescents could solve some problems by finding how to integrate the goals of self and another in a single plan of action. Suppose another child cheats in a game; a second child could cry, run away, hit the other, or it could suggest that the other has made an accidental mistake and the turn should be run again. Or a girl is on a bike hike with five of her friends. One of the girls, who has just moved into the neighbourhood, is very slow and is holding the group up. The other girls are all yelling at her and threatening to leave her behind. One solution might be simply to slow down to be with her (Dodge, 1990). Shure (1981) based a whole system of social skills training for children and parents on teaching them how to think up alternative solutions to social problems. We shall see later that many mental patients have difficulty in thinking of such solutions.

More difficult problems, requiring a very careful choice of

words, include reprimanding, explaining a decision not to promote a colleague, firing an employee, apologizing but making no concessions, rewarding A but not upsetting B, congratulating the winner without upsetting the loser, dealing with absurd questions from members of an audience, making complaints without damaging the relationship, giving bad news or dealing with a child who has been sent home from school. These are all problematic and need skilled delivery with supporting NVC to be successful.

### SPEECH AND CLASS

*Accent* It is well known that there are class differences in accent in Britain and some other countries; indeed accent is probably the strongest clue to social class in Britain. Research by phoneticians has tried to analyse exactly the class differences in pronunciation. Trudgill (1974) interviewed people in four areas of Norwich, judged to be of different classes, and recorded sixteen phonetic variables. Large differences were found (see Table 3.2);

|  | Lower working class | Middle middle class |
| --- | --- | --- |
| sound 'ing' as in 'workin' | 100 | 31 |
| glottal sounding, e.g. of 'bu'er' | 94 | 41 |
| dropping 'h' as in ''ammer' | 61 | 6 |

Table 3.2   Variations in pronunciation between classes in Norwich (Trudgill, 1974).

for example many more working-class people did not sound the final 'g' in 'working', 'jumping', etc. There were many other variations; for example middle-class speakers pronounced the 'a' in 'bath' as in 'staff', not 'maths'. There are also large regional differences between cockney, Scottish and other speech styles, but using any such accent is itself an indicator of class.

Labov (1966) studied accents in New York, for example by asking sales staff in different department stores (Kleins, Macy's,

Saks) a question to which the answer would be 'fourth floor', and found that 'r's were sounded in higher social classes.

However, working-class and uneducated people can speak in a more educated or 'middle-class' way if they wish or if they are asked to speak carefully. For example Trudgill asked his subjects to read word lists and found the number of dropped final 'g's was much lower (Figure 3.1).

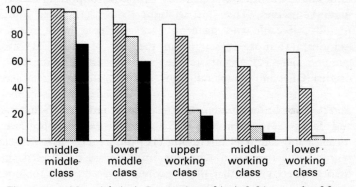

Figure 3.1 Norwich (ng). Proportion of (ng): [ŋ] in speech of five socio-economic classes in four styles: word list (white), reading-passage (hatched), formal (dotted), casual (solid) (based on Trudgill, 1974).

The shift from casual to formal speech produces the same accent changes that are produced by class or education. This leads one to ask: if most people know the 'correct' way to speak and are perfectly capable of doing it, why don't they do it all the time, since they know that the educated middle-class accent is more prestigeful? The answer is that a lower-class person who did this would be rejected by his own group. And we shall see below that regional accents can convey certain positive stereotypes.

How are speakers of different accents perceived? Research has been carried out with the 'matched guise' technique, whereby a versatile speaker makes tape recordings in several accents, which are rated by judges who think they are listening to different speakers. Such studies in Britain found that there is a social hierarchy of accents, from 'received pronunciation' (i.e. Southern, educated) at the top, to some acceptable local variants like Yorkshire and Scottish, and down to the stronger accents of industrial towns, including cockney, together with strong rural accents. The speakers of accents at the top of this hierarchy are judged to be of higher social class, and also to be more intelligent, ambitious, wealthy – even taller and cleaner. However, speakers of the lower-status accents are also believed to possess a number of desirable qualities, especially by people who speak in the same way themselves. They are thought to be: (1) more honest, friendly, likeable and generous, and to have more sense of humour; (2) more masculine in the case of males; (3) more genuine, since RP accents are seen as concealing a person's social origins (Giles and Coupland, 1991).

*Speech codes* Speech varies with class in other ways. Schatzman and Strauss (1955) in the USA interviewed people after a tornado and found an interesting class difference: the lower-class respondents, compared with the middle-class ones, used their own perspective, so that their accounts were difficult to follow unless the listener had been there too. They gave concrete information rather than using categories of people or acts, and they gave no illustrations. Bernstein (1961) took this further and argued that middle-class people in Britain use an 'elaborated' linguistic code, whereas working-class people use a 'restricted' one. He believed that the elaborated code makes fewer assumptions about the point of view of listeners, is less dependent on context and closer to 'correct' speech as taught in school. It uses more standard grammar, more subordinate clauses and a larger vocabulary.

These ideas led to many studies in which speech samples were elicited from middle- and working-class children, often with IQ held constant. It has usually been found as predicted that the working-class children used shorter sentences, fewer subordinate clauses and a smaller vocabulary, that their speech was more concrete, took less account of the point of view of the listeners and used more endings like 'didn't I' and 'you know'. However, as with accents, children were found to be perfectly capable of using either code: working-class children shifted to a more elaborated code on abstract or school topics, middle-class children to a more restricted code for informal chat (Robinson, 1978).

Uneducated speech is also less 'grammatical' – or we could say it uses a different grammar. Trudgill found that 70 per cent of his lower working-class subjects in Detroit used double negatives (for instance 'I can't eat nothing'), compared with 2 per cent of the upper middle-class speakers. In Norwich 97 per cent of lower working-class people left off the final 's' from verbs ('she like him very much'), compared with 2 per cent of middle middle-class ones. Other examples noted by Trudgill of lower-class English grammar are: 'I done it yesterday', 'He ain't got it' and 'It was her what said it'.

The origins of the two speech styles lie partly in the different ways that mothers speak to their children. Working-class mothers may reply to questions with 'because they do' or 'because I say so', while middle-class mothers provide carefully reasoned, sometimes very long, explanations. Working-class mothers control their children by threats, middle-class mothers by reasons explaining the consequences of actions (Robinson, 1978). Teachers have been found to address less complex utterances to working-class children, who are quite capable of more complex speech and may use it at home.

Is the elaborated code any more effective than the restricted code? In laboratory communication tasks, working-class children fare a little worse than middle-class children of similar IQ, mainly as a result of egocentric errors, such as giving incomplete information, rather like messages for oneself or a friend (Heider, 1971). Bernstein believed, however, that the restricted code developed for a quite different purpose – handling face-to-face relationships in a familiar group – and it may be equally good or better for this purpose.

Similar differences in speech styles are found in black people. Black English has its own 'grammar'. Examples are: 'The answers always be wrong', 'She nice', 'He kick ball' and 'I don't bother nobody'. Labov, Cohen, Robins and Lewis (1968) claimed that black English is complex and in some ways effective. It includes elaborate and imaginative ritual insults, and 'rapping', a lively form of repartee.

### GENDER DIFFERENCES

There are a number of interesting differences between the speech styles of men and women. To begin with, they talk about different things. Groups of men like to talk about money, work, sports and competition, and they like teasing one another, while women talk about family, friendships, feelings, clothes, health and food. Women engage in more self-disclosure and talk about more intimate topics, especially to other women. When men and women are together, men tend to talk more; they interrupt, speak more loudly and generally control the conversation. However, women are persistent and often return to the same topic. Women are co-operative and supportive, keep the conversation going, ask questions, give more back-channel responses: they are more polite. Men are mainly concerned with the task, women with the relationship, men with dominance, women with intimacy, but men too may achieve intimacy and have fun in other ways, by jokes or tall stories, and by mildly aggressive banter and teasing (Aries 1987).

Men and women use different vocabularies. Men might say 'Oh, shit' where women are more likely to say 'Oh, dear' (Smith, 1985); women say things like 'How adorable', men use expressions like 'What the hell is going on?'; and women use unusual colour words like 'turquoise' and 'lemon', which are not in the male vocabulary. Women's speech is more hesitant, with 'may' or 'might', and it intensifies, as in 'it was so beautiful'.

The main gender difference in voice quality is that women's voices are of higher pitch, partly for anatomical reasons, but partly because women tend to smile while they speak, which produces a higher-pitched sound. The resonance pattern is also different, male voices having more energy at the lower pitches. Women use more intonation, twice the pitch range of men in one study; women 'italicize' where men are 'deliberate'; women use sharp upward gradients, as in surprise – the bright and cheerful style, exaggerated when speaking to children (and parodied by the comedienne Joyce Grenfell). Men keep to the same steady pitch, or use a falling pitch.

Women have often been found to be more fluent than men;

they have fewer pauses or other speech errors. Their grammar is more correct, and their sentences more complete and complex, from an early age. Women use more standard RP speech, in these respects and in terms of accent. It has been suggested that the reason for women's 'better' speech is that, while men are judged by what they can do, women are judged by what they look like and what they sound like. This in turn could explain why uneducated accents in men are regarded as more masculine.

### FURTHER READING

Clark, H. H., 'Language use and language users', in G. Lindzey and E. Aronson, eds., *Handbook of Social Psychology*, Random House, New York, 1983.

Ellis, A., and Beattie, G., *The Psychology of Language and Communication*, Weidenfeld and Nicolson, London, 1986.

Giles, H., and Coupland, N., *Language Contexts and Consequences*, Open University Press, Milton Keynes, 1991.

## CHAPTER 4
# PERCEPTION OF OTHERS

In order to 'perceive' other people and social events, interactors use visual and auditory signals, verbal as well as non-verbal. Sherlock Holmes was very good at this. He perceived that Watson had returned to his medical practice in this way: 'If a gentleman walks into my rooms smelling of iodoform, with a black nitrate of silver upon his right forefinger, and a bulge on the side of his top hat to show where he has secreted his stethoscope, I must be dull indeed if I do not pronounce him to be an active member of the medical profession' ('A Scandal in Bohemia'). We have seen in earlier chapters how people decode target persons' facial expressions and other behaviour to infer their emotional state and attitudes to the perceiver. 'Perceiving' people is not at all the same as perceiving objects. Objects are seen as being pushed and pulled by physical laws; when we perceive people we are aware that they are to some extent responsible for events and initiating action, that they are conscious, have feelings, plans and intentions, which may be about us – we are often perceiving their perceptions. We are engaged in the whole process of interpreting and making sense of other people and the social events in which we are involved. This is important, because the way in which a person perceives (and interprets) events affects how he will behave. In an experiment by Kelley (1950) subjects who expected a person presented by the experimenter to be 'warm' interpreted his behaviour differently from those who expected him to be 'cold', and members of the first group talked to him more. Observers also make attributions about the causes of another's behaviour – did he jump or was he pushed, was he responsible? Again the decision will affect the perceiver's subsequent actions.

Both in forming impressions and in making attributions there are a number of common, but very important, biases and sources of error. Inadequate social performance can be partly the result of faulty person perception. It is particularly important for interviewers, doctors, personnel officers and others to avoid the various sources of error here. We shall see later that some kinds of mental patients have inaccurate perceptions of those around them.

### FORMING IMPRESSIONS OF OTHER PEOPLE

When we form impressions of other people's personalities we categorize them in various ways. Since we behave somewhat differently towards males and females, old and young, and other divisions of people, it is necessary to categorize them as soon as possible.

If subjects are asked to describe other people, they use various trait words. Everyone has a number of dimensions, or sets of categories, which are most important to him and which affect his behaviour. He may not bother about social class, but may be very concerned about whether another person is Catholic or Protestant (in Belfast, for example), or how intelligent he is. One way of finding out which categories are important to a person is the 'repertory grid' devised by George Kelly (1955). The technique is as follows: the subject is asked for the names of ten to fifteen people in certain relationships, such as 'a friend of the same sex', 'a teacher you liked' etc. The names are written on cards and presented to him three at a time. The subject is asked which two of the three are most similar and in what way the other one differs, thus eliciting one of his 'constructs'. When a number of constructs have been found, a 'grid' is made up in which all the target persons are rated on all the constructs. Statistical methods can be used to find the general dimensions which are most used by the subject.

It is found that people use three kinds of construct: roles (e.g. class, occupation), personality traits (e.g. intelligence, extraversion) and physical characteristics (e.g. attractiveness, height). Some of the most commonly used personality traits are:

  extraversion or sociability;
  agreeableness or likeability;

emotional stability;
intelligence;
assertiveness.

In many experiments subjects are asked to rate target persons on a number of seven-point scales, for dimensions like these.

Children, as they get older, come to perceive people in more complex ways. If asked to give free descriptions of those they know, older children make greater use of traits, values and motives, discover more regularities of behaviour and use organizing ideas about how traits work (Livesley and Bromley, 1973). Younger children do not use the traits familiar to psychologists, but rather different ones like 'silly', 'bossy' and 'naughty', though these are similar to adult traits like 'intelligent', 'assertive' and 'conscientious'. It is important not to impose our concepts on the people studied.

*The effects of physical cues* Our impressions of others are partly based on inferences from their appearance. People who wear spectacles are thought to be intelligent, though Argyle and McHenry (1970) found that the effect disappears after a person has been seen in action for a few minutes. The same may be true for the other traditional findings of this type, such as:

thick lips          – sexy;
thin lips           – conscientious;
high forehead       – intelligent;
dark or coarse skin – hostile;
    and so on.

These inferences are probably made by simple analogies: large heads are made for thinking, thick lips for kissing, etc. A more recent finding is that those with 'baby faces' are seen as less mature but more warm and submissive, which is attractive in females but not in males (Berry and McArthur, 1986). However, there is no evidence that people with any of these characteristics actually possess the qualities in question.

Voices are decoded mainly in terms of stereotypes: a person's accent is used to allocate him to a particular social class or nationality, and stereotypes are applied accordingly. Clothes raise other problems: they are under voluntary control (though choice is limited by occupational norms and income) and play an important part in self-presentation. We learn how the other person wants us to see him, which is not quite the same as how he really is (see Chapter 8).

*Physical attractiveness* This is a way of classifying people which is very widely used; a person's physical attractiveness has important effects on the way he or she is treated. It can be measured very easily by asking judges to rate an individual on a five- or seven-point scale, like this:

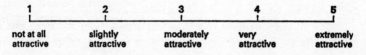

There is a high level of agreement between different judges of either sex on a person's physical attractiveness (p.a.) score. The individual, however, may not have a very accurate idea of his or her own attractiveness (as seen by others). There are quite low correlations, of the order of 0.25–0.30, for p.a. as rated by self and others; some people are over-modest, others the reverse. There are individual differences in preferences which are related to the personality of the beholder: extraverted males like pictures of girls with large bosoms and few clothes. It is possible that they are more prepared to admit these preferences than introverts. There are also cultural differences, in preference for thin or fat women and so on.

Attractiveness in females for many people in our society today appears to be based on the following elements (Wilson and Nias, 1976):

1 *Height* – shorter than partner, otherwise medium. Miss World winners average 5′8″.

2 *Physique* – 36–24–35 is the ideal; each of the three components is important; fatness is a very negative feature.

3 *Face* – regular features, full lips, clear skin, smiling expression.

4 *Hair and grooming* – long hair; 'frizzy wig' often used in experiments to make unattractive; careful grooming of skin.

5 *Health* – apparent healthiness, vivaciousness and arousal.

6 *Clothes* – in current fashion.

7 *Self-esteem* – people with high self-esteem get more attractive mates.

It is interesting that most of these features are under voluntary control, if we include ways of increasing height and changing real or apparent physique. To a large extent, personal appearance is a style of behaviour, which can be indulged in by those who choose to do so. Sex therapy and social skills training often include suggesting improvements to appearance, which are easier to make than improvements in social behaviour.

Attractiveness in men is not as important as in women, but it has its effects. It has similar components to those for females, but height is important and dominance is found attractive.

Experiments have shown that those who are physically attractive, of either sex, are thought to possess all kinds of other desirable attributes – the 'p.a. stereotype'. A meta-analysis of many studies found that attractive individuals are assumed to be sociable, dominant, in good mental health, sexually warm, socially skilled and intelligent (Feingold, 1992). Is there any truth in this stereotype? A further meta-analysis, mainly of studies with students, found that p.a. really does correlate with popularity with the opposite sex, which is not very surprising (average r = .29), with social skills, and with less social anxiety but greater self-consciousness with the opposite sex (Feingold, 1992).

There are great advantages in being attractive, especially for women. The most celebrated study in this area is the 'computer dance' at which Elaine Walster and colleagues (1966) invited 752 new students to a dance at which they were paired at random, except that the male was always taller than his partner. Ratings of attractiveness were made by the experimenters, and these proved to be the only predictor of how much each person was liked by their partner, for both sexes, but especially for attraction to females. Berscheid and colleagues (1971) found that attractiveness correlated 0.61 with the number of dates in the last year for females, 0.25 for males. It has been found that attractive females at an American university got better grades, and that they did it by staying behind afterwards and using their charms on the instructors (Singer, 1964).

Whether p.a. stereotypes have any truth in them or not, they certainly affect what happens to people. Several studies have presented various candidates for job interviews; the more attractive people are more likely to get jobs and attractive individuals earn higher salaries. Attractive girls get lighter sentences in lawcourts, and are likelier to be found not guilty – at any rate for less serious offences (Hatfield and Sprecher, 1986). The greatest effects are at the bottom end of the p.a. scale: those who are too fat, have bad teeth, facial scars, strawberry blotches, harelips or other stigmas are much less likely to get dates or some kinds of jobs; other people even stand further away from them on the pavement (Bull and Rumsey, 1988).

*Social stereotypes* Impressions of others' personalities are partly based on stereotypes. If we know someone to be a *female Oxford psychology undergraduate*, this draws our attention to four sets of stereotyped information, based on our past experience and contact with popular culture. Katz and Braly carried out a classic study in 1933, which was repeated in 1951 and 1967, on the stereotypes of Princeton students; 84 per cent thought blacks were superstitious, 79 per cent thought Jews were shrewd and 78 per cent thought Germans were scientifically minded. The percentage of Princeton students holding these views has fallen a lot since 1933.

A better method is to ask people *what percentage* of Xs are lazy etc., and this has been found to be a good predictor of evaluation of and contact with immigrant groups in Holland (Kleinpenning and Hagendoorn, 1991). In fact many people do hold stereotyped beliefs about the characteristics of, for example, old Etonians, sociology students and policemen. Although psychologists usually say that it is very wicked to hold stereotypes, these often contain useful summaries of the typical attributes of different sections of the population. Stone, Gage and Leavitt (1957) found that stereotyped ratings of a number of individuals simply described as 'students' were *more* accurate than the ratings given after interviewing them. On the other hand there is a lot more variation among, say, sociology students than the stereotype would suggest, and it is important to be able to recognize variations from the statistical average.

People use stereotypes because they contain information and save effort. Cognitive pressures exaggerate the supposed differences between, for example, men and women or blacks and whites, and also exaggerate the supposed homogeneity of both groups. There is greater perceived homogeneity of other groups (the 'out-group homogeneity effect'), mainly because we know more in-group than out-group members and so are more aware of the amount of variation in the in-group. This even works for old and young, men and women (Linville, Fischer and Salovey, 1989).

Stereotypes of other groups are often negative, as in racial stereotypes. The explanation may be that self-esteem depends partly on the properties of groups to which people belong; they can enhance their self-esteem by comparing out-groups unfavourably with the in-group (p. 193). Attitudes towards, and stereotypes about, other groups are more unfavourable when there is conflict with them, as in a war, or if the other group is thought to possess undeserved status or other benefits.

Stereotypes can have a massive effect on the way events are perceived. Duncan (1976) made videotapes of black people and white people having an increasingly violent argument, ending in individuals pushing one another. White subjects who saw the film categorized the behaviour of blacks who pushed as 'violent' in over 70 per cent of cases (as opposed to 'playing around' etc.), regardless of the colour of the victim; but only 13 per cent of whites who pushed were labelled as 'violent' (Figure 4.1(a)).

*Gender stereotypes* are particularly interesting. It is widely believed that men are more independent, assertive, self-confident, etc., while women are more affectionate, sympathetic, helpful, etc. (p. 128). Early studies found that these stereotypes led to biased judgements, for example that a male job applicant would do the

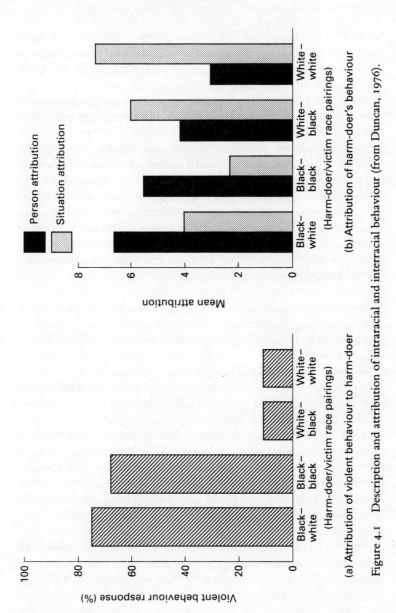

(a) Attribution of violent behaviour to harm-doer

(b) Attribution of harm-doer's behaviour

Figure 4.1   Description and attribution of intraracial and interracial behaviour (from Duncan, 1976).

job better, or that an article was better if apparently by a male author. It has been found that these gender stereotypes are used more by those who see themselves as definitely masculine or definitely feminine. However, more recent studies in the USA have found that this kind of prejudice has now almost disappeared, and Locksley et al. (1980) found that gender stereotypes affected judgements of others only in the absence of any useful information about them.

Stereotypes are partly created by the media. For example British TV advertisements often portray women as half-witted, unqualified housewives, worried about making things clean, and submissively obedient to assertive men in white coats (Livingstone and Green, 1986). A recent analysis of obituaries of managers in European papers found that between 1974 and 1986 there had been a decline in descriptions of female managers as kind and adorable; they were increasingly described, like male managers, as intelligent and decisive (Kirchler, 1992).

*Names and nicknames* Rom Harré (1976) has drawn attention to the importance of names in social behaviour. People think of themselves and others by their names, as when asked 'Who are you?' A person's name often has clear indications of social class (Sebastian Digby-Vane-Trumpington), race (Moses Levi) or regional origins (Stuart McGregor). First names, though usually given by parents, also carry certain images – Charity, Horace, Robin and Joan for example.

Children are given nicknames by their parents, sometimes as many as eight different ones being used in the family. They are also given nicknames by their peer group, and this signifies acceptance into a social group and often some social role within it. These names may be based on personal qualities (Fatty); on particular incidents (Sneaky); or on the person's real name (Sherlock, surname Holmes). The society of childhood contains a number of traditional roles, perpetuated by school stories and comics, such as that of Piggy the fat boy, Twit and Thinker. In these various ways a person's name and nickname contribute to impressions formed about him.

A title is a kind of appellation which is achieved – for

instance, ranks in the army, Dr and Professor, Sir and Lord. The niceties of British titles – of the different kinds of Lady, for instance – are most important to those concerned, as are such German academic labels as 'Dr Dr'. In a number of countries, such as Wales, it is the custom to refer to people by their profession (Jones the Spy), in this case because so many people have the same name.

*Forming a simplified and unified impression* When forming an impression of someone we tend to produce an over-simple picture of them; we assume that they are highly consistent. Asch (1952) carried out some very clever experiments with lists of words – though we now regard these studies as rather artificial. He found that given a list of trait words – intelligent, skilful, industrious, warm, determined, practical, cautious – subjects had no difficulty in inferring that such a person was also happy, strong, honest, reliable, generous and serious. Each trait affects the meaning of other traits: 'strong' is different if combined with 'good' (forceful) rather than with 'bad' (ruthless). More recently Asch and Zukier (1984) found that people could quite easily form impressions of someone who was 'brilliant' and 'foolish', or 'strict' and 'kind'.

The traits which are presented first affect the interpretation of those given later. For example a target person said to be 'intelligent' and 'envious' is also rated as 'humorous' by 52 per cent of subjects, but only by 21 per cent for the reverse order. If the word 'cold' was included rather than 'warm', many of the ratings inferred were different: warm–cold is a 'central trait', which has an effect on many other traits. All good things are assumed to go together, a phenomenon familiar to interviewers as 'halo effect' – when an interviewer forms a generally favourable impression of a candidate for some reason and makes all ratings on specific scales very favourable. This leads to a lot of inaccuracy. If we think about it, people are very complex and not always consistent; the best individuals sometimes do things which are less admirable, and have their weak points, and vice versa. We shall take up this theme again in the next chapter.

However, the warm–cold dimension does not lead to

inferences about ability – showing that people have definite ideas about which dimensions go together. We bring our social knowledge and expectations to help us interpret others, which saves a lot of effort and makes the world seem more predictable. It has been said that we are 'cognitive misers'. However, my colleague Mansur Lalljee says that much of the research in this area has treated people as 'cognitive hermits', since it has been carried out on subjects in isolation rather than in true social situations.

These expectations, cognitive constructs or 'schemas' take several forms. They may be dimensions in which we are particularly interested, because of our orientation to social interaction, e.g. as dominant or submissive; or because of our job, e.g. teachers look for ability and diligence, psychiatrists for signs of mental disorder. An important source of schemas is the way we see ourselves, the 'self-schema'; others are then seen as similar to the self or contrasted with it (Markus, 1977). People become most accurate at assessing whatever qualities concern them most – anti-Semites are better at identifying Jews, for example. The categorization needs to be made because an anti-Semitic person will use quite different social techniques with Jews and Gentiles, and he wants to know which to select. Precisely the same is true of a person for whom differences of social class, or of intelligence, are of importance. When others are assessed on such favourite schemas, not only is there greater accuracy for this dimension, but judgements are made faster, more inferences are made and there is better memory for schema-consistent behaviour of the other (Fiske and Taylor, 1991).

Women focus on overall evaluation (i.e. whether they like a person) and social style, men concentrate on abilities, achievement and status, except when judging romantic partners.

The constructs an individual uses may be extremely weird and private. Whole groups have their constructs, like *saved–not saved*. Some people use very simple category systems, with only one or two dimensions, such as *nice–nasty, in the army–not in the army*. Others may use a considerable number of independent dimensions; a teacher might classify pupils as *intelligent–unintelligent, creative–uncreative, hard-working–lazy, neurotic–stable, socially skilled–socially unskilled*, etc. Those who use only a few dimensions will collapse the other possible ones and suffer from 'halo effect'. A more complex impression makes it possible to handle the other person in a more effective way; for example, if a teacher decided that a pupil was *intelligent, lazy* and *unstable*, this would enable him to select appropriate social skills. Thus people differ in 'cognitive complexity', which may be defined in terms of the number of independent dimensions they use.

Another way of categorizing others is in terms of types, not only as male or female, black or white, but in terms of a whole hierarchy of sub-types (Andersen and Klatzky, 1987). It is found that people use intermediate levels, i.e. several kinds of extravert, of black person or religious person. These are not exclusive categories but 'fuzzy sets', represented by prototypical members or by a number of actual examples of the type (Fiske and Taylor, 1991). Types can also be based on significant others, in close relationships.

Different constructs are used in different situations. Forgas, Argyle and Ginsburg (1979) found that members of a psychology research group, for informal chat over coffee, used *extraversion* and *evaluation*. At seminars, on the other hand, they categorized each other in terms of *dominance, creativity* and *supportiveness*. Furthermore, different traits are used to describe different groups of people, such as girlfriends, children, sporting friends and professors (Argyle, Ginsburg, Forgas and Campbell, 1981).

Research on schemas draws attention to the effect of preconceived ideas, producing perceptions of others biased towards stereotypes. However, our perceptions of others do take account of the individual properties of target persons. They are 'data-driven' as well as governed by 'top-down' inferences. Stereotypes are less important the more information is available.

Impressions of others are more or less subject to bias, depending on the mood of the observer. Forgas (1992) has found that induction of happy or depressed moods by hypnotism or other methods has a strong effect on how people view videotapes of themselves and others. In a happy mood people 'saw more positive, skilled and fewer negative, unskilled behaviours than did sad subjects, both in their own and in others' performance'. However, sad subjects also saw their own behaviour as much worse than the behaviour of others. We shall see later that depressed patients think that they are rejected by others more than is the case (p. 236). Forgas also found that these effects of mood were greater in judging the behaviour of atypical persons, where more cognitive work was needed to make judgements.

Expectations have a similar effect. We saw earlier that a target person who is expected to be 'warm' is perceived more favourably. These errors can be 'self-fulfilling' – the target person behaves in the expected way. Snyder, Tanke and Berscheid (1977) asked male subjects to talk over the phone to a female who was described as very attractive, or not; in the attractive condition the voice styles elicited from the females were rated as those of attractive women. However, if a target person initially behaves in a manner which is clearly different from what was expected, there can be a contrast effect; if warm was expected, he or she is now seen as definitely cold (Zebrowitz, 1990).

*The accuracy of person perception* Forming accurate impressions of others is important in all social situations, because we need to know how to handle people and how they will react. For professional interviewers and clinical psychologists, however, forming accurate impressions is their job. What is meant by 'accurate' here? It is possible to compare the judgements of interviewers or observers with results obtained from psychological tests or from self-ratings and questionnaire. The main sources of error in person perception in general are as follows:

1 Paying too much attention to physical cues – beards, attractiveness; etc. Any inference made should be checked against relevant samples of the target's behaviour.
2 Applying stereotypes based on class, race, age or membership of particular groups.
3 Halo effects, based for example on the other person coming from the same school or college as oneself; trying too hard to construct a consistent picture of the other; thinking all good things go together; being unwilling to recognize that he may be intelligent *and* lazy, neurotic *and* generous.

4 Assuming a person will behave in the same way in other situations, overlooking situational causes of his observed behaviour, including the behaviour of the observer himself.

5 There is a tendency for negative points about a person to be given more weight than positive ones. Bad acts are taken as evidence for general badness, failures given more importance than successes.

6 An error common in mental patients and other socially inadequate individuals is simply not looking enough at, paying enough attention to or being sufficiently interested in, other people.

Accurate person perception may be impaired by the efforts of the target person to present a favourable impression, for example in an interview, though the same applies to many other situations. In a selection interview the interviewer can pursue the truth about a candidate with persistent follow-up questions to get a detailed account of his or her performance in relevant past situations.

One problem here lies in separating *differential* accuracy from simply knowing the right average score for the population. Cook (1979) measured differential accuracy and found that judges could place target persons in nearly the right order for extraversion, after seeing a short sample of their behaviour on videotape, but could not do the same for neuroticism, which evidently is not so easily visible. Cline and Richards (1960) showed judges films of target persons being interviewed and asked them to predict, or rather *post*dict, the behaviour of these rather carefully studied target persons in a number of situations. They found that some judges were consistently better than others.

A more basic problem is that people vary greatly in their behaviour in different situations, as will be shown in the next chapter; extraverts are not extraverted all the time.

One kind of prediction of great practical importance is that of success at jobs, each job involving a range of situations. We shall discuss the accuracy of personnel-selection interviewers later (p. 253). These results can be summarized by saying that interviewers can add a lot to other sources of information, but that their predictions are far from perfect and that interviewers disagree a lot with each other.

### INTERPRETING BEHAVIOUR

As well as perceiving behaviour, we go further and decide what caused it, who was responsible. This is important because the interpretation may affect our future actions. Did X fail the exam because he didn't work hard enough, wasn't clever enough, was badly taught, or because the examiners were unfair? Different actions will follow on the part of parents or teachers, for example, depending on the interpretation chosen. This is not necessarily an accurate assessment of the true cause of the behaviour, but is simply what those involved believe it to be. Individuals are not making attributions all the time, but they do it when something unexpected happens and especially when things go wrong.

Early research on attribution was mainly about how people decide that someone acted from an internal cause – that an act was due to a disposition rather than to external causes, such as social pressure. 'Attribution theory' puts forward the factors which indicate someone is acting from internal causes:

1 He behaves in a way which is against his interests, such as being rude to the boss.

2 He appears to be free of social pressures; for instance, when a high-status person conforms he is seen as freely deciding to change his mind; when a low-status person conforms he is seen as yielding to social pressure (Thibaut and Riecken, 1955).

3 His behaviour is consistent, e.g. he is nice to the secretary in a variety of ways and places.

4 His behaviour is distinctive, e.g. he is nicer to one important person than to another with whom he has the same formal relationship.

5 He is the only person to behave in this way.

A number of systematic errors or biases have been found in the way people make these internal–external decisions:

1 It is assumed that behaviour is mainly due to persons rather than to situations; behaviour is thought of as generated by personality traits even when it isn't. Ross, Amabile and Steinmetz (1977) found that subjects, chosen at random to ask quiz questions to which they happened to know the answers, were thought to be cleverer than those, also chosen at random, who tried to answer them. Thinking in terms of persons and their traits, rather than situations and *their* traits, may be a pervasive feature of Western culture.

2 Performers are likelier to think that their own behaviour is more due to situational causes ('I fell over because it was slippery') than is that of others but performers are as likely as observers to think the person factors are important ('I slipped because I was clumsy') (Watson, 1982). This is because the performer is attending to the environmental situation, while an observer is attending to the performer's behaviour.

3 Success is attributed by an actor to his own ability or efforts, while failure is attributed to the difficulty of the task (Weiner, 1980).

4 If a member of the in-group does something good, this is thought to be due to him; if he fails or does something bad, it is attributed to situational factors. The opposite happens for the activities of out-group members (See Figure 4.1 (b)). Racial discrimination (by whites) is thought by blacks to be mainly due to the behaviour of whites; whites think it is due to both blacks and whites (Hewstone and Jaspars, 1982).

Attributions are often more complex than just deciding whom to blame. If subjects are presented with a puzzling piece of behaviour they make up possible explanations, based on their own experience and common sense. 'X is found standing on his head': this could be because he is doing yoga, has been hypnotized, has been sponsored for charity, etc. (Lalljee, Lamb, Furnham and Jaspars, 1984).

*The effects of attribution* After a traffic accident, a family row or any other social event it is often found that people report what happened differently, or have different ideas about whose fault the accident was, who started the row or why people acted as they did. Deciding on responsibility and blame is what the law is all about, and different groups may see the same events differently. Hastorf and Cantril (1954) studied a football game between Dartmouth and Princeton. The game became very rough and several players were injured. After the match 36 per cent of Dartmouth students and 86 per cent of Princeton students interviewed thought that the Dartmouth team had started the rough play. This shows that interpretations can be different in important respects, and are influenced by group memberships or attitudes of perceivers. This is a basic problem in all conflicts between groups.

Football fans and the authorities also see things differently. A study of British football fans by Marsh et al. (1978) found that they see their behaviour on the terraces as an orderly, rule-governed affair, where they have fun making threats and rude gestures at supporters of the other side but have no intention of inflicting any bodily harm. The press and authorities, on the other hand, see football 'hooligans' as extremely violent, uncontrolled savages, who need to be kept in order by large numbers of police, wire cages and £1,000 fines. This situation has become complicated by the fact that the fans pretend to themselves and others that the official theory is true, and gain some satisfaction from the enhanced image of themselves as a frightening menace to society.

Differences of attribution affect the smaller battles of marriage too. Distressed spouses each think that the main cause of the trouble is the other spouse's behaviour – their selfishness, negative intentions or personality failures. Longitudinal studies have found that these negative attributions, especially those held by women, cause later marital distress (Bradbury and Fincham, 1990).

A person's attributional style also has consequences for himself. It is well established that depressed people blame themselves for bad things that happen to them, and expect these to keep on happening. It has been found, however, that this self-blaming style is not the cause of depression but rather a result or aspect of it. 'Attributional therapy' has nevertheless been developed, in which clients are persuaded to stop blaming themselves for

everything that goes wrong, to look for other causes, especially
ones that are controllable, and to take credit for things that go
well. Success has been reported with students who do badly at
college, people at work and depressed patients (e.g. Wilson
and Linville, 1982). Our happiness research has found that
happy people do not blame themselves for bad things, but on
the contrary think that they are responsible for the good things
that happen to them. We are trying to find out whether this
is a cause or effect of happiness, or simply part of the
condition.

Attributional style affects several other areas of behaviour.
Achievement motivation may be the result of attributing one's
failures to lack of effort rather than to lack of ability, so that the
individual tries harder next time (Weiner, 1980). Attributional
styles affect health behaviour: if a person thinks that his illness is
due to controllable aspects of his life or environment, he is better
able to cope with it successfully than someone who thinks it is
due to some unalterable aspect of his personality (like smoking
seen as an addiction) or is due to fate and has no known cause.
Health beliefs, such as whether a treatment will be effective and
how likely one is to get a certain disease, have been shown to be
predictors of whether someone will for example have a flu
injection or a health check-up, or stop smoking or excessive
drinking.

Attributions can affect emotional states in several interesting
ways. An experiment by Schachter and Singer (1962) showed
that people use situational cues to interpret a state of physiological
arousal – 'misattribution' of a physiological condition. Valins
(1966) played amplified sounds of heartbeats to subjects, and
found that he could influence how much young men thought
they liked slides of nude females by speeding up the heartbeats
they heard – making them think that they were more emotionally aroused than they were. In another experiment he made
subjects feel less afraid of snakes, by the same method. While
misattribution techniques can certainly reduce anxiety in laboratory experiments, they have not been found so successful in
patients, and there is an alternative explanation – that subjects in
the feedback experimental groups are simply better informed

about which symptoms to expect, which reduces their anxiety (Cotton, 1981).

Facial expression also affects the emotions we experience. Izard (1971) has put forward the view that it plays an important part in this process: a situation produces a biological response at lower levels of the nervous system, causing a facial expression which provides information resulting in the subjective experience of emotions. This theory has been supported by a number of experiments in which subjects adopt a facial expression for a few minutes and are then found to be experiencing the appropriate emotion (Laird, 1974) – 'Smile, and you will feel happy'! Lanzetta et al. (1976) found that subjects asked not to show pain in their faces felt less pain from electric shocks and experienced a smaller physiological reaction. Similarly, people find jokes funnier if they have been aroused by pedalling on an exercycle and if they hear canned laughter (preferably in the right ear). They find erotic films more exciting after an exercycle ride, especially with a four-minute delay, so that they don't realize that their state of arousal is responsible (Zillman, 1983).

## FURTHER READING

Hewstone, M., *Causal Attribution*, Blackwell, Oxford, 1989.
Zebrowitz, L. A., *Social Perception*, Open University Press, Milton Keynes, 1990.

## CHAPTER 5

# THE EFFECT OF PERSONALITY AND SITUATION ON SOCIAL BEHAVIOUR

It is common experience that individuals differ in their style of social behaviour in a number of ways, and it is usual to interpret this variation in terms of personality traits, like extraversion and assertiveness. Furthermore, the old and the young, schizophrenics and criminals, have their distinctive social styles. Social behaviour also varies between situations – people are noisier and more talkative at pubs than in church, and they engage in quite different behaviour at seminars, Scottish balls and cricket matches. It is sometimes easier to influence behaviour by changing the situation than by trying to change the people. A prison governor stopped inmates fighting by finding out where conflicts occurred – in this instance at the corners of corridors – and modifying these areas, by rounding off the brickwork so that hurrying prisoners didn't bump into one another, a prime cause of fights.

In this chapter we shall examine how features of persons combine with features of situations to generate social behaviour.

## PERSONALITY TRAITS

The first dimension to be studied by psychologists was intelligence. It was found that a person is fairly consistent in his ability to tackle different kinds of problems, and tests were constructed which sampled this ability over a number of domains – verbal, numerical, etc. The population was found to be distributed in a 'normal' way, as with height and other biological variables. This model has been followed in the analysis of dimensions of personality like extraversion and neuroticism.

Factor analysis is an important part of the procedure. A number of measures are assembled, which may be self-report ratings of behaviour in different situations, experimental tasks or ratings by others, all related to the dimension being studied. Factor analysis then shows how many underlying dimensions there are.

Personality traits are often measured by questionnaires, which are very convenient and may themselves be based on factor analysis of the items. There are other kinds of measure, and we described projection test measures of motivation in Chapter 1. However, tests need to be validated against better measures of the trait in question – tests for neuroticism against the judgements of psychiatrists, for example. Tests of extraversion, assertiveness or other social traits need to be validated against observation of behaviour. It follows that successful tests of such dimensions will be predictive of social behaviour. It should be emphasized that personality is not the only predictor of such behaviour, since this depends also on the situation and the other individuals present.

What are the origins of personality traits? How do some people become extraverted or assertive? Many of these traits have a genetic component: children resemble their parents, even when adopted by other families, and identical twins are more similar to each other than fraternal twins. Socialization experiences in the family are a second source. We showed earlier how aggression is partly the result of rejection and physical punishment in childhood, combined with permissiveness for aggression (p. 16); We shall examine the childhood origins of extraversion shortly. Personality can undergo changes at major life crises, such as adolescence, and it can change and develop further in later life. For example work experience of powerlessness and lack of autonomy leads to a high level of 'external control', based on the belief that one cannot control what is going to happen (Kohn and Schooler, 1983). Various forms of psychological treatment can alter personality too.

Sometimes the psychological basis of a trait is understood. Internal–external control is fairly straightforward: it is a set of generalized expectancies, based on past experience, as to how far one can control things (Rotter, 1966). We shall meet this dimension later, since it is one of the most important sources of 'hardiness', the capacity to stand up to stress. We saw earlier that achievement motivation is probably a kind of secondary drive, in which the goals of success and achievement acquire reward properties and can energize and direct behaviour (pp. 20–21).

## HOW CONSISTENT ARE INDIVIDUALS ACROSS SITUATIONS?

For many years psychologists believed that personality traits could enable them to predict an individual's social behaviour. It was gradually discovered that tests give quite modest predictions of social performance in any particular situation, rarely above .30. Personnel selection often does better than this, but again there seems to be an upper limit of about .60 for such predictions (de Wolff and van den Bosch, 1984). This realization caused a minor revolution in thinking about personality in the 1970s, and led to new research.

There is not much consistency between different single acts by the same individual. However, aggregation, i.e. averaging behaviour over a number of occasions, produces more stability, so that average lateness over seven days is an excellent predictor of average lateness over another seven days. The same applies to aggregates of different but related behaviours, such as forms of aggressiveness, extraversion or different religious behaviours. Such aggregates are stable over time and correlate with relevant questionnaire measures – which are themselves aggregates of items (Ajzen, 1987).

However, the way to understand variability between situations is to analyse and take account of the situation. To give an example of the way personality and situation might jointly affect behaviour, consider three mythical people, Tom, Dick and Harry, who have different tendencies concerning lateness. If persons and situations are equally important, their typical lateness might be like this:

| minutes late for | lecture | tutorial | coffee | person means |
|---|---|---|---|---|
| Tom | 0 | 3 | 6 | 3 |
| Dick | 3 | 6 | 9 | 6 |
| Harry | 6 | 9 | 12 | 9 |
| situation means | 3 | 6 | 9 | 6 |

Table 5.1   How personality and situation might affect lateness.

However, there is a further problem. The table above shows our three friends as consistently late: Tom is always earliest, Harry always latest. We now know that people are not nearly as consistent as this. Harry might be keen on lectures and always arrive early, while Tom is very bored by lectures and is always late.

The traditional trait model has been replaced by the interactionist model of personality (Endler and Magnusson, 1976). This model recognizes the existence of stable, underlying features of personality, but says that these interact with the properties of particular situations to produce behaviour. This is quite different from the earlier model; it is not saying that a person has a typical or average tendency to dominance which he generalizes across situations, for example, but that he has certain drives and other aspects of personality which may or may not produce dominant behaviour on a particular occasion. Authoritarian personalities illustrate the point. An authoritarian bullies less powerful or important people and is submissive to more powerful people; there is no question of the generalization of similar behaviour.

Attempts have been made to test these two models by finding the relative importance of persons, situations and P × S interaction. This is done by observing, or asking for reports of, the behaviour of a number of individuals in a number of situations, and calculating how much of the variation can be explained by persons and situations. The averages for a number of studies are as follows:

persons      31.6%
situations   21.5%
P × S        46.9%

(Furnham and Jaspars, 1983)

The overall results are very clear: persons and situations are both important, but P × S interaction is more important than either. It is now recognized that this kind of research cannot establish whether personality or situation is more important, for various reasons (Argyle, 1976). Nevertheless, the results clearly favour the interactionist position.

In order to predict how a particular person will behave in a particular situation we need to know something else: the equation showing how P and S interact, which is of the general form

$$B = f(P,S)$$

This states that the amount of some form of behaviour is a mathematical function of personality and situation variables. Such equations can be given by graphs showing how behaviour is a function of person and situation. Below is an example, from a study of reactions to role conflict (Figure 5.1). Notice that only people with high neurotic anxiety are affected by role conflict. Notice also that experienced conflict is greater when actual role conflict is high (situation), and for people with high neurotic anxiety (personality), but is most affected by an interaction between the two (P × S).

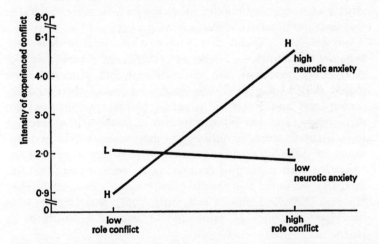

Figure 5.1   Effect of role conflict and neurotic anxiety on intensity of experienced conflict (Kahn, Wolfe, Quinn and Snoek, 1964).

A further part of the story is that traits are manifested in some situations but not in others. Kenrick and colleagues (1990) found that subjects thought they could demonstrate intellectual traits in academic settings but not in athletic or play settings, while dominance could be displayed in sport and business but not in church or in the street.

*Which people are most consistent?* Is it not the case that some people are more consistent across situations than others, so that there are at least some individuals for whom the trait model works? To begin with, individuals at the extremes of any dimension are more consistent than those nearer the middle: very intelligent people can get all the tests right for example, while less intelligent people get only some of them right. Persons high in internal control are found to be less affected by social pressures, though they are influenced by reasoned arguments; they engage in more cognitive activity, such as being alert, asking questions and trying to find out about situations. They will stick to their beliefs and values, but do not necessarily display the same social behaviour in different situations; coping successfully with a situation may require social moves which are specific to that situation (Phares, 1976).

Snyder (1979) found that people who monitor their own behaviour carefully, and who are consequently very aware of their effect on others, are less consistent, but generally more highly skilled, than those who make a point of their straight-forwardness and sincerity (p. 218). Mental patients, perhaps surprisingly, are *more* consistent than normals; as they recover they become more inconsistent – they adapt to the requirements of different situations better. Women are somewhat less consistent than men, thus confirming an ancient piece of folk-lore, and we found that the British are more consistent than the Japanese (Argyle, Shimoda and Little, 1978), mainly because of the elaborate rules of etiquette for particular situations in Japan.

So personality does affect how people behave, though they behave differently in different situations. However, it is more complicated than this, because personality operates in more than one way. In the first place, people do not usually enter situations because psychologists put them there, but because they choose to enter them, and their choice reflects their personality. An example of this is the choice of situations made by extraverts: they select leisure occasions involving social interaction, like parties and dances, much more often than do introverts, and they spend more time playing games, walking and pursuing other physical activities (Furnham, 1981). Another example of choice is the selection of occupation: people decide on jobs where they can be creative, help others or make money, and this reflects their pattern of interests and values (Argyle, 1989). Authoritarian students at American universities often leave to join military academies.

When a person has chosen a situation or a series of situations in this way, it also affects his personality. Runyan (1978) has shown how the stages through which a person becomes a drug addict can be traced as a series of choices of situations, each of which has implications for the next condition of the personality. For instance, at the period of regular use, the drug is readily available, most friends are drug users and the desire for the drug is intense. Each step that is taken creates a quite new P × S equation, by changing the situation, and eventually changing the state of the personality. It is possible to anticipate such changes, or to bring them about deliberately, by committing oneself to a series of situational experiences, such as going to one kind of educational establishment or another, one kind of job or another, or a course of encounter group meetings.

A second problem is that, as well as choosing situations, people can change them once they are there. Some people turn every situation into a party, or try to. Informal situations, where a wide range of behaviour is permitted, can be modified, or 'redefined', quite a lot in this way; more formal situations cannot be changed much. Very often, individuals are not aware of the extent of their impact on others. They think that they are constantly encountering others who are bad-tempered, shy or very friendly, for example, without realizing that they themselves are the real cause of this behaviour (Wachtel, 1973). We will discuss below the problems of predicting the behaviour of two people in combination.

Behaviour sometimes cannot be understood apart from the

situation in which it occurs, and the same is true of the personalities of those involved. The behaviour of, for example, John McEnroe and Arthur Scargill takes place in certain very distinctive settings. In order to understand or predict their behaviour we need to appreciate the properties of these settings. Traits like extraversion, or categories of behaviour like amount of talk, don't help very much.

### THE ANALYSIS OF SITUATIONS

It is now clear that the situation is an important factor in the generation of social behaviour. We need to measure, classify or otherwise analyse situations, in order to explain and predict the behaviour that occurs in them.

We can look at situations in terms of their elements, and this helps in understanding their different properties. Socially unskilled people often fail to understand them. Situations are rather like games: they have goals, rules and repertoires of moves, and they require special skills. If someone wanted to play, for example, American football, he would want to know how to win, what the rules are and so on. Clients for social skills training often seek similar instructions about parties, interviews or other occasions which they find difficult.

Social situations probably exist as regular events in the culture because they enable common needs to be met. The rules and other component features of situations are functional because they make this process easier. The main components of situations are listed and discussed below.

*Goals* In all situations there are certain goals which are commonly obtainable. It is often fairly obvious what these are, but socially inadequate people may simply not know what parties are for, for example, or may think that the purpose of a selection interview is vocational guidance.

We have studied the main goals in a number of common situations by asking samples of people to rate the importance of various goals, and then carrying out factor analysis. The main goals are usually:

social acceptance;
food, drink and other bodily needs;
task goals specific to the situation.

There may be conflicts between the goals of different people, for example between salespersons and customers, managers and union representatives, interviewers and candidates. There may even be some conflict between the goals of *one* person, for example between task goals and the social goal of keeping on good terms with the other person (Argyle, Furnham and Graham, 1981).

*Rules* All situations have rules about what may or may not be done in them. Socially inexperienced people are often ignorant or mistaken about the rules. It would obviously be impossible to play a game without knowing the rules, and the same applies to social situations.

By a rule we mean a shared belief that certain things should or should not be done. Figure 5.2 shows a cluster analysis of the rules we found for Oxford psychology students. The top cluster consists of those which apply to nearly all situations: should be friendly, should be polite, etc. The last cluster shows those for sherry parties and similar occasions: should dress smartly, should keep to cheerful topics of conversation, etc. There were two specific rules for going to the doctor: make sure you are clean and tell the truth. Some of these rules are clearly functional in relation to the goals of situations.

*Repertoire of elements* Every situation defines certain moves as relevant. For example, at a seminar it is relevant to show slides, make long speeches, draw on the blackboard, etc.; if moves appropriate to a cricket match or a Scottish ball were made, they would be ignored or regarded as totally bizarre. We have found sixty-five to ninety main elements used in several situations, like going to the doctor. We have also found that the grouping of elements varies between situations. For example, asking questions about work and about private life are quite similar on a date, but totally different in the office (Argyle, Graham and Kreckel, 1982).

108     *The Psychology of Interpersonal Behaviour*

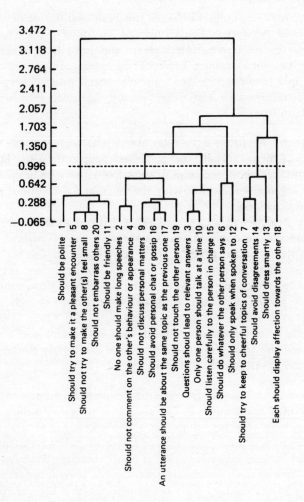

Figure 5.2   Clusters of rules for Oxford psychology students (from Argyle et al., 1979).

*Environmental setting* Environmental psychologists sometimes assess situations in purely physical terms. It has been found, for example, that if people meet in a room at a temperature of 93.5°F, or with four square feet per person, they will like each other less than in a larger and cooler room (Griffitt and Veitch, 1971). However, the physical features of the environment work in another way, by their symbolic meaning. A room decorated in red and yellow suggests a warm emotional mood; placing some people at a greater height, as on a high table, suggests dominance; a room with a concrete floor, battered furniture and a bare light-bulb suggests prison or interrogation, not love, work, social life or committee meetings. Many situations involve special props; a lecture needs a blackboard and slide projector, while a party needs quite different equipment.

*Concepts* In order to play cricket one must know the meaning of 'innings', 'over', 'out' and so on. In order to carry out psychotherapy one needs to know about 'resistance' and 'transference'. As a chess player becomes more experienced he acquires more elaborate concepts, like 'fork', 'discovered check' and so on. Similar knowledge is needed in social situations proper, and perhaps the kinds of concepts introduced in this book provide what is necessary for many of them. Examples are 'mutual gaze', 'terminal gaze', 'synchronizing', 'reinforcement', 'remedial sequence', 'informal speech' and 'self-presentation'. There are concepts to describe different kinds of person, and different kinds of situation, as well as ongoing social interaction. There are also concepts related to the task, such as 'amendment', 'straw vote' and 'nem con' for committee meetings.

*Roles* In most situations people adopt roles specific to the occasion, like those of doctor and patient, salesman and customer. The goals can be similar, but the rules different, for those in distinct roles, like the chairman, secretary or treasurer of a club. There may be roles created by the situation, like those of guest and host, and also more general ones, created by age and sex for example.

*Special skills* In order to play games like ice hockey, polo or water polo, certain skills have to be mastered. Many social situations require special skills, as in the case of various kinds of public speaking and interviewing or such everyday situations as dates and parties. A person with little experience of a particular situation may find that he lacks the necessary skills.

This method of analysing situations opens the way to a number of useful applications. Some forms of crime are most easily tackled by situational modifications; for example, shoplifting can be greatly reduced by closed-circuit TV and by chaining up the goods, vandalism by buildings which have better lighting and surveillance, stronger materials and rougher surfaces (Clarke and Mayhew, 1980). Social skills training for mental patients can be focused on the situations which they find troublesome (p. 230). Difficult situations anywhere can be modified by altering the physical setting, the rules or other components (Argyle, Furnham and Graham, 1981).

## SELECTING SOCIAL BEHAVIOUR TO DEAL WITH THE OTHER

We have already seen that the same person varies his behaviour from one situation to another – parties, interviews, etc. – in keeping with their different rules and conventions. People also vary their behaviour according to the age, sex and social class of those present, and in accordance with other role-relationships. Some people behave so differently towards men and women that they seem to undergo a personality change when moving from one kind of encounter to the other. A young man may be very relaxed with other men but terrified of women, or aggressive and competitive towards men and very amorous and at ease with women. Such differences of behaviour are learnt in the course of relations with parents, and later with male and female members of the peer group during adolescence.

Age is a more differentiated variable than sex: some people have alternative ways of behaving towards young children, older children, teenagers, young adults, etc., with any number of fine variations; others may use broader divisions, e.g. between those who are older or younger than themselves.

Social class, especially in Britain, is an important dimension for the classification of others. We discuss social interaction between classes in the next chapter (p. 157).

Social class and age each have two separate effects on the social techniques adopted. Firstly there is the question of whether the other person is higher or lower, older or younger, secondly of how great the distance. There may be certain age or class groups for which a person has virtually no social techniques at all – he is simply unable to interact with members of them. This can be observed among some adults in relation to children, some upper middle-class and working-class people in relation to each other, some adolescents in relation to adults, and many children in relation to adults outside the family circle. This no doubt reflects a lack of experience with the groups in question, combined with the discovery that the familiar social techniques are completely useless.

Introverts and extraverts need to be handled differently; experiments with schoolchildren show that introverts respond better to blame while extraverts respond better to praise. Different motivations in others means that they will strive for different goals in social situations and can be rewarded in different ways. One may need a strong leader, another a submissive follower, a third needs acceptance of his self-image, and so on. For those very low in affiliative needs the usual social rewards will not be satisfactory.

Variations in anxiety, or neuroticism, mean that some people will be very ill at ease in social situations. When with them it is important to adopt social techniques which will reduce their anxiety, such as being very friendly and relaxed, and keeping to harmless topics. Experienced interviewers may spend a large part of an interview doing just this.

Attitudes to authority and to the peer group are important. Juvenile delinquents are often very hostile to authority but behave quite differently with members of their peer group. Those in authority can only handle such boys and girls if they adopt the manner of an older member of the peer group and make special efforts to win their confidence, such as taking them into their confidence or granting special privileges.

### THE CO-ORDINATION OF SOCIAL BEHAVIOUR

Two people may meet, each with his own social drives and social skills, but there will be no proper interaction unless the two sets of techniques mesh together in a synchronized and co-ordinated manner. If both talk all the time, or if both shout orders or ask questions, to give three obvious cases, there cannot be said to be social interaction at all. Between such extreme cases and a well-conducted interview or a conversation between friends, there are degrees of co-ordination of behaviour. Rather low on the scale, for example, would be conversation with a schizophrenic, with long pauses, irrelevant remarks and inappropriate emotions being expressed. Synchronization is necessary along a number of different dimensions for smooth and motivationally satisfying interaction to take place.

1 *Amount of speech* In most conversations between two people there is enough talk for nearly all of the time to be filled. If they speak more than this, there will be interruption and double-speaking; if they speak less than this, there will be periods of silence.

There also has to be synchronizing of the speed or tempo of interaction − the actual rate of speaking in words per second, the shortness of the interval before replying and the rates of movement of eyes, facial expression and other parts of the body.

2 *Dominance* This is a matter partly of who speaks more and partly of the degrees of deference with which A and B treat each other − of whose ideas are to be taken more seriously and of who shall for purposes of the encounter be regarded as the more important person. If A and B both want to be the dominant member there is incompatibility of styles; both may give orders but none are obeyed.

3 *Intimacy* This we have discussed previously (p. 30) and shown to be a matter of physical closeness, eye contact, conversation on personal topics and so on. If A uses techniques correspond-

ing to greater intimacy than B, A will feel that B is cold, formal and standoffish, while B will feel that A is intrusive and over-familiar.

4 *Emotional tone* If A is elated and euphoric while B is anxious or depressed, there is incongruity; to everything that happens A and B are likely to react in quite different ways, involving incompatible reactions and remarks.

5 *Role-relations and definitions of the situation* Two people must agree on the role-relation between them. If one is to be a teacher the other must behave like a pupil; if one is to be an interviewer then the other must behave like an interviewee.

6 *Task, topic and definition of the situation* Two people must agree on what the encounter is for, just as they must agree to play the same game, not different ones. They also have to agree on the different phases or episodes of the encounter.

There are a number of forces internal to social interaction which help to produce co-ordinated behaviour. One is *accommodation*, whereby people shift towards similar speech styles if they want to be accepted and understood by the other (pp. 68–9). Interaction may lead to *imitation* of one another, and the unwitting *rewarding* of behaviour that is liked.

Can we predict how two people will relate to each other, for example who will talk more? It is found that A's talkativeness is related, rather weakly, to his talkativeness in other similar situations; it is also *inversely* related to the normal talkativeness of B, i.e. a normally silent person talks more with silent people, a normally talkative person talks less with normally talkative people (Borgatta and Bales, 1953). Clearly people often have to shift from their average behaviour in order to accommodate others. But who will shift the most? There may be a 'struggle for the floor', in which they interrupt or try to shout each other down. When A does this he frustrates B; he may make B less friendly or even cause him to leave the situation. However, A can interrupt B safely under two conditions:

1  if A has sufficient power over B;
2  if A has sufficient skill to interrupt without upsetting B.

How can we predict the dominance relations between A and B? Dominance consists partly of need (e.g. for power) and assertiveness skills; it includes taking decisions, influencing the other and controlling the pattern of behaviour, as well as usually talking more. Simply measuring A's 'dominance' gives a rather poor prediction of his dominance in relation to B. A better prediction can be made from role variables: the person who is older, male rather than female, or of higher social class is likely to be dominant (Breer, 1960), though the dominance of males seems to be diminishing. If these variables are held constant the person with the highest score on questionnaire measures of extraversion, intelligence and dominance, or who knows most about the task in hand, will dominate.

Let us consider a more complex prediction of both dominance and intimacy. We will take account of the motivations of A and B in the figure below. This shows that A is strong in both dominance and affiliative needs, and prefers to be in a warm and superior relation to others. B prefers a warm and submissive relation, so they would get on smoothly together. C and D are also in equilibrium: both are hostile and C is slightly superior to D.

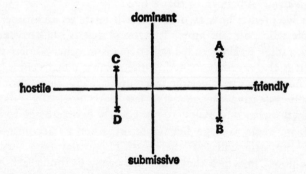

On the other hand, in the next diagram X and Y are not in equilibrium – X is friendly while Y is hostile, and both want to dominate. If Y is able to get more of his way than X, they might move to X'Y'.

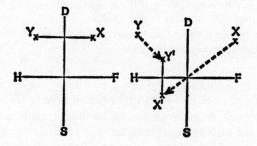

Let us take another case, where A and B play incompatible roles. For example an inexperienced interviewee thinks he has come for a pleasant chat, or to receive free vocational guidance. If one person adopts a certain role it may force the other to adopt the complementary role ('altercasting'), particularly if the first person is powerful and is in charge of the situation. In this example, if one person plays the role of interviewer the other person is more or less compelled to behave like a candidate. The interviewer can use other methods to modify the candidate's behaviour: (a) using NV signals and reinforcements to control the candidate; (b) explaining the normal procedure; and (c) controlling the candidate by the content of his remark, e.g. 'Could you tell me, *very briefly*, what you do in your spare time?'

These methods do not always work. Here is an example of someone *not* accepting the proffered role, in a situation of attempted altercasting.

PLAYBOY: How do you get your kicks these days?

DYLAN: I hire people to look into my eyes, and then I have them kick me.

PLAYBOY: And that's the way you get your kicks?

DYLAN: No. Then I forgive them, that's where my kicks come in.

PLAYBOY: Did you ever have the standard boyhood dream of growing up to be President?

DYLAN: No. When I was a boy, Harry Truman was President. Who'd want to be Harry Truman?

PLAYBOY: Well, let's suppose that you were the President. What would you accomplish during your first thousand days?

DYLAN: Well, just for laughs so long as you insist, the first thing I'd do is probably move the White House. Instead of being in Texas it'd be in the East Side of New York, McGeorge Bundy would definitely have to change his name and General McNamara would be forced to wear a coonskin cap and shades.

(Brackman, 1967)

When A is in charge he can use explicit, verbal negotiating signals about how he wants the other to behave. In most other situations such instructions would be unacceptable and ineffective; it is not usually possible to tell one's friends or colleagues to talk less or to be less dominating. Here NV negotiating signals are normally used; they have the advantage that they are small and tentative, can be easily withdrawn, can be used to explore other possible relationships without embarrassment, and operate away from the focus of conscious attention of either party (cf. Mehrabian, 1969).

### SOCIAL COMPETENCE

By social competence I mean the ability, the possession of the necessary skills, to produce the desired effects on other people in social situations. These desired effects may be to persuade the others to buy, to learn, to recover from a psychological problem, to like or admire the actor, and so on. These results are not necessarily in the public interest – skills may be used for social or antisocial purposes – and there is no evidence that social competence is a general factor: a person may be better at one task than another, e.g. interviewing v. lecturing, or in one situation than another, e.g. parties v. committees. In this section I shall discuss a variety of social competences.

There are several ways of assessing an individual's social competence. For some professional skills it is possible to use objective measures of effectiveness, like sales or other outcomes. Other measures are ratings by subordinates, role-played performances of analogue work roles as in Assessment Centres, or responses to work problems presented on video. For assessing everyday skills by patients and others there are a number of

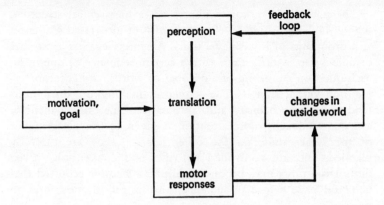

Figure 5.3   Motor skill model.

questionnaires (reviewed by Spitzberg and Cupach, 1989), though none have been widely accepted. We have used lists of up to thirty difficult everyday situations, which the client rates for difficulty or avoidance (such as 'going to parties', 'complaining to a neighbour about noise'). Clients can be asked to role-play simple social situations and their performance carefully studied; they can be interviewed to find out what they say their problems are.

Social competence has a number of components.

*The social skill model* I want to suggest that there is a useful analogy between motor skills, like riding a bicycle, and social skills, like making friends, conducting conversations and interviewing. In each case the performer seeks certain goals (e.g. make other talk a lot), makes skilled moves (e.g. asks closed questions), perceives the effects of this (e.g. short replies) and takes corrective action (e.g. asks more open-ended questions). The model emphasizes the goals of interactors, the specific social behaviour used, and the perception of and reactions to feedback. In the example above, the questioner modified the kind of questions asked, just as a driver might adjust the steering-wheel of a car. There is continuous flexibility of behaviour in response to the behaviour of the other.

The pattern of motor responses has a hierarchical structure, where the larger, high-level units consist of integrated sequences and groupings of lower-level units. An interview has a number of phases (pp. 250ff.), each with a certain sequence of questions, each question consisting of a number of words, and accompanying non-verbal signals. The sequences making up small units tend to become habitual and 'automatized', i.e. independent of external feedback; more attention is given to the performance of the larger units on the other hand – they are carefully planned, and are controlled by rules and conventions. Even quite large units may become habitual; a lecturer reported that he could 'arise before an audience, turn his mouth loose, and go to sleep'.

In a continuous skills or 'tracking' task, feedback can be seen very clearly. A beginner motorist tries to steer the car down the road, he sees that he is about to hit the kerb, so he corrects the steering to the right; when he is more competent the same process takes place with greater speed and accuracy. The social-skill performer corrects in a similar way: a teacher who sees that his pupils have not understood the point will repeat it slowly in another way; a person who realizes that she is annoying someone by her behaviour will usually change her style of behaviour. Often the translation processes are completely unverbalized and lead to automatic sequences of behaviour with little conscious awareness – as in riding a bicycle. Or they may start as conscious rules and deliberate decisions but become automatic later, as with changing gear in a car.

Social interaction also depends on the existence of a learnt store of central translation processes. In the course of socialization people learn which social techniques will elicit affiliative or other responses from those they encounter. Research has shown how these can be improved upon in many cases; for example, to get another person to talk more the best techniques are (a) to talk less, (b) to ask open-ended questions, (c) to talk about things he is interested in, and (d) to reward anything he does say. In Chapter 10 an account will be given of the rather specialized styles of response for professional social skills.

This model has led to emphasis on the specific elements of

social performance, particularly non-verbal ones, like facial expression and gaze. However, it has become clear that verbal elements are also important, and that global aspects of performance, such as rewardingness and assertiveness, may be more important than any specific elements. We also know that a number of further processes need to be taken into account; some of these are about particular goals (e.g. assertiveness), others about particular behaviours (e.g. non-verbal communication) or about other parts of the model (e.g. cognition) (Argyle, 1993).

*Rewardingness* Social psychologists have often regarded this as the key to friendship and interpersonal attraction. Jennings (1950), in a classic study of 400 girls in a reformatory, found that the popular girls were the ones who helped, protected, cheered and encouraged others. Several theories of interpersonal attraction are based on findings like this. Leadership skills include a dimension of 'consideration', i.e. looking after the needs of group members. Marital therapy has often consisted of training spouses in providing greater rewards for each other. Mental patients, especially schizophrenics and depressives, are found to be very unrewarding, 'socially bankrupt'. Children are more likely to be popular, rather than rejected or neglected, if they produce positive social actions (e.g. affection, co-operation and concern for others), have positive social traits (e.g. being attractive, humorous and happy) and are not disruptive or aggressive (Newcomb, Bukowski and Pattee, 1993).

The effect of reinforcement in social situations is (1) to keep others in the situation or relationship; (2) to increase the others' attraction to ego; and (3) to make greater influence possible, when reinforcement is contingent on the desired behaviour.

Rewardingness can take a variety of forms. Verbal reinforcement includes praise, approval, acceptance, agreement, encouragement, sympathy. Non-verbal rewards are smiles, head nods, gaze, touch (in some situations) and tone of voice. Rewards can also take the form of help, presents, meals, advice and information. Engaging in enjoyable shared activities is also rewarding – sport, dancing, music and parties, for example (Hargie, Saunders and Dickson, 1987).

*Empathy, taking the role of the other* This has a cognitive aspect – seeing the other's point of view – and an emotional aspect – sharing and being concerned about his or her feelings. Both are important and lead to greater success, as a teacher or psychiatrist, in romantic relations and making friends. It is also an important source of helping behaviour. Davis and Oathout (1992) argued that seeing another's point of view leads to behaviour which minimizes disruption, and thus to positive reactions from others. Undue attention to self, including an inability to take much interest in others or their point of view, is found in all kinds of mental patient. In psychotherapy, interviewing and many other skills, it is important to pay careful attention to the views and feelings of others, and to display this by questions, 'reflection' and other techniques.

Empathy is linked to co-operativeness. Co-operation is taking account of the goals of others, as well as one's own, and co-ordinating behaviour so that both shall be reached. All social activities take more than one to do them, whether play (see-saw, tennis), leisure activity (dancing, singing, talking, sex) or work of most kinds. Many kinds of social skill failure can be seen as failure of co-operation.

*Social intelligence, and problem-solving* There are a number of areas of social performance where knowledge and thinking are important. We have discussed the importance of understanding the nature of social situations and their rules in this chapter. Some inexperienced individuals don't understand what a party is for or what is supposed to happen at a job interview. The same is true of relationships and their rules, to be described in Chapter 6. Some people don't understand friendship or love, don't realize the importance of loyalty, commitment or concern for the other. Professional social skills like teaching, negotiation or therapy require knowledge of the ins and outs of these relationships. Inter-cultural skills require knowledge of the other culture.

On the other hand, as we have seen, social behaviour consists partly of lower-level processes, which are partly automatic, partly outside consciousness. People cannot tell us how they manage to take turns, follow the rules of grammar, respond to small non-verbal signals, fall in love or manage other relationships, any more than they can explain how they walk or ride a bicycle. In both cases the lower levels are automatic, the higher ones governed by plans and rules.

There is fluctuation in the level at which conscious control takes over: during training, clients are made unusually aware of, for example, turn-taking cues or gaze patterns, though attention later passes to higher-level concerns. An important part of the social skill model is called 'translation', the process of using feedback information to modify behaviour: what to do if the other doesn't talk enough, becomes hostile or presents some other problem? Some tests of social skill provide a sample of problems requiring the skill, to see how the client would cope with them. One method of SST is based on problem-solving: trainees are taught how to tackle problem situations by thinking up solutions to scripted problems (Shure, 1981). Other methods of SST make use of educational methods, to increase knowledge and understanding of, for example, social relationships, or behaviour in another culture.

*Assertiveness* was discussed earlier as a form of motivation (p. 13); and the special skills involved will be described later (p. 135ff.). In a sense all social skills involve some degree of assertiveness, though this is only one aspect of social competence. The reason that it is important is that it enables people to control what happens in social encounters, to influence people without aggression and without damaging the relationship.

Another component of social competence is *non-verbal communication*; we showed in Chapter 2 that there is a general factor of positive NVC which makes individuals more rewarding and more effective in most social situations. Another component is *verbal communication*, which lies at the heart of most social behaviour; some of the complexities of verbal skills are described in Chapter 3, and the different ones needed for various professional skills in Chapter 10. *Self-presentation* is important in many skills, especially professional ones, and is discussed in Chapter 8. Some general personality traits are correlated with social competence: *extraversion* is associated with competence, and is described next; *neuroticism* and social anxiety go with social inadequacy, and are described in Chapter 9 (Argyle, 1993).

### EXTRAVERSION

In the analysis of personality in general, and not just of social behaviour, a number of general dimensions have been found. Two of these are extraversion and neuroticism. We shall deal with the social behaviour of neurotics and different kinds of mental patients in Chapter 9. There are other dimensions, which describe other aspects of social behaviour, such as assertiveness and self-consciousness, and these are described elsewhere in this book.

Extraversion is probably the most important dimension of personality for social psychology, since it is about overall sociability. It was originally thought of by Jung in a quite different context, and extensively studied by Eysenck, again with no reference to social behaviour. Eysenck developed a widely used questionnaire measure of extraversion, together with neuroticism, in the Eysenck Personality Inventory. The original version of the extraversion scale included a number of impulsiveness items, but the revised version is now all about sociability (Eysenck and Eysenck, 1985).

Extraverts are sociable, in a number of different ways:

1 Given a free choice, extraverts choose social situations and those involving physical activity. This suggests that there is a motivational factor here: extraverts enjoy and seek social situations.

2 The extravert social style is distinctive, especially with strangers. Thorne (1987) put pairs of extraverts in a room and found that they engaged in frenetic social activity; when she put two introverts in a room, they often sat in total silence. I have replicated this in practical classes. It is as if extraverts

confidently expect to get on well with people, and enjoy themselves.

3 Thorne also found that extraverts talk more, agree more, compliment others, discuss pleasant things, tell jokes and tall stories, and try to find what they have in common with each other.

4 Extraverts have a distinctive non-verbal style: they smile more, look more, speak more, faster and at higher pitch, stand nearer, are more expressive generally, and laugh more.

5 Extraversion is a source of happiness, especially in social situations. We tried to discover why, and in one study found that this was partly because they had enjoyable leisure activities of certain kinds – going to parties and dances, and belonging to teams and clubs (Argyle and Lu, 1990a). The happiness of extraverts is also partly due to their greater social skills: they are more assertive and more co-operative (Argyle and Lu, 1990b, 1991).

6 Extraverts have other social skills: they have more friends, become leaders of groups and have more social influence than introverts (Morris, 1979).

A word in praise of introverts. They have their social life too, though it is less noisy and with friends rather than strangers. Introverts have consistently been found to do better at school and academic work than extraverts. With the earlier Eysenck measure introverts were found to be less delinquent, drink and smoke less, have less sex and were less likely to take drugs; however, this may reflect the impulsive part of the scale, now removed.

The origins of extraversion lie partly in the genes, about 50 per cent according to the massive study of 12,898 pairs of twins in Sweden, by Floderus-Myrhed, Pederson and Ramuson (1980). How do these genes lead to social behaviour? Eysenck's theory of extraversion is that extraverts have low levels of cortical arousal, and seek a lot of stimulation; but it is hard to see how this could explain the pattern of social behaviour described above. The best-supported theory is by Gray (1982). He proposed that differences in the hypothalamus and hippocampus make extraverts more sensitive to rewards; other people are the most important source of reward, which gives an explanation of why extraverts seek company and are happier than introverts. This theory has some support from studies with drugs and on the effects of brain lesions.

The origins of the other 50 per cent of extraversion must lie in the environment somewhere. Studies of adopted children show that relations with the (adoptive) mother are important, more so than relations with the father or siblings. Early warm relations with mothers at twelve to eighteen months – 'secure attachment' – are found to lead to the children being friendly and socially outgoing, and co-operating with unfamiliar peers, at two and a half to three years of age (Sroufe et al., 1983). It might be expected that children from large families would be more extraverted; in fact there is a small difference in the opposite direction – only children are the most extraverted. Perhaps they get more practice with strangers, or with the peer group.

Extraversion is fairly stable over time, and predictable over long time periods. However, it can still change. In a four-year longitudinal study in Australia, happy events with friends and at work predicted increases of extraversion (Headey, Holstrom and Wearing, 1985).

Is extraversion a collection of habits, a group of skills or a kind of motivation? It is probably all three. There is evidently a motivational aspect, similar to the needs for affiliation and intimacy, described earlier (p. 10): Extraverts choose social situations and they want to interact with people. They have certain social skills, for making friends and influencing people. And their behaviour is partly learnt – a set of learnt ways of dealing with people and situations, a set of learnt expectations.

### GENDER DIFFERENCES IN SOCIAL BEHAVIOUR

There are quite marked differences in the social behaviour of men and women. We looked at some of the differences in NVC in Chapter 2. Women smile a lot more (50 per cent more in some studies), laugh more, look more, touch each other more are generally more expressive, have higher pitched voices, take much more trouble over their appearance, use more self-touching nervous gestures and finer hand movements; and others approach them more closely. Men use more expansive bodily movements, adopt postures which take up a lot more space, have louder voices and interrupt more. Women are more accurate decoders, but are also 'polite' decoders; that is, they see what they are intended to see, and either fail to see or choose to overlook 'leakage' of suppressed emotions or attitudes (Argyle, 1988).

We dealt with gender differences in speech in Chapter 3, and described how men are more concerned with the task or topic, women with the relationship and keeping the conversation going. There are also gender differences in vocabulary, grammar, accent and some of the minutiae of conversation.

In some ways women appear to be more extraverted in their behaviour, though this does not show up in questionnaire scores. They smile and look more, are more responsive, ask more questions, disclose more, give more social support and seek close relationships in a style of 'relaxed sweetness'. Men are extraverted in a different way: they tell jokes and tall stories, engage in friendly banter or teasing and may provide concrete help (as opposed to just sympathy).

The differences between men and women can be described in part by saying that men are more assertive, women more co-operative. Men tend to dominate women and try to dominate each other, forming dominance hierarchies even in groups of small boys. Adult males do this by talking more and louder, interrupting, arguing, challenging; even friendly teasing has an aggressive edge to it. Men seem comfortable with social hierarchies, can give and take orders; women prefer equality and co-operation. In childhood boys play in larger groups, which are inevitably hierarchical, while little girls prefer to talk to close friends, getting to know each other and exchanging self-disclosures. Girls do play competitive games, but in a friendly way, which means that they usually lose if they play against boys. The female subculture has a positive, trusting quality, which may explain why women take others' non-verbal signals at face value while men look to see what is being concealed. Women score much higher on empathy, concern for others and responsiveness to others' feelings, and they are usually found to be more rewarding, both by men and women (Argyle, 1991).

Women's friendships are closer and they talk a lot about personal matters, while male friends do things together, like playing golf and squash, or in working-class culture going angling and to football matches. Women are more helpful inside the family, especially, of course, in looking after children, and in being sympathetic listeners and providers of social support for husbands (Vanfossen, 1981). Within the wider family it is women who hold the whole structure together, by keeping in contact with each other, giving presents, remembering birthdays and looking after family members. Women are more often employed in the helping professions, such as nursing and social work, do voluntary work in the community and occupy 'helpful' jobs in organizations, such as secretaries and research assistants.

Women do not often get promoted to the higher levels of many occupations, partly as a result of prejudice, partly diversion of time and energy to the family. As leaders women have a more democratic participatory style, are more employee- and less task-centred (Eagly and Karan, 1991). Attempts have been made to explain the relative lack of success of women in terms of personality differences. Men are more aggressive, have greater self-confidence and higher career aspirations; there is no difference in power motivation, and it is not clear whether there is any difference in achievement motivation; and, as we have seen, women are more rewarding and have greater empathy (Ragins and Sundstrom, 1989). The great difference between male and female success remains to be explained.

*The explanation of gender differences* Could they be innate, or partly innate? Throughout the animal kingdom females look after children and males form dominance hierarchies. In all primitive human cultures females look after families while males co-operate over large tasks and in governing the community.

It is possible that there are some innate, evolved differences here.

The greater aggressiveness of males may well be innate, as may their approach to mate selection. We shall see later that men look for girls who are young and attractive, while girls look for men who are strong and rich, in all cultures (p. 49). Some of the non-verbal differences may be innate; for example girls show an early interest in faces, and are better than boys at decoding them at an early age.

Parents treat boys and girls differently, and this is probably the main source of gender differences. It has repeatedly been found in Britain and the USA that parents allow boys greater independence, have higher expectations for independent task performance, encourage them to compete and discourage them from showing their feelings. Parents are warmer towards girls and closer to them, punish them less, encourage physical activity less and look after them more closely (Huston 1983). Girls are more fluent at an early age, and they become more expressive, probably because their mothers talk to them more and encourage expressiveness, which is *dis*couraged in boys.

Men, in the past at least, have usually been dominant and more powerful, and their style of behaviour reflects this. There has traditionally been a major division of labour, where women's work is in the house, men's is outside, men's talk and behaviour are centred on work and decision-taking, women's on looking after members of the family (Aries, 1987). However, this situation varies between cultures. In Pakistan and Algeria there are very traditional ideas about these sex roles, in Israel much less so; they tried to abolish them entirely in the kibbutz. There have also been major historical changes, in that many more women now go out to work and they have more power in the home than before, though they still do most of the housework.

*Masculinity and femininity* There are differences not only between sexes but also within sexes, in what is commonly understood as masculinity and femininity. Individuals can rate themselves, and each other, on this dimension. However, Sandra Bem (1974) discovered that masculinity and femininity may be two independent dimensions. She asked people to say which traits are more desirable for women, which for men. Some of them are:

| *Males* | *Females* |
|---|---|
| aggressive | affectionate |
| assertive | sensitive to the needs of others |
| competitive | sympathetic |
| independent | understanding |
| self-sufficient | yielding |

Women rate themselves higher on the feminine items, men on the masculine ones. Subjects of either sex with high scores on femininity were more helpful, for example looking after a lonely student, playing with a kitten or holding a baby. Those scoring high on masculinity were more independent and less conforming.

However, these dimensions were later found to have little or no relation with self-related masculinity or femininity; they are rather two unrelated dimensions of expressive and instrumental styles of behaviour. Those who score high on both scales, formerly described as 'androgenous', really have two sets of desirable attributes (Brown, 1986); the male ones are about leadership qualities, the female ones about sympathy and concern. Sandra Bem thought that special merit was attached to being 'androgenous', that is, having the good qualities of both sexes. This was an ideological point, and all that has really been found is that there are two sets of desirable qualities, which members of either sex may possess, and that it is desirable to have each set of qualities.

There was no evidence that the two sets of qualities interact statistically, to produce new qualities, but in a quite different research tradition, the study of social skills, it has been found that both dimensions are often needed in combination – in leadership, for example (p. 279). Research on social interaction has therefore provided support for Bem's claims about the advantages of 'androgyny', though without any reference to gender (Argyle, 1991).

## FURTHER READING

Argyle, M., Furnham, A., and Graham, J. A., *Social Situations*, Cambridge University Press, 1981.

Hampson, S., *The Construction of Personality*, 2nd edn, Routledge, London, 1988.

## CHAPTER 6
# TWO-PERSON RELATIONSHIPS

In this chapter we move from the study of short-term encounters to long-term relationships. Much of our social behaviour, and most of that which is important to us, is with family, friends, workmates, neighbours or others whom we have known for some time. Many problems presented by mental patients and clients for social skills training are in this area. Many people can't make friends, and a third of marriages in Britain end in divorce.

#### HOW TO WIN FRIENDS AND INFLUENCE PEOPLE:
#### I MAKING FRIENDS

All relations depend on some degree of attraction between those concerned, and some relations, like friendship and love, are formed simply because people like one another. How does this happen?

*Proximity and frequency of interaction* Frequent interaction can come about from living in adjacent rooms or houses, working in the same office, belonging to the same club and so on. Interaction can lead to liking, but liking leads to more interaction; in other words, a positive feedback cycle is started, which is halted by competing attractions and the increasing difficulties of accommodation with greater intimacy – like two hedgehogs trying to keep warm. Only certain kinds of interaction lead to liking, as has been shown in research on interracial contacts.

Two people should be of equal status, preferably members of the same club, church or other group. Students who share rooms or offices usually come to like each other, adult neighbours more rarely – because they are not similar enough, in age, class or attitudes, the next most important factor.

*Similarity* People like others who are similar to themselves in certain respects. They like those with similar attitudes, beliefs and values, who have a similar regional and social-class background, and who have similar jobs or leisure interests – but not necessarily those who have similar personalities. Among students, traditional v. non-traditional masculinity or femininity also has some effect. Duck (1973) has produced evidence that similarity of cognitive constructs is important, i.e. the categories used for describing other people (pp. 81ff.). As far as other aspects of personality are concerned, it now seems that neither similarity nor complementarity have much effect on friendship. However, Rosenbaum (1986) found that disliking people because they are different was more important than liking people because they are similar – the 'repulsion hypothesis'.

*Reinforcement* The next general principle governing liking is the extent to which one person satisfies the needs of another. This was shown by Jennings (1950) in a study of four hundred girls in a reformatory. She found that the popular girls helped and protected others, encouraged and cheered them up, made them feel accepted and wanted, controlled their own moods so as not to inflict anxiety or depression on others, were able to establish rapport quickly, won the confidence of a wide variety of personalities and were concerned with the feelings and needs of others. The unpopular girls, on the other hand, were dominating, aggressive and boastful, demanded attention and tried to get others to do things for them. This pattern has been generally interpreted in terms of the popular girls providing rewards and minimizing costs, while the unpopular girls tried to get rewards for themselves and incurred costs for others. The activities of the popular girls could also be interpreted in terms of 'social support'.

Studies like this led to belief that reinforcement is the key to interpersonal attraction. It is certainly important, and some marital therapy is based on increasing the rewards which spouses give one another; however, it has been found that 'communal' relationships, like close friendships and love, work differently. Hays (1985) found that the early student friendships which survived were the ones where the sum of rewards *plus* costs was greatest, i.e. doing things for the other was a positive factor. Clark (1986) found that in communal relationships people were more concerned with the other's needs than with their own rewards.

These findings suggest that in close relationships people do not count the cost to themselves, or assess the rewards received. But according to 'equity theory' they are concerned that they receive a fair share of rewards in relation to their contribution to the relationship, and are happier when neither under- nor over-benefiting. Rook (1987) found that reciprocity of rewards, though not in a tit-for-tat manner, led to satisfaction with a relationship, and to less loneliness in the case of friends (but not for kin); we shall see later that equity also affects romantic relationships.

*Reciprocated liking* If B likes A, A will probably like B. B's liking is signalled by the non-verbal signs we have described in Chapter 2 – facial expression, proximity, tone of voice, etc. Being liked by another combines with other factors, such as physical attractiveness and similarity of attitudes, and has a powerful effect on interpersonal attraction.

*Emotional state of the chooser* If A is in a good mood when he meets B, he will probably like B more. Thus people get on better if they meet in an attractive room rather than an ugly one, in a room which is pleasantly warm rather than one which is very hot and humid, when they have just seen a funny rather than a sad film or when they have heard good rather than bad news. If people share emotional experiences they are drawn together. The most dramatic cases of interracial attitudes being improved have occurred under conditions of high arousal, such as fighting side by side and serving on ships together (Amir, 1969).

*Self-disclosure* As two people get to know one another more, they disclose increasingly intimate information about themselves. Self-disclosure can be measured on a scale (1–5) with items like:

the types of play and recreation that I enjoy (1.01);
how often I have sexual experiences and the nature of these
experiences (4.31).

(Jourard, 1971)

Taylor (1965) studied pairs of students who shared rooms at
college. The amount of self-disclosure increased during the first
nine weeks and then levelled off, but at quite different degrees of
intimacy for different pairs (see Figure 6.1). The main increase
was at the most superficial level; there was not much increase of
disclosure about intimate matters and basic values.

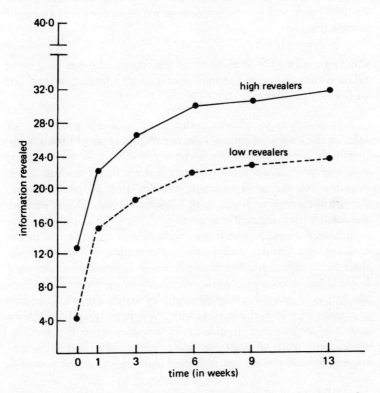

Figure 6.1   Amount of disclosure over time of high- and low-revealers
(Taylor, 1965).

We recently found that for many relationships there is more disclosure in some areas than others, e.g. what we are prepared to tell the doctor and the bank manager is quite different. Australian students told their fathers a lot about how hard up they were and how well their work was going, but nothing about their love life; they told their romantic partners everything, and their tutors nothing (Argyle, Trimboli and Forgas, 1988).

More disclosure is possible when people come to trust each other; they know that the other will not laugh at or reject them, or pass on their confessions to others or use them to his or her own advantage (Naegele, 1958).

Self-disclosure is more important to females than males; they disclose more and are disclosed to more, as in the case of pairs of female friends.

*Building a shared life* In the case of marriage and other long-term relationships there are further sources of attachment, arising out of shared activities.

1 In addition to self-disclosure there is also a great deal of talk, in the course of which a shared cognitive world is built up, in which there is confidence because it is shared. Women friends talk a great deal, disclose more and drink a lot of tea and coffee together; so do most married couples and people at work, though the range of topics here is more limited. This is perhaps the main female form of attachment.

2 Many activities which are important to us, at work, in the home or for leisure, require the co-operation of other people; their behaviour is needed in conjunction with our own, so they become necessary to us. Male friends *do* things together, such as playing golf or squash; married couples share domestic jobs; and at work there is division of labour. When daily and important activities are sustained regularly in this way there is a sense in which the other is part of one's personality, and it is not surprising that people are distressed when such a relationship is ended.

3 Two people are usually part of a larger social network, so that their relationship is supported by the others in the network,

e.g. their children, kin and neighbours. They are also part of a shared environment – a house, garden or office – which helps to sustain their relationship.

### HOW TO WIN FRIENDS AND INFLUENCE PEOPLE: II INFLUENCING PEOPLE

In any relationship it is not enough to agree with the other person all the time, since this would lead to frustration and eventual discontent. Special skills are needed to be sufficiently assertive without damaging the relationship. These are suggested by Table 6.1, which shows how dominant and affiliative styles are related. It is the top right-hand corner, warm and dominant, which is most effective.

One of the keys to successful leadership is consultation: it is found that people act with more enthusiasm if they have been consulted and have helped to make a decision. This principle applies to all face-to-face social influence, and means that the other person has to be persuaded and agree with what he is to do.

'How many psychologists does it take to change a light-bulb? One, but it has to want to change.'

|  | dominance | |  |  |
|---|---|---|---|---|
|  | analyses | | advises |  |
|  | criticizes | | coordinates |  |
|  | disapproves | | directs |  |
|  | judges | | leads |  |
| low affiliation | resists | | initiates | high affiliation |
|  | evades | | acquiesces |  |
|  | concedes | | agrees |  |
|  | relinquishes | | assists |  |
|  | retreats | | cooperates |  |
|  | withdraws | | obliges |  |
|  | dependency | |  |  |

Table 6.1   Combinations of dominant and affiliative techniques
(Gough, 1957).

*Non-verbal signals* Requests need to be made in a sufficiently assertive manner. We discussed these non-verbal cues earlier – talking loudly and most of the time, in a confident tone of voice, interrupting others, adopting an attentive but unsmiling facial expression, and an erect posture with the head tilted back, shoulders squared and hands on hips. For most situations rather small amounts of these signals will be enough, and again these social techniques must be combined with sufficient warmth and rewardingness. Friendly and dominant attitudes are difficult to combine in the face, and rather easier for the voice.

There is a clear difference between assertive and aggressive behaviour; aggressive behaviour may or may not produce the desired influence, but it damages the relationship.

*Reinforcement* It is possible to influence another's behaviour in the immediate situation by systematic rewarding of the desired behaviour immediately it takes place, and non-reward or punishment of other behaviour. Rewards based on the need for affiliation include smiling, looking, agreement, head nodding, etc. Punishment could consist of frowning, looking away, looking bored, looking at a watch, disagreeing, etc. It may be easier to influence another person in this way if he is of higher status, where direct influence might be inappropriate. Members of groups often conform because they want to be accepted rather than rejected. Endler (1965) found that conformity could be increased if the experimenter reinforced it, and reduced if the experimenter reinforced nonconformity.

*Using the personal relationship* It is easier to influence another person if they like you, because they do not want to lose your approval or damage the relationship. This is the basis of ingratiation.

*Reciprocation of favours* This is similar to the above. If A does something for B first, B is more likely to do what A asks. Regan (1971) found that subjects bought twice as many raffle tickets from a confederate who had previously bought them a Coke, compared with other confederates. This kind of reciprocity or exchange of gifts plays an even more important part in African countries, where officials often have to be bribed (as we call it) before they will be helpful.

*Persuasion* The design of persuasive messages has been studied mostly in connection with the mass media, but some of the principles apply in face-to-face situations. It is necessary to appeal to the needs, values or interests of the other in some way, and then show that what you want him to do will satisfy one of those needs: 'Come and do the washing-up while I change, then we will be able to go out to the pub earlier'; 'If you do some work during the holidays, you'll get better A levels and be more likely to get into university.' This may require some initial exploration of what the other does want, as when a salesman tries to find out the customer's needs. The objections to the behaviour being requested may be neutralized by appealing to higher loyalties, denying that injury will result, or other ways of changing the way the act or the situation is perceived (Sykes and Matza, 1957): 'It's nothing, just a matter of taking a small present to a friend of mine in Amsterdam.' Moral exhortation on the other hand is no good if the exhorter is seen not to be behaving in this way himself (Bryan and Walbek, 1970). The very words used can create certain assumptions or ways of defining the problem; politicians may manage to make the public think primarily in terms of unemployment and the problems of social inequality, or alternatively of national prosperity and the creation of collective wealth. Similarly, face-to-face persuasion may be achieved by using the right rhetoric, making the other think in terms of your concepts.

*Power* Persuasion is more effective if the source of it is regarded as an expert – on university entrance, to take the earlier example. There are other kinds of power, such as the power to reward and punish, possessed by most formal leaders. Power makes influence easier, particularly if the influencer is thought to be a *legitimate* source of directions, in view of his ability, experience or sheer rank in a hierarchy. In the well-known experiments by Milgram (1974) it was found that 65 per cent of subjects gave what they thought were 450-volt shocks to what they thought were other subjects, who gave signs of intense suffering and apparent collapse, because the experimenter ordered them to do so as part of a learning experiment. There was less obedience when the experiment was done away from the lab, and when the victim was within touching distance. The explanation of the main finding may lie in the experimenter sending signals indicating that he was in charge and that there was nothing to worry about. However, the experiment also shows the very high degree of obedience which can be commanded by a legitimate leader, with no power to reward or punish.

*Persuasive strategies* By a 'strategy' I mean a planned sequence of at least two moves. These may be conscious and deliberate, as in some sales techniques, but they may also be acquired and used with little conscious awareness of what is being done. Interviewers commonly ask questions in a carefully prepared order; the more intimate ones come last, the most harmless ones first. A salesman may offer the most expensive objects first and then produce cheaper ones, depending on the customer's reaction. This is similar to starting negotiations with exaggerated claims, with the intention of making concessions and extracting reciprocal concessions from the other party; this doesn't work if the initial demands are seen as bluffing. The foot-in-the-door technique consists of making a small request which is followed by a larger one; Freedman and Fraser (1966) found that if housewives had been asked earlier to answer a few questions, 53 per cent agreed to allow a survey team into their houses for two hours, compared with 22 per cent who had not been asked those questions. Another technique, known in the USA as 'low-balling', involves obtaining an initial agreement and following it with a series of extra charges or conditions. Cialdini, Caciapopo, Bassett and Miller (1978) found that 55 per cent of subjects turned up for a 7 a.m. experiment if they had already agreed to take part without knowing at what time it would be, compared with 25 per cent of those who were invited directly to come at this hour.

## THE RANGE OF RELATIONSHIPS

In all human cultures there is the same set of social relationships, though they can take varied forms (for example, some allow more than one wife). They are:

friends
spouse, and other kinds of cohabitant
parent–child relations
siblings and other kin
work relations, especially mates and supervisors
neighbours.

These relationships are very different from one another. For example, the relationship with a spouse usually involves sharing property and bed, and producing children; this does not apply to other relationships.

They all provide satisfaction, of different kinds and degrees. Argyle and Furnham (1983) asked subjects to rate their degree of satisfaction with a number of relationships on fifteen satisfaction scales. Factor analysis of these scales produced three orthogonal factors:

I    Material and instrumental help
II   Social and emotional support
III  Common interests.

The average scores for each relationship on these three dimensions of satisfaction are shown in Figure 6.2. It can be seen that the spouse is the greatest source of satisfaction, especially for Factor I.

Another way of comparing relationships is in terms of the rules which it is generally thought apply to each. Argyle and Henderson (1985) surveyed nearly 1,000 people in four cultures about the rules of twenty-two relationships. We predicted that relationships would be grouped into intimate and less intimate in respect of the rules which apply. A cluster analysis of the twenty-two relationships using only the thirty-three common rules produced the clusters shown in Figure 6.3. The first cluster consists of intimate relationships: here the rules are for expressing

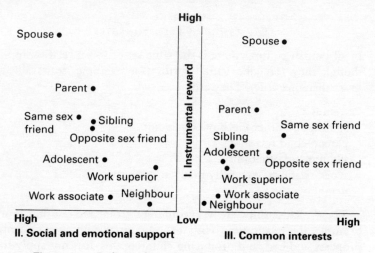

Figure 6.2    Relationships plotted on satisfaction dimensions.

and maintaining intimacy. The other cluster was of less intimate, work relationships: here the rules were for avoiding intimacy and for the efficient performance of tasks.

Since similar relationships are found in all cultures, and some of them in animals, it is possible that there is an innate basis, derived from evolution. Systems of behaviour may have evolved which promote the welfare of genes by helping the production and care of children, and looking after other close kin. In animals the giving of help is proportional to the genes shared with the other animal; do these principles apply at all to humans? There is some evidence that they do: help of an exceptional nature, like donating parts of the body, is almost entirely to close kin (Fellner and Marshall, 1981), and children seem to be pro-grammed to communicate with their mothers from a very early age. Some of the differences between men and women are culturally universal, and can be explained biologically: women seek a reliable and supportive mate, men look for an attractive one, and are interested in fertilizing females as well as looking after them.

Social relationships can be seen as little social systems, like games, where all the elements are functional in making

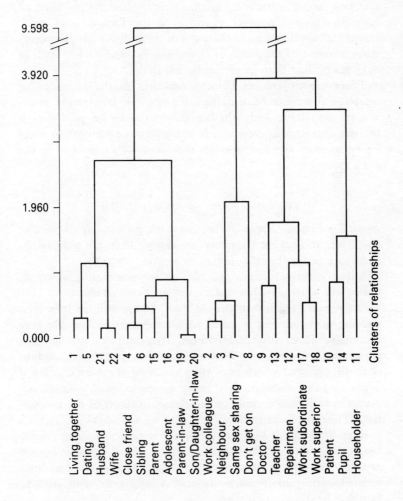

Figure 6.3   Clusters of relationships (Argyle and Henderson, 1985).

attainment of goals possible. The rules of each relationship reflect the nature of that relationship and help in the attainment of the goals. In work relations, for example, the rules are about avoiding undue intimacy, and the efficient and fair conduct of business. Here is another example of the functions of rules: Harris (1968) offered an explanation of the Indian rules protecting cows in terms of the value of cow dung as fertilizer and fuel, of oxen for pulling farm implements, and so on.

There are differences between cultures in the character of marriage and other relationships, for example how many wives a man may have and whether they have to be paid for. It follows that socialization and learning about relationships must be taken into account, though these are all variations on the same themes.

THE MAIN TYPES OF RELATIONSHIP

*Friendship* Friends can be defined as those people whom we like and trust, and whose company we enjoy. They are outside the family, but we have a lot in common with them and are attracted towards them. Friends are symmetrical and equal, unlike kin, who are often of different age or social class.

How many friends do people have? It depends on how you put the question, but if asked to list their friends people give around seven to fifteen. However, friendship choices are not always reciprocated. In Wellman's survey (1979) in Toronto only 36 per cent of choices were returned. Friends don't just come in pairs, though; they form networks, with cliques and chains, which can be more or less dense, in terms of the proportion of possible linkages taken up.

Friendships don't last for ever; children's friends change quite fast, and among adults friendships may end when one person moves to another town or changes his job. However, close links formed during adolescence may last a long time, and are also found to be the most intimate.

Friends come from work, leisure groups, the neighbourhood, or from school or college. The importance of different factors varies between classes and cultures. For working-class populations, material help and proximity are most important; for middle-class people, shared interests, especially belonging to the same leisure groups, are important, and proximity less so.

What do friends do together? For one thing, they talk a lot; teenagers will spend several hours with their friends, and then have long telephone conversations with them. Argyle and Furnham (1982) asked sixty people to report on the frequency with which they had taken part in twenty-six kinds of activity with others in eight different relationships. Very large variations were found; the characteristic activities for three relationships are shown in Table 6.2.

It can be seen that this Oxford sample went dancing, played tennis and attended sherry parties with their friends. This is not entirely frivolous, since joint leisure ties people into a supportive network, and the companionship gives social support.

Our own study of the satisfactions derived from friendship found three main sources (see Figure 6.2).

1 *Common interests* (doing things together/joint leisure, talking about things of mutual concern, sharing common beliefs and values) provided nearly as great a source of satisfaction for same-sex friends as for spouses, with all other relationships well behind in this respect.

2 *Social and Emotional support* among friends was less important than between spouses but just more so than in other relationships, e.g. with members of the family or people from work.

3 On the *instrumental reward* scale however (financial support, advice, working together, etc.), friends were quite low compared with spouses and parents.

There are different kinds of friends, too. Bochner, McLeod and Lin (1977) found that foreign students in Hawaii had Hawaiian friends (for instrumental reasons, e.g. showing them the ropes) and friends from the same country (probably for emotional support and shared values).

Friends are expected to provide help when needed. This may be important for the young, but for adults the level of help provided by friends is quite low compared with that from kin. Friendship has been described as too fragile a relationship to

| Spouse | | Work Colleague, liked, same status | | Friend, similar age | |
|---|---|---|---|---|---|
| mean ratio 1.64 | | mean ratio 1.11 | | mean ratio 1.26 | |
| *situations above this ratio* | | *situations above this ratio* | | *situations above this ratio* | |
| watch TV | 2.61 | attend lecture | 2.11 | dancing | 2.00 |
| do domestic jobs together | 2.48 | work together on joint task | 1.56 | tennis | 1.67 |
| play chess or other indoor game | 2.31 | together in a committee | 1.55 | sherry party | 1.63 |
| go for a walk | 2.28 | morning coffee or tea | 1.50 | joint leisure | 1.63 |
| go shopping | 2.15 | casual chat and telling jokes | 1.35 | pub | 1.60 |
| play tennis or squash | 2.03 | one helps the other | 1.31 | intimate conversation | 1.52 |
| informal meal together | 1.93 | | | walk | 1.50 |
| intimate conversation | 1.92 | | | | |
| have argument or disagreement | 1.84 | | | | |

Table 6.2 Situations/activities most chosen for certain relationships (Ratios to mean frequency for all relationships; Argyle and Furnham, 1985).

stand the strains of giving major help, such as providing money or accommodation, looking after sick children, helping to find jobs or dealing with the police (Adams, 1967). On the other hand, people do more for friends than for strangers. Friends also provide 'social support', i.e. can help to deal with stresses by giving emotional support, acting as confidants or providing some material help.

Friendship provides a number of benefits. Social support is good for physical and mental health. In an Australian study it was found that neurotics had far fewer friends than normal controls and did not belong to social networks (Henderson, Duncan-Jones, McAuley and Ritchie, 1978). Perhaps the greatest benefit is that being with friends puts people in a positive mood, as shown in a study by Larson (1990) in which subjects were 'bleeped' on random occasions and asked to record their mood. They were much happier when with friends, followed by being with family, and least when alone. How is this joy created? It is partly due to the enjoyable things that friends do together (see Table 6.2). In addition, friends send each other a lot of positive NV signals – smile, gaze, touch, tone of voice and so on – which produce immediate positive reactions (Argyle, 1987).

Being lonely is a source of depression. It is partly due to not having friends, but partly to not engaging in sufficient self-disclosure with them. However, many people value some degree of solitude, not only poets and religious recluses but also adolescents who need time to develop their independence and identity, and anyone who wants to get away from the pressures of people.

Friendship has its rules, and if they are broken there is a danger of losing friends. We asked a sample of people about friendships which they had lost, and asked if this was because they or the other person had broken one of the rules found in our rules study. In many cases this had happened, as shown in Table 6.3. It is interesting that what may be called 'third-party' rules were so important here – such as keeping confidences, not criticizing each other in public, standing up for the other in their absence. Friends come not one at a time but in networks, and

| | moderately or very important in breaking up friendship | slightly important in breaking up friendship |
|---|---|---|
| Being jealous or critical of your other relationships | 57% | 22% |
| Discussing with others what was said in confidence to him/her | 56% | 19% |
| Not volunteering help in time of need | 44% | 23% |
| Not trusting or confiding in you | 44% | 22% |
| Criticizing you in public | 44% | 21% |
| Not showing positive regard for you | 42% | 34% |
| Not standing up for you in your absence | 39% | 28% |
| Not being tolerant of your other friends | 38% | 30% |
| Not showing emotional support | 37% | 25% |
| Nagging you | 30% | 25% |

Table 6.3   Friendship rules and break-up of friendships (Argyle and Henderson, 1985).

networks have to be handled with great care (Argyle and Henderson, 1985).

It is also necessary to *understand* what friendship is. In a study of disturbed and isolated teenage girls it was found that they had concepts of friendship like those of young children, thinking about benefits to themselves but lacking the ideas of commitment, loyalty and concern for the other's welfare (La Gaipa and Wood, 1981). We showed earlier that close friendships, like love, are 'communal' relationships, and there is a lot of concern for the other.

Many people have difficulty in making friends. A number of social skills are needed, and these will be described later.

*Love*   Loving is not the same as liking, although it includes it. In this section we shall be concerned with 'falling in love' among the young; the equally intense but rather different attachment between the married will be discussed under Marriage.

Courtship, like friendship, develops over time. Mate selection is an important biological process. The biological basis of love is to attract and retain mates, reproduce with them, and for the female to find a mate who will look after her and the infants (Clark and Reis, 1988). And while romantic, sexual love does the job for a limited time, it is later replaced by companionate love.

Falling in love, having love affairs and living together occur mainly among individuals of opposite sex, between the ages of eighteen and thirty, and may or may not lead to marriage. Love usually involves sexual attraction, is more intense than liking, shows a rapid build-up and then declines slowly. There is a great need for the other, a caring for him or her, and a high level of intimacy and disclosure. Its presence can be measured by questionnaires like Rubin's (1973) with items such as 'I would do almost anything for . . .' and 'If I could never be with . . . I would feel miserable.'

The nature of the love relationship varies between different cultures and historical periods, with young people learning how they are supposed to feel and behave. Simon, Eder and Evans (1992) carried out in-depth interviews and recorded conversations among teenage girls; there was frequent talk about love and what was supposed to happen. It was agreed that love was very important, that one should always be in love, with one boy at a time, and to one who was unattached.

Traditionally there are two public rituals – engagement and marriage – which proclaim the stages in the relationship and result in others treating the couple in a new way. The effect of cognitive labelling is shown in a study by Rubin (1973), who found that couples who accepted the love mythology fell in love more rapidly than those who didn't. He also found that married couples had a more realistic view of love. People often try to find out, for example by writing to women's magazines, if they are 'really in love'. On the labelling theory there is no difference between love and infatuation, except perhaps that infatuation is what love is called when it's over.

We saw earlier that males and females look for rather different things when choosing a partner, though physical attractiveness is important for both, and couples in steady relationships have *similar* levels of p.a. (Feingold, 1988). Several experiments show that heightened arousal of various kinds leads to sexual attraction. Dutton and Aron (1974) arranged for an attractive girl to stop young men in the middle of a high and dangerously swaying suspension bridge in Vancouver; 50 per cent of them accepted her invitation to phone her and hear more about the experiment, compared with 13 per cent of those asked on a very low bridge. (I have been to that bridge and noted that not everyone will go over it; perhaps those daring enough to cross are also more willing to phone strange girls.)

Couples who are in love spend many happy hours in a combination of sexual activity and intimate conversation. They also have an increasing number of things to argue about as they get to know each other better, and they have to work these disagreements through (Braiker and Kelley, 1979). Love is a form of 'bonding' or attachment, and is found to take a similar form to the earlier attachment to parents, i.e. 'secure' (find it easy to get close to others), 'avoidant' (uncomfortable being close to others) or 'anxious/ambivalent' (worry that my partner doesn't really love me). A series of studies has found that young people who describe their romantic relations in these terms also report similar childhood relationships with their parents, and with people at work (Hazan and Shaver, 1987).

Being in love is probably the greatest source of joy among young people (followed by having a baby and being promoted); it is also associated with distorted perception of the other – 'Love is blind' – and a great deal of altruistic concern for them.

Freedman (1978) compared the benefits of living together with the benefits of marriage. People who were living together were less happy than married people but a lot happier than those who were single. They also reported that they were somewhat more satisfied with sex than marrieds, but less happy with love.

Many love affairs break up. Hill, Rubin and Peplau (1976) studied 105 student affairs and found that half of them broke up within two years of starting. The causes given were that the partners were bored with the relationship, had different interests or backgrounds or had different ideas about sex. Couples were more likely to break up if they differed greatly in age, education, intelligence or physical attractiveness. The males fell in love faster but the females fell out of love faster, and the breakup usually took place in the long vacation – which may itself have been one of the causes of the rift. It has also been found that young people who are low in self-esteem fall in love more often and more deeply (Dion and Dion, 1975), and that love is accompanied by distorted perceptions of the other.

*Marriage* is 'a holy mystery in which man and woman become one flesh . . . that husband and wife may comfort and help each other . . . that they may have children . . . and begin a new life together in the community' (Alternative Service Book, 1980). These are some of the central features of marriage – sharing bed, food and property, producing children and caring for one another; it is a commitment to a biological partnership.

Our satisfaction study showed that a spouse is by far the greatest source of satisfaction in all three dimensions, but especially in that of *instrumental reward*. A spouse is also the greatest source of both kinds of conflict, just as arguing is one of the most characteristic marital activities (Table 6.2). Married people are in better physical and mental health and live longer, especially if the marital relationship is supportive; the divorced are in the worst health (Burman and Margolin, 1992). The better health of married people has two causes: their immune system is more active, and they engage in better health behaviour, e.g. smoke and drink less, do what the doctor orders, through looking after each other better.

While many studies have shown the great importance of 'social support', it is still not clear exactly of what it consists. Being a confidant (i.e. a sympathetic listener), offering helpful advice, providing emotional support and social acceptance, giving actual or financial help, and simply doing ordinary things together, like eating and drinking, are the main possibilities (see p. 226). Some of these require definite social skills, such as offering necessary but unpopular advice and handling the NV components of emotional support. There is some evidence that social support works best when it is a two-way affair, the recipient doing something for or with the donor rather than passively receiving help (Cohen and McKay, 1984).

Most people get married, though in Britain a third of those who do so also get divorced. An increasing number live together without marriage over a long period. Pairs of friends may also live together, with or without sexual involvement, as may siblings, and these relationships share some of the properties of marriage.

In the traditional family there was a clear division of roles: the husband was the main provider while the wife looked after the household and children; he was task-oriented, she was expressive. This has changed quite a lot, in that wives now earn more and husbands do more in the home. But marriage has changed in more ways than this. To begin with, families are smaller than before. There has been pressure from women for an equal say in decisions, for the chance to have careers, and for husbands to share the housework. Dual-career marriages are stressful and difficult to operate however, especially when there are children. Marriages have become more 'symmetrical' in other ways too, especially in that couples share decision-making, leisure interests and friends.

We have found that the main activities in marriage are being in bed, watching TV, doing domestic jobs, eating, talking and arguing (Table 6.2). We found that many rules are believed to apply to marriage, but the most important one is 'be faithful', together with 'give emotional support', 'show affection', 'engage in sex' and 'keep the friendship rules'.

A lot of the findings about marriage can be explained in terms of reinforcement. Marriages are happier, and last longer, when there is more sex, more shared leisure, and more positive verbal and non-verbal acts by the partner, like compliments and kisses. This principle has been made good use of in marital therapy (Argyle and Henderson, 1985).

It has been proposed that marital partners are more satisfied, and stay together longer, if the relationship is seen as *equitable*, which is better than 'underbenefiting' but also a little better than perceived 'overbenefiting'. VanYperen and Buunk (1990), in a longitudinal study, found that perceived inequity caused later dissatisfaction, and the same authors (1991) found greater discontent over equity among people with egalitarian rather than traditional ideas about sex roles. It is found that more women feel underbenefited, and more men overbenefited. Sprecher (1992) found that subjects, and especially women, thought that underbenefiting would make them feel depressed and angry, while overbenefiting would make them feel guilty; in both cases they thought they would try to restore equity.

There is a high level of bonding in marriage, as shown by the intense distress when marriages break up. Divorce and bereavements are two of the most damaging experiences as sources of mental ill-health (p. 224). In unhappy marriages there is a lot of 'negative reciprocity', e.g. she says or does something horrid and he responds likewise. However, those who are more committed to the relationship often do not react in this way but respond constructively instead. This is very beneficial for the relationship, especially when done by male partners (Rusbult et al., 1991).

It is easy to see why marriage is so difficult: it is because there are so many things, large and small, to be agreed about. One of the characteristic marital activities, we found, was 'arguing' (see Table 6.2). Part of the solution is for the partners to be better negotiators, able to arrive at constructive, co-operative solutions. Marriages are happier when the partners can see the other's point of view; for example, 'Before I criticize my partner I try to imagine how I would feel in his/her place' (Long and Andrews, 1990). Certain conflicts are very common in marriage – those arising from the need for very close co-ordination of behaviour, the different roles and spheres of interests, conflict with in-laws, and different beliefs or values.

Marriages break up for a number of reasons. Many do so in the first five years, especially in the case of early or hasty marriages and if there are difficulties with money, accommodation or sex, the basic affective bond having never been made. During the next twenty years difficulties may arise when the wife grows to greater independence, if the two develop in different directions and as a result of trouble with the children.

Some marriages break up later, after the children have gone, if there was only a social alliance to raise the children, without a strong affective attachment. Adultery, violence and alcohol are often additional sources of trouble (Dominian, 1980).

*Kinship* In Western Europe and North America a person's main kin are his siblings, parents and children. Parents and children make up the nuclear family, which lives together until the children leave home. Relationships with cousins, uncles, aunts and other kin outside the nuclear family may or may not be taken up in our culture. Elsewhere, such as in Africa and the East, kinship is more important and relationships with a wider range of kin are maintained. Compared with purely friendly connections, kinship links are less optional and last much longer. People who are unmarried or widowed spend more time with, or actually live with, their own children or siblings. Kin do not usually share leisure activities, as friends do; they tend to meet for regular meals or visits, or at Christmas, birthdays, weddings and funerals (Adams, 1968; Firth, Hubert and Forge, 1969).

When kin meet, they eat and drink and talk, spend time together, take an interest in each other's health and welfare, and pass on family news. They may also provide regular help, such as with babysitting or shopping. Kin, unlike friends, are prepared to provide major forms of help, such as money, accommodation and care for others when ill (Adams, 1967). Sociobiological 'selfish gene' theories offer one explanation (p. 18). Hewstone, Argyle and Furnham (1982) asked subjects how they would divide money between themselves and others; they were most generous to a spouse, followed by child, friend and workmate, while women were more generous than men.

Women are more active than men in maintaining kinship links, this being especially noticeable between sisters and between mothers and daughters. In middle-class circles the link with father and father-in-law can be important, e.g. for financial help, while the mother–daughter link may be weaker if the daughter has established herself independently before marriage (Bell, 1968). Kinship ties last a long time and the nature of each relationship changes greatly over time. Parents start by looking after their children, who then live away from home for years but in turn may end up looking after their parents. Siblings start by playing and quarrelling but may eventually live together, in old age. They have a strong initial bond based on their shared, intimate experiences, but there is often jealousy and rivalry as well. Sisters are especially close but also quarrel a lot.

Working-class people have fewer friends but spend more time with kin, partly because they often live quite near; and they do invite them home, or rather they invite themselves. Working-class husbands are often poor confidants, so sisters do the job.

Kin are especially important to old people, many of whom live with or near one of their offspring, and most of whom have seen a son, daughter or sibling during a given week and are regularly helped by their children. Telephone calls and letters are mainly to kin. Working-class old people are in closer touch with kin than the middle-class elderly, since middle-class families are more dispersed. The latter are, however, less lonely, because they have greater access to telephones and cars, write more letters, see their friends more often and in addition value privacy and can cope better with isolation (Shanas, Townsend et al., 1968; Atkinson, 1970).

The bonds between kin are strong and long-lasting. Another reason for this may be the sense of shared identity with another person of the same family name (apart from mother–daughter etc.) and some common physical features. Sharing the intimacies of family life is probably a source of bonding. Kin are part of a network of relationships which sustains links between pairs of individuals (Schneider, 1968). These bonds to a large extent survive separation by distance, or differences of age or social class. Kinship, unlike friendship, does not need to be sustained by regular and rewarding meetings.

*Parent–child* This is the first and most basic relationship to be experienced, and it affects later ones. Children are innately programmed to relate to and interact with a female caretaker; they enjoy interaction even over closed-circuit television at the age of two months; by twelve months they can engage in primitive turn-taking (Murray and Trevarthen, 1985). During infancy, a child is a part of a joint biological system with its mother.

Most children in Britain are brought up in families, with an average of 2.3 children, though an increasing number live with one parent or with one parent and a step-parent. This is a relationship which begins when the child is born and usually endures to the death of the parent, taking quite different forms at each stage. For some years children are completely dependent for food, care and protection. Gradually they become more independent, and at adolescence partly break the bond by various kinds of rebellion and hostility. Soon the grown-up child resumes a close but now more equal relationship, and eventually it may be the parent who is dependent.

The main activities of parents and children are feeding, supervision of play, conversation (which is at first very primitive and teaches language), showing affection and enjoying each other's company; later, children help a bit in the house (or, in some cultures, help a lot). An important parental skill is discipline and the training of children in acceptable ways of behaving. The expression of sufficient warmth is most important, has desirable influences on many aspects of the child's personality, increases sociability and reduces the likelihood of later mental disorder or delinquency. The most successful style of discipline is the use of reasoning and explanation of the consequences of behaviour rather than 'because I say so', physical punishment or love-withdrawal. There should be clear and consistent discipline, somewhere between strictness and permissiveness. Adolescents are very hard to manage, but most success is obtained with a democratic-persuasive style, plenty of explanation and reasoning, and sustained warmth – though all this is easier said than done.

A powerful attachment develops between children and parents or other caretakers, and this explains why the relationship is so enduring. Its power is probably partly due to shared genes: parents and children on average share 50 per cent. Attachment also depends on the nature of mother–child contact, and is strongest when the caretaker feeds the child, plays and engages in social stimulation, involving bodily contact, looking and smiling.

The benefits of children to parents are obvious: a great deal of joy and satisfaction, help on the farm in rural communities, and the fact that people with children live a little longer. There are also costs in the form of stress and hard work; marital satisfaction – and probably happiness – hits low periods when there are babies in the home, and is even worse when babies become adolescents.

During adolescence less time is spent with parents, and there is often a period of increased conflict and decreased warmth in the relationship with them, especially between mothers and daughters, though later this is usually the strongest relationship (Paikoff and Brooks-Gunn, 1991). However, the low period during adolescence is followed by the time of the 'empty nest', which is often surprisingly happy, especially if the children are still in close touch; after this there is lifelong attachment on more equal terms.

*Workmates* Most men, and many women, are at work between the ages of about twenty and sixty-five for eight hours a day. They sustain relations with peers, subordinates and superiors, and often with clients, customers, etc. Work relationships are the result of people being brought together by the work, for example as workmates on assembly lines or in offices, as members of teams such as aircrews, or where one is a supervisor, assistant, inspector, technical adviser or client.

Work relations overall are weaker than the others we have discussed. On the other hand, they take up a lot of the waking hours and are an important source of job satisfaction and support in dealing with work stress (Payne, 1980; Cohen and McKay, 1984). Are work relationships superficial or not, then? Several kinds of work relations can be distinguished: those who become friends in the normal sense, those who are often seen over lunch or coffee at work but not outside, those who are quite liked but not seen in this way, and those who are disliked. We asked a sample of workers to report their frequency of various activities with workmates in each of these categories, with the results shown in Table 6.4. It can be seen that in the closer work relations there was a higher occurrence of various forms of help

| | With | | | |
|---|---|---|---|---|
| | Social friend | Friend at work | Work colleague | Disliked colleague |
| Helping other with work | 52% | 32% | 18% | 8% |
| Discussing work | 49% | 52% | 32% | 17% |
| Chatting casually | 72% | 63% | 26% | 15% |
| Joking with the other | 72% | 54% | 24% | 13% |
| Teasing the other | 46% | 32% | 18% | 20% |
| Discussing personal life | 30% | 19% | 13% | 11% |
| Discussing personal feelings | 26% | 10% | 5% | 5% |
| Asking for or giving personal advice | 33% | 19% | 8% | 6% |

Table 6.4   Percentage of workers who engaged in work and social activities (Argyle and Henderson, 1985).

and co-operation at work, but also of a lot of pure sociability – games, jokes and gossip (Henderson and Argyle, 1985). Other studies have described the high level of joking, teasing and fooling about, entirely unrelated to work, on the part of workers. This is the basis of a major component of job satisfaction, social satisfaction and supportive social relationships at work.

Work superiors and associates can be an important source of social support, and are able to reduce the harmful effects of stress at work more than a spouse or friends. This is perhaps because they are in a better position actually to remove the source of stress (Payne, 1980). Furthermore, relationships with people at work are one of the main sources of job satisfaction (Argyle, 1989).

Many work relationships, perhaps most of them, consist of easy co-operation but go no further than this. And a few have to be sustained even though people dislike each other. There are often conflicts between those at work, arising out of opposing roles (e.g. management and unions), competition and rivalry, or conflicting views about policy.

Work relationships, like others, have their rules. The main rules are about being fair in the division of rewards, being helpful and co-operative, and preventing too much intimacy.

## VARIATIONS WITH CLASS, CULTURE, GENDER AND AGE

We have described some of the universal principles governing relationships. Now we come to some of the very interesting ways in which they vary between different groups.

*Social class* Friendship is more important for middle-class people: they have more friends and call on them rather than kin for help, compared with working-class people. Middle-class friends have similar interests and attitudes, and come from work, leisure groups, voluntary work or other activities, Working-class friends are chosen more because they live near and can provide help when needed; they form tight-knit groups, with neighbours, and see each other in social clubs and pubs.

Kin are seen much more often in the working class, partly because they live near; they are regular sources of domestic help, advice and social support. This is particularly true for female kin, who used to form a 'female trade union' to help cope with unhelpful husbands.

Working-class individuals have much more premarital intercourse, often without contraception, so the girls marry when young, and often when pregnant; middle-class couples marry four years later on average, and delay longer before having children. Middle-class marriages are more 'symmetrical' – there is more companionship, shared friends and leisure, conversation and sharing in decisions – and the husbands provide a greater amount of support. It is not surprising that middle-class marriages tend to be happier; working-class couples are three and a half times more likely to get divorced.

Middle-class families are more child-centred, with the father playing a larger part in child-rearing, and there is more likely to be a father in the home. Working-class parents are more authoritarian, perhaps reflecting the way they themselves are treated at work; there is a higher incidence of physical punishment of children, and discipline is directed towards respectable behaviour, obedience and conformity. Middle-class parents are more accepting and egalitarian, make more use of explanation, and emphasize the importance of achievement and responsibility; however, lower-class child-minders may introduce different values.

Middle-class individuals at work have a lot of independence and responsibility; they receive little supervision themselves, but are in charge of others. They get a lot of affiliative satisfaction from social contacts at work. Manual workers work in groups, often in noisy conditions, and this may not lead to very positive social bonds.

The overall pattern of social relationships is quite different in each class, the middle class making more use of friends and having happier marriages, the working class more often using kin. However, the total amount of social support is found to be greater for the middle class (Argyle, 1994).

*Culture* Friendship is found in all cultures, but it can be more formal than in ours. Australian 'mateship' developed in the early days among miners and stockmen, isolated in the bush with very few women; they needed a friend who could be trusted to stand by them. Blood brothers are another variety; this creates a bond so that the other can be relied upon as a brother. Friendship networks, like the Mafia, are sources of mutual help in cultures where the official institutions can't be relied upon and the official channels don't work. Social life is different in Japan and some other parts of the East, because of the importance of saving face and of harmony in groups; there is no teasing or public disagreement, for example.

Buying a bride with 'bride price', e.g. camels, is a very widespread custom, especially in Africa, where the wife is a kind of property like an animal or servant. Marrying for love began in Europe in the Middle Ages, and even today, in much of India and Japan, most marriages are arranged; love comes later. Marriage takes a variety of forms: up to four wives for Muslims, a concubine for the Chinese, 'open' and 'swinging' marriage for some Californians.

The family has become much smaller in the modern world; the nuclear family is believed to be a response to the need for mobile labour in an industrialized age. Children in Third World countries are still reared in extended families. Popenoe (1988) has documented the 'decline of the family' in Sweden during recent decades: fewer marriages, increased divorce, smaller families, less joint activity, family routines or conversation with the children, weak family subculture, less contact with kin, less care of old people, more working mothers and children in day care. In early agricultural communities children had to be obedient and responsible; aggression, achievement and co-operation are handled in different ways, reflecting the values of the culture.

Kinship networks are much more extensive and important in Africa, India and the rest of the Third World. If you want a job, or want almost any kind of help, the kinship network is the best place to turn. In parts of Africa it is difficult to become rich or start a business because so many 'brothers' want a share. In China respect is paid to elderly parents, as is a substantial proportion of the income of unmarried children.

China and other parts of the East have been described as 'collectivist', compared with Western 'individualism'. In collectivist cultures people subordinate their own goals to those of the group, especially family, neighbours and close friends, for example sharing material resources (Triandis et al., 1988).

Work relationships in most of the world outside Europe and North America are more hierarchical, with paternalistic styles of leadership at best. In Japan managers are trained for obedient behaviour in hierarchies by management courses in which they are compelled to go on twenty-five-mile route marches by night, on little food, and ordered to shout or sing the company song, and to learn and recite meaningless texts. There is often emphasis on working in groups, and these may be kept intact; there is a high degree of conformity and co-operation. In less developed parts of Africa, as in Britain before the Industrial Revolution, work is done in groups of relatives and neighbours, and is not separated from leisure (Argyle and Henderson, 1985).

*Gender* Women friends *talk*, drink coffee, disclose confidences and provide social support; men friends play squash, help each other and in a number of ways *do* things together – there is less disclosure and intimacy, though men often drink together and talk about work. As well as having fewer intimate friendships, men have fewer friends altogether, especially in middle age. The reason for these sex differences is not agreed upon; it could be male fear of homosexuality, male competitiveness at work and sport, or because work contacts meet the same needs.

Research at the Rochester Interaction Record includes obtaining information about every social encounter of subjects lasting more than ten minutes over a period of time. One finding is that feeling lonely is correlated with a low frequency of interaction with women, for young people of both sexes. Interaction with men is felt, on the whole, to be less intimate, rewarding or meaningful than interaction with women (Wheeler, Reis and Nezlek, 1983).

We have seen that males and females look for different things in a partner (p. 49), following their different biological interests. Men are trying to propagate their genes, so they are promiscuous, but they will settle down with a woman who has good prospects of child-bearing. Women want a mate who will look after them and the children; we saw that they are attracted to men who are strong and have good financial prospects. It has been found that girls are cooler and more cautious in matters of love; in one study some males thought they were in love after the first date, but 40 per cent of girls were not sure after the twentieth (Kephart, 1967).

For a long time, and in all cultures, men have dominated in marriage and been the main providers, while women have done most of the work in the house – especially childcare and cooking. The greater education of women has led to greater equality of spouses and more employment for women, but they still do most of the housework and childcare. And it is husbands who benefit most from marriage; married people of both sexes are happier, and in better mental and physical health, than singles, but men benefit more, probably because wives are more sympathetic confidantes.

For men, relationships at work are important, and, as we have seen, some workmates become friends while others are regularly seen for lunch or coffee at work, though not outside. Relations with work colleagues may last for many years. Women at work tend to have more social jobs – secretaries, teachers, nurses and social workers – and they enjoy the social side of work more. Women in senior positions usually handle their subordinates in a more caring and democratic way than the corresponding men, but they have more difficulty in being promoted to these positions, partly as a result of prejudice, partly because of the diversion of their energies to family duties.

*Age*  Friendship is very different at different ages. Between adolescence and the age of twenty-five, friends may spend hours a day together; in middle age they may only meet once a month, family and social contacts at work seeming to have replaced friendships. Middle-aged people also find it more difficult to make new friends than when they were younger (Nicholson, 1980). Old people who are widowed or retired may spend time with their friends, but they are more likely to take up with their siblings or grown-up children. They have less social life than before, but often do not feel lonely, partly because reduced social contact is expected and does not affect their self-esteem, as it would for a younger person (Shute and Howitt, 1990).

Romantic love is for the young, and starts at about seventeen. Marriage goes through definite stages, now often preceded by a living-together period: the honeymoon period, lasting until the arrival of the first child; the child-rearing period; the period after the last child has left home; and finally widowhood. Sexual activity declines in frequency and importance, and the nature of the relationship changes to a level of greater security and commitment. Marital satisfaction is greatest before and after the child-rearing stage.

Kin are important to children while they are still at home, and of least interest when they are between the ages of twenty and thirty, but kin are especially important to old people, many of whom live with or near one of their offspring, and most of whom have seen a son, daughter or sibling during a given week and are regularly helped by their children. Telephone calls and letters are mainly to kin. Working-class old people are in closer touch with kin than the middle-class elderly, since middle-class families are more dispersed.

Young people at work have to be 'socialized' into the ways of work; they have to learn how to work as a member of a group and under the direction of a supervisor. For young people at work the peer group is important; and for older workers, especially those who have not been very successful, or those whose main achievements are behind them, the social contacts may again be more important than the work itself.

### HOW TO SUCCEED WITH RELATIONSHIPS – RULES, SKILLS AND KNOWLEDGE

In this section I shall put together some of the main implications of research for the successful management of relationships.

*Friendship* We have seen that it is generally believed that certain rules should be followed by friends, and that breaking some of them, especially third-party rules (p.145), leads to the loss of friendships.

Making friends requires certain social skills, and these are often taught on social skills training courses to lonely and isolated individuals. The main skills are:

1 Non-verbal communication, especially more use of smiling, gaze and friendly tone of voice.

2 Conversational skills, especially initiation of conversation, taking an interest in the other, self-disclosure – which indicates trust – and finding things in common.

3 Being more assertive, less passive, more rewarding and less egocentric.

Lonely people often have an inadequate understanding of friendship. They sometimes do not realize that it involves concern for the other. They may also have a negative attitude to others, not expecting to enjoy their company.

For those who want to make more friends there are some very simple, practical steps they can take. Friends are most likely to be found in leisure settings, at work or in the neighbourhood. Joining a club in the neighbourhood realizes the conditions of similarity and proximity; but the third principle, rewardingness, is needed too.

*Marriage* The problem is not so much getting married, which is achieved by most people, but staying married, where about 40 per cent now fail, with much distress to themselves and their children. We found a long list of rules for marriage that were widely endorsed. Which are the rules leading to trouble when broken? Studies of distressed and divorced couples have found that the following are most often mentioned:

adultery
neglect of home and children
physical or verbal abuse
drinking
lack of love or appreciation
not enough sex

(Argyle and Henderson, 1985)

Marriage requires some special social skills, and these are taught in marital therapy; for example:

1 Increasing rewardingness, verbal and non-verbal, having 'love days', keeping records of positive and negative behaviour. There is a lot of evidence that in unhappy marriages there are more negative acts than in happy ones, both verbal and non-verbal, and that these are reciprocated (Gottman, 1979).
2 Better negotiation of disagreements, by willingness to compromise to meet the needs of the other. One technique is quid pro quo contracts, e.g. he agrees to take her out two nights a week while she agrees to sex games of his choice once a week. This idea is derived from exchange theory (see p. 150).
3 Improved communication, especially non-verbal expression

of emotions and attitudes. It would probably be useful to concentrate on the husband's skills.

4 Improved problem-solving, particularly the capacity to discuss relationship problems. However, nothing is known about the form such discussion or negotiation normally takes.

Some people have a poor understanding of marriage. They may not appreciate the high probability of disagreements between two different individuals living so closely together; they may not realize that marriages often go through temporary bad patches, for example with teenage children; and they may not understand the strength of bonding created by marriage, and the consequent distress if the relationship is lost. There are some simple steps that can be taken, which may make marital therapy or guidance unnecessary:

1 Since attachment is based on joint activities which are important and rewarding, the range of these could be expanded, e.g. to include both leisure and domestic tasks.
2 Since attachment is partly due to building a shared cognitive world, through talk and self-disclosure, it follows that spouses should talk and disclose more.
3 Since environmental and social network supports are important, spouses should establish more joint social contacts.

*Work* There are generally agreed rules for all work relationships. Table 6.5 shows the rules for dealing with co-workers.

> 1 Accept fair share of the work.
> 2 Co-operate over physical conditions.
> 3 Help when asked.
> 4 Co-operate despite dislike.
> 5 Don't denigrate to supervisor.
> 6 Ask for help and advice.
> 7 Don't be over-inquisitive about private life.

Table 6.5   Rules for workmates (Argyle and Henderson, 1975).

There is a wide range of work skills, and some of the main ones will be described in Chapter 10: supervision, negotiation, chairmanship, interviewing and selling.

## FURTHER READING

Argyle, M., and Henderson, M., *The Anatomy of Relationships*, Penguin, Harmondsworth, 1985.
Duck, S., *Handbook of Personal Relationships*, Wiley, Chichester, 1988.

## CHAPTER 7
# GROUPS, ORGANIZATION, CLASS AND CULTURE

In the previous chapters, problems of social interaction have been simplified by concentrating on encounters between two people. In this chapter, social situations and relationships involving more than two people will be considered. First, interaction may take place between members of small social groups with three, four or more members. Second, there may be differences of power, status or role in social organizations. Third, people are steeped in a cultural and social-class background, which prescribes the verbal and non-verbal means of communication, as well as the rules governing behaviour in different situations. We shall consider how to improve relations between groups, including how to train people to cope with another culture.

### MEMBERSHIP OF SMALL SOCIAL GROUPS

We have seen that most animals live in groups; many human activities are also carried out in groups between three and fifteen in size. There are several rather different kinds of small group; families, work-groups and groups of friends are the most basic. There are also decision-taking and problem-solving groups, committees of various kinds and groups invented by psychologists, like T-groups and encounter groups.

Some processes of social interaction are similar in all kinds of group – all form norms and have leaders; on the other hand there are distinctive forms of social behaviour in each kind of group. Much research on small groups has taken the form of laboratory experiments; these have the advantage of being able to test hypotheses rigorously, but they tend to omit important features of real-life groups and are stripped down to those elements of group life which the experimenter knows about already.

The basic theory of groups is simple, there being two motivations for joining one: to carry out a task, play a game, etc., and to enjoy the social interaction and sustain relationships. All groups have activities, though the balance varies. People often join a group for economic or other non-social reasons in the first place; they then become involved in group activities, find these satisfying and become attached to the group. A group of friends may want to enjoy each other's company, but they have to do something, i.e. a task must be devised; leisure groups provide a solution to this problem.

The social behaviour in groups can be divided up as shown in Table 7.1.

|  | *Task* | *Sociable* |
|---|---|---|
| *Verbal* | Information and discussion related to the task. | Gossip and chat, jokes and games, discussion of personal problems. |
| *Non-verbal* | Task performance, help, NV comments on performance, NV signals conveying information. | Communicating interpersonal attitudes, emotions, self-presentation. |

Table 7.1 The two basic dimensions of group behaviour.

*Group formation* A group, by one definition, is a number of people who are attracted towards the group, either to the activities or to each other, usually both. Such 'cohesiveness' can be measured by the proportion of choices, as friends, which are made of other group members, or by the frequency with which the word 'we' is used as opposed to 'I'. A group will become cohesive under the following conditions:

physical proximity, e.g. sharing an office;
similarity of background, values, interests;
rewarding experiences in the group, including success at tasks;
activities which require co-operation;
a skilled leader, who can preserve harmony;
the absence of hostile or disturbed personalities.

Cohesiveness has important consequences: the members co-operate and help each other, enjoy the group, and have high job satisfaction in working groups, which as a result have low absenteeism and turnover, and greater productivity at tasks which require co-operation. On the other hand, there may be too much social activity at the expense of work, and there may be hostility to other groups – the in-group is favoured at the expense of out-groups (Argyle, 1989).

Group formation is different in groups of various sizes. Groups of three are different from groups of two. The addition of a third member to a dyad, even as an observer, changes the situation entirely. Each of the original participants now has to consider how his behaviour will be seen by the new member, and his behaviour will be affected differently if this is, for example, an attractive girl, his mother or his tutor. A and B may have worked out their dominance relationships and the proportion of the time each will speak; C now has to be fitted into this hierarchy, and he may dominate both, be intermediate or be dominated by both.

In groups of three there are various kinds of internal competition and jockeying for position. With three males there is usually a straight battle for dominance, and the weakest becomes excluded. If there are two males and one female, the males will compete for the attention of the female. Females behave rather differently: if there are three females and one begins to get left out, the others will work hard to keep her in (Robson, 1966). If there is one powerful and dominating member of a triad, the others may form a coalition in which they combine together against him. The collaboration of the weak against the strong is observed in small-group experiments and in real life; it has been summarized by the proposition 'in weakness there is strength'.

As group size increases from four to ten or more, the character of interaction changes. It is less easy to participate, both because others want to take the floor and because of greater audience anxiety; it is less easy to influence what the others will do; there is greater discrepancy between the amount of interaction of different members – in large groups the majority scarcely speak at all; the variety of personality and talent present is greater and there is greater differentiation of styles of behaviour; discussion is less inhibited and there is ready expression of disagreement; and if the group has work to do there is a greater tendency to create rules and arrange for division of labour (Thomas and Fink, 1963).

The development of cohesion may be made difficult by the combination of persons in the group. Haythorn (1956) created groups of four, where one member was designated the leader, and where different combinations of authoritarian and non-authoritarian leaders and followers were compared. The groups ran most smoothly, with least conflict between leader and followers, when both were authoritarian or both were non-authoritarian. In each case leader and followers were using social styles which fitted in a complementary way.

*Norms* All groups develop norms, i.e. shared ways of behaving and thinking, including ways of working and dressing, common beliefs and social behaviour, and especially shared ways of doing and thinking about the main group activity. Religious conversion, the adoption of new drugs by doctors, and many other changes of behaviour or beliefs are partly the result of conformity to group norms. Norms affect much of our life, and embarrassments are caused by our unintentionally violating these norms: walking into the wrong rest room, clapping at a pause during a symphony, arriving at a party in the wrong clothes (Myers, 1993).

Members of a group will have something in common from the beginning, and there is further convergence towards shared norms, particularly on the part of individual deviates. Such norms will govern the styles of social behaviour which are approved and admired. Anyone who fails to conform is placed under pressure to do so, and, if he continues in his non-conforming behaviour, he is rejected. Numerous experiments show that a deviate becomes the object of considerable attention, and of efforts to persuade him to change his behaviour. This is particularly likely to happen when his deviation is on some matter which is important to the group, which may affect the success of the group or which challenges deeply held beliefs. Deviates may conform for two quite different reasons: to avoid looking silly and being rejected, or because they regard the group's views as a valuable source of information. The other group members might be more expert, while consistent behaviour on the part of the group may be taken to indicate the operation of some unknown rule; this may explain why subjects in conformity experiments are prepared to go along with the group when it gives, unanimously, an apparently wrong answer. It is important that people should deviate from time to time in a constructive way and lead the group to adopt a better solution to its problems in response to a changing external situation.

Characteristic interaction sequences take place in connection with norms. A member may deviate because he does not like a norm, is conforming to another group or has thought of a better way of doing things. Deviation is often greeted with surprise, non-verbal signals of disapproval, verbal attempts at influence and finally by rejection and exclusion from the group. Sometimes it leads to laughter, sometimes the easiest thing is to ignore it and sometimes it is recognized as a possibly useful innovation. Originality and independence are especially valued in fields such as science, art and fashion, though still within certain limits. Independence is not simply a failure to conform, but rather a positive choice and one that risks disapproval by the rest of the group. It is more likely to arise if there is some positive reward for being right. Innovators are more likely to be successful if they are persons of high informal status, in virtue of their past contributions to the group. Hollander (1958) has suggested that they earn 'idiosyncrasy credit' and that the group gives them permission to deviate, their behaviour being seen as a possible new line of action rather than a failure to attain the approved standard.

A persistent minority, even of two, may be able to change the norms. One deviate can be seen as an eccentric failure, but two deviates are taken more seriously. A second person disagreeing with the group casts doubt on the correctness of group norms and may open up disagreements within the majority. A minority who are unanimous, and who display conviction, offer an alternative view of things. Moscovici (1980) has found that such a minority can bring about real conversion, at first indirectly via inferences from the new ideas and later through a change of heart after a time interval. Another view is that sub-groups exercise influence in proportion to their size, but a minority can sometimes trigger a general change in opinion if the group has lost touch with the true state of affairs outside (Latané and Wolf, 1981), whereas a majority can only produce public compliance.

*Hierarchies and roles* All groups of animals and men form hierarchies, there being advantages in having leaders who are able to direct task activities and prevent conflict in the group. It is probably functional to have such hierarchies since groups, especially large ones, with clear leadership structures are more effective. During the early meetings of a group there is a struggle for status among those individuals strong in dominance motivation. Several members carry out task functions and thus become seen as potential leaders, one of these candidates finally being adopted (Stein, Hoffman, Cooley and Pearse, 1980). When leaders need to be appointed quickly, as in a jury, the group members are influenced in their choice by the age and apparent social status of those present, and also by an assertive non-verbal manner, of posture and voice, and the convincing and businesslike nature of what is said by the potential leader.

When the order has settled down, a characteristic pattern of interaction is found. The low-status members at the bottom of this hierarchy talk little, they address the senior members politely and deferentially, and little notice is taken of what they have to say. A person's position in the hierarchy is primarily a function of how useful he has been in the past; thus the hierarchy is maintained in equilibrium – people are allowed to talk and are listened to if their contributions are expected to be useful. Position in the hierarchy bears little relation to personality traits, but is connected with ability at the group task. The group uses techniques of reward and punishment to maintain this system: a person who talks too much is punished, while high-status members who feel sleepy are stimulated to speak. When people at different positions in the hierarchy interact, the pattern of relationships between them is part of the total scheme of group structure (Bales, 1953).

In addition to having different degrees of status and influence, group members adopt styles of behaviour which are differentiated in other ways. Slater (1955) first noted this effect and found that in discussion groups there was usually a popular person, or 'socio-emotional' leader, and a task leader. It is interesting that the same person did not do both these things – reflecting contrasting types of motivation among the members. Each kind of group has a characteristic set of roles which are available, though the roles of task and socio-emotional leader may occur in every kind of group. A role of 'leader of the opposition' is often found in juries and work-groups. There may be a number of other roles, such as secretary, treasurer, committee member and member responsible for the coffee rota.

*The effect of the group on behaviour* Simply being in the presence of others increases the level of physiological arousal and general activity and causes one to emit common, well-learnt responses; for example, one does better at familiar tasks, worse at unfamiliar ones (Zajonc, 1965). This is true of ants and rats as well, but for humans the effects are probably only produced by others who are evaluating or judging in some way; the presence of blindfolded people does not increase arousal (Cottrell et al., 1968). At tasks like tug of war or cheering, the more people there are the less effort they each put in – 15 per cent less in groups of three in one experiment – which has been called 'social loafing'; it happens when individual efforts can't be identified.

Working in groups has advantages for some kinds of task – where co-operation is needed, to catch large animals or build houses in primitive societies, and where a number of different skills are needed in modern ones. Many decisions are taken in groups; are these any better than those taken by individuals? Groups do better on average if the work can be divided into sub-tasks, though they take longer over it. In addition, committee members feel committed to the decisions taken and are motivated to help carry them out.

However, groups can sometimes make very bad decisions. In laboratory experiments it has been found that groups often move towards extreme positions, through the members reinforcing each other's initial prejudices, if these were widely shared in the first place. Janis and Mann (1977) suggested that certain unwise political decisions, like supporting the Bay of Pigs invasion of Cuba, were due to such a process. They called this 'groupthink', and put it down to conformity pressures, where criticism and deviation are suppressed, leading to excessive optimism, risk-taking, and interference with cognitive efficiency and moral judgement. Tetlock and colleagues (1992) analysed ten case studies of political decisions, including the Cuban missile crisis and Chamberlain's Cabinet between 1937 and 1940. They found that it was useful to classify these decisions as 'groupthink' or 'vigilant', and that groupthink led to poor decisions. However, this was not due to conformity or situational pressures, but more to defective procedures in the organization.

In some group situations individuals behave without the usual restraints, engage in aggressive or other antisocial behaviour, and cannot remember clearly who did what. This is known as 'deindividuation', and occurs in lynch mobs, and in experiments in which subjects are made anonymous by wearing masks and white coats (Zimbardo, 1969). However, not all crowds are aggressive or uncontrolled – e.g. music festivals, religious meetings and most cricket matches.

#### DIFFERENT KINDS OF GROUP

So far we have been concerned with the properties of groups in general; we shall now look at some of the special features of particular kinds of group.

*Families* differ from other kinds of group in having a distinctive role-structure of father, mother, sons and daughters. In every culture there is a culturally prescribed relationship between husband and wife, with some differentiation of the roles, and between mother–son, older–younger daughter, etc. There is variation between families, as a result of the personalities and abilities of the members. Family life takes place in the home and centres round eating, sleeping, child-rearing, other domestic jobs, watching TV and further leisure activities. The pursuits of the different members have to be co-ordinated within the space and with the facilities available. Members share the same financial fortunes and position in society. Interaction inside the family has a special quality of great informality; there is almost no self-presentation and little restraint of affection or aggression. In other kinds of group the members do not usually take their clothes off, laugh uproariously, cry, attack, kiss or crawl all over each other, as family members often do – nor do they quarrel so violently.

The special features of family relationships were described earlier (p. 149ff.).

*Groups of friends* are different in many ways: they have no formal structure and no task, but consist of people of similar age, background, values and interests, who come together primarily for affiliative purposes. Members also obtain social support, advice and help with common problems. For young people between fifteen and twenty-five the peer group is of great importance; it gives them a social milieu, where they can be independent of the home, meet members of the opposite sex and develop new social skills and an ego–identity (Muuss, 1962). In a large study of Italian teenagers it was found that those who identified both with family and peer group did better in solving problems like loneliness, lack of life values, and making the transition to adulthood (Palmonari, Kirchler and Pombeni, 1991).

Friends and acquaintances spend several hours a day in conversation, in a number of encounters. Much of this is 'gossip', about self or others. A lot of information is exchanged, and socially skilled people can acquire knowledge which is useful to them, and also send information which influences their reputation (Emler, in press). Friendship groups have no 'task' in the usual sense, but they devise activities which generate the desired forms of social interaction – eating and drinking, dancing, playing games and just talking.

The sociometric structure is important – who likes whom, who is in and who is out. Acceptance depends on conforming to the group norms and realizing the group values, as well as being kind and helpful. However, friends usually form networks rather than closed groups, containing some very popular people, some tight-knit cliques, and chains of communication.

*Work-groups* Most work is done in groups, because of the need to carry out large and complex tasks. The task partly creates the relation between people – how often they meet, whether they must co-operate, their relative power. However, a pattern of informal social life develops as well; it takes place at coffee and lunch breaks, and also during the work, and includes gossip, jokes and other pure sociability (p. 156). Homans (1950) showed how this 'secondary system' affected the work; for example, relationships enjoyed over gossip and games led to help and co-operation over the work. And if cohesiveness is very low there will be little co-operation and output will fall; in addition, there will be a lot of absenteeism and labour turnover.

We now have a fairly clear idea how work-groups should be designed to ensure maximum productivity and maximum job satisfaction. They should be fairly small – not more than fifteen members; cohesiveness should be high; they should work as a co-operative team for shared rewards; status differences should be small; and there should be the optimum style of supervision (pp. 279ff.), with participation in decision-taking (Argyle, 1989).

The technology and work-flow system influence work groups and their effectiveness. Workers may, for example, be on an assembly line, which means that they interact only with their neighbours but are dependent on the whole group for their pay. They may be in a group under a foreman on individual piece-work, or may be isolated at control points in an automated system. These arrangements have definite effects on the relations between people; they may make them love or hate each other, depending on whether they are helping or hindering one another, and may make communications easy or impossible. The Tavistock Institute of Human Relations has shown that it is possible to devise improved social arrangements with exactly the same technology. For example, Trist and colleagues (1963) found that the Longwall method of coal-mining could be employed with greater productivity and less absenteeism if the three main jobs were done on all of the three shifts; previously the jobs of cutting, filling and stonework were done by different shifts, who never met, resulting in a lack of co-operation.

An important development in this tradition is the formation of flexible and autonomous work-groups, which can organize the work as they like. The Volvo assembly plant is a famous example, and an analysis of fifty-three such cases showed increases in productivity, quality of work and safety, and reduced absenteeism and turnover (Pasmore, Francis and Halderman, 1984).

*Leisure groups*  Much adult friendship takes place in leisure groups – for sport, dancing, music, voluntary work, church, etc., or for purely 'social' purposes. Each club has its social niche, in terms of what it does and the age, class and sometimes gender of those who are acceptable. The activity determines the nature of the relationships – intimate, co-operative, competitive or extraverted, for example. Typical groups meet once a week, though keen members may gather several times a week. Leisure groups are different from other friendship groups in that they are based on a single activity (e.g. tennis, Scottish dancing) or set of beliefs (Church, politics), a concern which is shared by the members and important to them. They are different from work-groups in that there is no material reward and, perhaps as a result, little competition for any particular benefits.

We find that these clubs produce high levels of enjoyment and social support, and that the friendships formed are sometimes said to be closer than other friendships. Leisure groups have some features which make them different from most other groups: they are positive, often generous, to outsiders, and they are often quite undemocratic. They are a force for social integration, since the common interest to some extent overrides other social differences, such as age or class. They can be a force for higher standards of behaviour, for example in music, sport or charitable activity.

*Groups invented by social scientists* The groups described so far can be found in all cultures and periods of history. In the modern world there are groups which have been invented by psychologists and others. Therapy groups were created to increase the productivity of therapists and to help patients understand themselves by seeing their own problems in others. Mutual-support groups were established to help alcoholics and many others, by giving help and support to deal with their common problems. T- (training) groups were devised by social psychologists so that clients could receive feedback on their social performance and thus gain in social competence; the experience proved too traumatic for many people, and the movement has faded away. Encounter groups use exercises which give experience of intimacy and other relationships, often involving bodily contact and self-disclosure. Clients find this a powerful experience, but some become worse rather than better.

A careful follow-up study was carried out involving 206 Stanford students who attended encounter groups, T-groups, etc., using 69 control subjects. Success was estimated by a combination of criteria – self-ratings, ratings by friends and so on. The results were as shown in Table 7.2.

| | Percentage group members | Percentage controls |
|---|---|---|
| drop-outs | 13 | — |
| casualties | 8 | — |
| negative change | 8 | 23 |
| unchanged | 38 | 60 |
| moderate positive change | 20 ⎫ | 13 ⎫ |
| high positive change | 14 ⎭ 34 | 4 ⎭ 17 |

Table 7.2   The effect of T-groups and encounter groups.

About a third of the group members and 17 per cent of the

controls improved, while 8 per cent of the group members were harmed by the experience (for example, needing psychiatric help afterwards), in addition to the drop-outs and those who showed negative changes. There were no consistent differences between encounter and non-touching groups; variations between individual group leaders were more important (Lieberman, Yalom and Miles, 1973).

Despite the lack of success of these groups, methods derived from this tradition have been incorporated in a number of therapeutic packages and adopted by quasi-religious sects, along with meditation and other Indian practices. None of these packages has been subjected to follow-up study, and it is very likely that, as with encounter groups themselves, some people benefit, many are unchanged and some become worse.

## SOCIAL ORGANIZATIONS

A great deal of social behaviour takes place against a background of social organization – in schools, industry, hospitals and elsewhere. 'Social organization' means the existence of a series of ranks, positions or offices – such as teacher, foreman, hospital sister, etc. – which persist regardless of particular occupants. Behaviour in organizations is to a considerable extent *pre-programmed*, having been worked out by previous members. The roles interlock: doctor–nurse, patient–nurse, and so on.

*The growth of organization* As groups become bigger and their tasks more complex, a formal structure gradually develops, with a leadership hierarchy and divisions of function. Since it is difficult for one person to supervise more than ten to fifteen others, a second level of management becomes necessary for groups larger than this.

Social organization is an essential part of modern life, because it would be impossible to co-ordinate the activities of the numbers of people involved in large-scale enterprises without extensive division of labour and a hierarchy of leadership. As a small workshop expands to become a factory, or when a guerrilla band becomes an army, the paraphernalia of social organization become necessary. To manufacture motor cars, for example, thousands of different parts must be made by a large number of different people and fitted together; there is thus a great deal of labour division, several levels of leadership, lines of communication and committees for decision-taking.

Social organization is essential, but the precise forms which we have are not necessarily the best, and are in fact found to be dissatisfying by many who serve in them. They have developed slowly. Industrial organizations as we know them today, for example, have been derived from the first small factories established during the Industrial Revolution, by trial and error methods. The first factories were hierarchical and authoritarian, partly modelled on the army of the time. New ideas have led to changes: the Human Relations movement emphasized the importance of supervisory skills, relations within groups and job satisfaction. More recently ideas about industrial democracy have led to changes in hierarchies.

There are several different kinds of social organization. Etzioni (1961) distinguished between:

*coercive* organizations, e.g. prisons and mental hospitals, in which people do what they are told because they have to, through fear of punishment, and are unable to leave;

*utilitarian* organizations, e.g. industries, in which members work in exchange for rewards;

*moral* organizations, e.g. churches, hospitals and universities, members of which are committed to the values and goals of the organization.

The senior members have quite different kinds of power in the three cases – by punishment, reward or appeal to shared goals respectively. Power can also be based on a leader's expertise, or on the desire of subordinates to identify with him ('referent power'). By power is meant the capacity to influence the behaviour of others, and those low in a hierarchy also have this: they can act collectively, as in strikes, and they can withdraw co-operation or other rewards from their superiors.

Behaviour in organizations differs from that in small social groups in a number of ways. Interaction patterns are not so much a product of particular groups of personalities, but are part of the organizational structure. People come to occupy positions of influence or leadership not through the spontaneous choice of their subordinates but because they are placed there by higher authority.

Not all doctors or nurses behave in exactly the same way; there are variations due to personality and past experience. However, deviation from official practices goes a lot further than this. It has long been known that industrial workers engage in a wide range of unofficial practices, including ingenious forms of scrounging and time-wasting, in order to make life tolerable. The same has been reported of life in the army and in mental hospitals. Elizabeth Rosser has studied the underworld of English schools. She found that the pupils have their own procedural ideas and 'rules' for teachers derived from these; if a teacher breaks these rules – for example, by being unfair, too strict or boring – she is punished. What appears to be uncontrollable chaos from the point of view of the authorities turns out to be the operation of another set of rules (Marsh, Harré and Bosser, 1978).

*Positions and roles* Organizations consist of a set of related positions, whose occupants play interlocking roles. A role is the pattern of behaviour shared by most occupants of a position, and which comes to be expected of them. In a hospital, for example, there are obvious differences between the behaviour of patients, doctors, nurses, visitors, etc. Roles include a variety of aspects of behaviour: the work done, ways of interacting with other members of the organization, attitudes and beliefs, and style of clothing.

The pressures to conform to a role can be very strong. Zimbardo (1973) paid a number of normal, middle-class student volunteers to play the roles of prison guards and prisoners, assigned arbitrarily, with appropriate uniforms in an imitation prison. Many of the guards became brutal, sadistic and tyrannical, and many of the prisoners became servile, selfish and hostile, and suffered from hysterical crying and severe depression. The experiment had to be stopped after six days and nights.

Why do people conform so strongly to roles? There are

various pressures to do so, not the least being that someone who deviates will be regarded as eccentric, mad or not 'right' in some way. In addition roles are *interlocking*, so that, if doctors and nurses play their roles, patients have no choice but to play theirs. In any case a role may provide the most effective means of doing a job; teachers, for example, traditionally have a loud, clear and didactic voice, and adopting the same may save someone new to the profession much trial and error. Furthermore, only certain kinds of people want, or are able, to become, say, bishops or barmen, so only particular types of person are found occupying these positions. Newcomers learn a role by imitating senior members and may be given special practice in role-playing during training courses.

Many members of organizations experience *role conflict*, which can take various forms. A person may be under conflicting pressures from different groups of people in the organization. For example, different demands may be made on foremen by managers and by workers, and female students may be expected to be hard-working and intellectual by their teachers but not by the male students. In such cases there may be withdrawal from those exerting the pressure.

Role conflict often leads to anxiety, tension, illness and reduced levels of work. There may also be ambiguity about what a role entails, when a job is not clearly defined or when a new role is created. There can be conflict between role and personality, for example, if an authoritarian personality is a member of a democratic organization. A person may also find himself playing two incompatible roles, e.g. a military chaplain or a teacher whose own child is in the school.

Organizations can be assessed in similar ways to personalities, to show the preferred motivation and styles of behaviour; individuals whose personality matches the organization are found to be under less stress and have lower levels of absenteeism (Furnham and Walsh, 1991).

*Interaction in organizations* Social organization introduces a totally new element, which has not so far been considered. To predict how A and B will behave towards one another it may be much more useful to know their positions in the organization than to know about their personalities or preferred styles of interaction. In the extreme cases of church services and drill parades the whole course of interaction can be 'predicted' by knowing the formal procedure. Even a person's popularity may be more a function of his position than of his personality; it depends whether he has a rewarding role, like awarding bonuses and giving out free buns, or a punitive role, like inspecting work, or the military police.

It is impossible to understand why the members of an organization interact as they do without knowing their organization chart. There have been many studies of the communication between the members of industrial management hierarchies, like that shown in Figure 7.1 (see Argyle, 1989). The main findings are as follows:

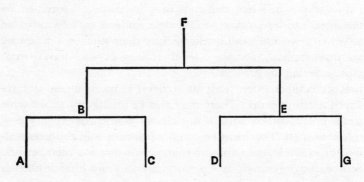

Figure 7.1    Organization chart.

*A and B* Relations with the immediate superior are often rather strained and formal. A may ask B for help, information or advice; he may also have to report progress, possibly delaying and distorting the news if it is bad; and he may want to make suggestions or complaints, which B might not be very eager to hear. B may give orders, advice, expert information or comments on A's performance.

*A and C* Relations with immediate colleagues can vary from

close co-operation in a team, through carefully reciprocated helpfulness, to cutthroat competition.

*A and D* Lateral relations with equal-status people outside the group are often friendly and relaxed. They are useful in producing rapid information-flow and co-operation, and are the basis of the 'grapevine'. Friendship choices are often in A–D relationships.

*A and E* Relations with those of different status but outside the line of command are easier than direct superior–subordinate links and can act like an A–D relationship.

*A and F* It is difficult for F to communicate with persons two or more steps below him in the hierarchy. If he goes through B, four encounters have to take place before some delayed and distorted feedback reaches him, yet if B is left out he will be upset. If notices or other mass media are used there is no feedback.

Since a person's behaviour varies with the rank or position of those with whom he comes into contact, it is important to be able to categorize people; many organizations have uniforms, and members of others can usually be placed by more subtle aspects of their appearance. When an outsider enters an organization, even for a short visit, there is great pressure to find out his 'equivalent rank' so that everyone shall know exactly how to treat him.

Nearly all organizations have a hierarchical structure and this seems to be necessary to provide the necessary administration and co-ordination. However, there are a number of difficulties about hierarchies. As we showed above, there are difficulties of communication up and down hierarchies; these become more acute when there are many levels in the hierarchy or if relationships are authoritarian. It is often found that while those at the upper levels are very satisfied, strongly committed to the organization and work very hard, those at the bottom may be completely alienated, do the least they can get away with, and may even behave destructively by putting a spanner in the works, or its equivalent.

There are several ways of changing organizations to minimize these effects:

1 the style of leadership can be changed so that it is more democratic, leaders delegating and encouraging participation in decisions (cf. p. 281);

2 the number of levels can be reduced by increasing the span of control and decentralizing the organization into smaller units;

3 formal arrangements can be made for consultation as in 'industrial democracy' and for student representation.

Industrial democracy can take a variety of forms: trade union representation and joint consultative committees (Britain), workers' councils (Holland and former Yugoslavia), worker directors (Germany), quality circles (Japan). Follow-up studies have found that such consultation works better if all levels are represented (especially first-line supervisors), if the joint committees are not just advisory but have real power, and if management take it seriously and don't simply push through their own plans. It has been shown to lead to increased productivity, less absenteeism and labour turnover, better decision-taking and improved relations between management and workers (Argyle, 1989).

## CULTURE

Social interaction takes place within a cultural setting. By the culture of a group of people is meant their whole way of life – their language, ways of perceiving, categorizing and thinking about the world, forms of non-verbal communication and social interaction, rules and conventions about behaviour, moral values and ideals, technology and material culture, art, science, literature and history. All these aspects of culture affect social behaviour, directly or indirectly.

Infants are born with basic biological needs and a certain amount of intrinsic equipment. However, human beings have greater powers of learning than animals, as well as a longer period of dependence on their parents, so that different solutions to life's problems can be learnt. As a result of the development of language, humans can communicate their solutions to these problems to one another, and there is continuous modification of the cultural store.

We described cultural differences in non-verbal communication in Chapter 2 – facial expression, gesture, bodily contact and proximity; and we described cultural differences in relationships in Chapter 6 – friendship, kinship, marriage and work relations. We now turn to some other cultural differences in social behaviour.

*Rules* The rules and conventions of social behaviour vary a lot, and it is easy for visitors to get into trouble by breaking them. We have seen that rules are part of social systems which enable people to attain goals, but that there can be alternative ways of solving the problems, as with driving on the right or the left. Here are some of the rules which often cause problems for people working abroad:

1 *Bribery* In many parts of the world it is normal to pay a commission to civil servants, salesmen or professional people who have performed a service, although they are already receiving a salary.

2 *Nepotism* In African and other countries people are expected to help their relatives, and this is the local equivalent of social welfare. Sometimes relatives have contributed to an individual's education; when he gets a good job as a result they expect some return.

3 *Gifts* In all cultures it is necessary to present relatives, friends or work colleagues with gifts on certain occasions, but the rules vary greatly. The Japanese spend a great deal of money on gifts, which must be bought from standard gift shops.

4 *Buying and selling* There are several alternative sets of rules here: barter, bargaining, fixed-price sales and auction. In cultures where bargaining is used it is normal to establish a relationship first, perhaps while drinking tea, and there are conventions about how the bargaining should proceed.

5 *Eating and drinking* One of the main problems in intercultural communication is that there are rules in all cultures about what may not be eaten or drunk, especially certain kinds of meat – like pork, beef or dog – and alcohol.

6 *Rules about time* How late is 'late'? This varies greatly. In

Britain and North America one may be five minutes late for a business appointment but not fifteen, and certainly not thirty minutes late, which is perfectly normal in Arab countries.

One may encounter totally new situations, with their rules; for example, visitors to Oxford University may have to cope with the procedures surrounding dessert, vivas, collections and other strange events. In developing countries there are often two sets of rules corresponding to traditional and modern attitudes – about time, gifts, parental authority and the position of women, for example (Dawson, Whitney and Lan, 1971).

Goffman (1963) has shown how these rules penetrate to the key processes of social interaction, and govern, for example, the detailed sequences of eye and other bodily movements. Kissing one's wife goodbye is done quite differently at a bus-stop and at an air terminal, for example. Such rules are usually unverbalized, and we are only dimly aware of them when someone breaks them.

*Language* This is one of the most obvious differences between cultures. However, when a new language has been learnt there are still problems about its use. In several cultures there is polite usage, words being designed to please rather than inform. Americans often give instructions or orders as if they were questions – 'Would you like to . . .?' Cultures vary in the use of exaggeration: 'if an Arab says what he means without the expected exaggeration, other Arabs may still think that he means the opposite' (Shouby, 1951). English upper middle-class speech includes considerable understatement; a person who fails to follow this convention is regarded as boastful. And in every culture, in many situations, there are special forms of words, or types of conversation, which are thought to be appropriate – for example, to ask a girl for a date, to disagree with someone at a committee, to introduce people to each other, and so on. Americans prefer directness, but Mexicans regard openness as a form of weakness or treachery, and think one should not allow the outside world to know one's thoughts. Frankness by Peace Corps volunteers in the Philippines leads to disruption of smooth social relationships

(Brein and David, 1971). In Japan it is rude to say 'no', as it would lead to loss of face by the other; it is therefore wrong to ask a question for which this might be the answer. Saying 'no' may be avoided simply by changing the topic, while 'yes' can mean 'no' or 'perhaps'. The episode structure of conversations varies a lot: Arabs and others have a 'run-in' period of informal chat for about half an hour before getting down to business.

The language also carries the categories of thought which are important in a culture. For example, the colours of the rainbow are divided up differently in different cultures; Zuni Indians have difficulty in recognizing an orange stimulus shown them previously because they have no word for orange. The Inuit have fifty-six words for snow, where we would need several words to describe each variety (Brown and Lenneberg, 1954). Special styles of social behaviour are labelled, such as *machismo* (Mexico – flamboyant bravery), *chutzpah* (Yiddish – outrageous cheek). When a concept or distinction is important in a culture this becomes reflected in the language, which in turn helps people to deal with situations common in the culture, and in the production of relevant behaviour. Old concepts and words disappear and are replaced by new ones. A long time ago an uncle of mine advised me about tipping, saying, 'A half-crown is a gentleman's coin.' Since then, however, both concepts in this statement have disappeared.

*Motivation* The goals pursued in different cultures vary and sometimes we can see how this has come about. For example, tribes which are constantly at war with their neighbours encourage aggressiveness in young males (Zigler and Child, 1969).

Achievement motivation is created by strong independence training of children, and results in hard work and risk-taking in order to make money, increase status and build up large enterprises. McClelland and Winter (1969) succeeded in improving achievement behaviour in Indian managers, with the result that they increased the size and turnover of their firms.

Assertiveness training is much in demand in the USA, particularly from women; in Britain people want to learn how to make friends, while in Indonesia submissiveness is valued more than assertiveness. Extraversion scores are higher in the USA, Australia and Canada than in Britain, and in the East great value is placed on maintaining good relationships and not losing face (Noesjirwan, 1978).

*Ideals and values* Cultures vary in their moral rules governing sexual behaviour, use of drugs and other matters. Even within modern societies there are great variations between different groups of people in the extent to which alternative moral values and ideals are accepted. They are taught by parents, teachers, clergymen, politicians and others, and are learnt by children brought up in the culture. Values and ideals function as restraints which control and inhibit certain spontaneous patterns of behaviour. While aggressive and sexual behaviour are among the main targets of these controls, the whole style and strategy of social behaviour may also be affected.

Telling the truth is valued in most cultures, but the truth is often not told. In our own culture it is also thought important not to hurt people's feelings, and in some cultures there is a great desire to please the hearer.

It has been found by Triandis (1972) that there are great cultural variations in what is most valued. In parts of India, for example, wealth is not desired because it can lead to arrogance and fear of thieves. In Greece, punishment is valued because it leads to justice. In Japan, serenity and aesthetic satisfaction are most valued. Wealth and health are greatly valued in the West but not in parts of the East.

Moral codes may be learnt as simple sets of rules – 'It is wrong to tell a lie' – or as rather high-level principles such as 'Do unto others as you would they do unto you.' They may be expressed as attitudes which should be adopted – 'Love your neighbour.' Most moral codes in fact recommend behaviour which is more affiliative, less dominating and less aggressive than social behaviour often is.

*Co-operation and competition, collectivism and individualism* Some primitive societies, like the Zuni Indian, are very co-operative; the members help each other with their work in the fields and in building houses, and there is almost no private property. Some tribes, such as the Kwakiutl of Vancouver Island, are very competitive, their lives dominated by the quest for material possessions and social status. Others, like the Greenland Inuit, are (or were) very individualistic, families being isolated and self-sufficient, relationships quarrelsome (Mead, 1937).

Modern cultures can be contrasted with each other on a dimension of individualism–collectivism. China is a collectivist culture, and individuals are expected to subordinate their own interests to the group of kin, immediate neighbours and close friends; there is a high level of conformity, co-operation and social support, but everyone outside this group is regarded as out-group (Triandis et al., 1988). Wheeler, Reis and Bond (1989) provided a clear example of some of these differences in a comparison of social encounters reported by samples of students in Hong Kong and an American university. The Chinese had fewer social interactions a day on average (2.45 v. 5.99), but these were more often with groups, lasted longer, were more task-oriented and involved more disclosure.

Our study of relationship rules showed the much greater concern for group harmony in Japan compared with Britain and Italy. In Japan in particular, though also in Hong Kong, there is greater concern with rules for maintaining harmony in groups. There is more endorsement of rules for obedience to authority, not joking or teasing, keeping up positive regard, avoiding public criticism and restraining emotional expression (Argyle et al., 1986).

Surveys by Hofstede (1984) and others have found that the most collectivist cultures are China, South America, Portugal, Pakistan, Greece and Turkey; the most individualistic cultures are the USA, Australia, Britain and other European countries.

A number of experimental procedures have been devised to see how far children are prepared to co-operate, to win marbles for example. South American children are found to be much more co-operative than US children. Children from a number of primitive cultures are very co-operative, and rural children more co-operative than city children; Israeli kibbutz children are also very co-operative (Madsen, 1971).

### Greetings and other rituals

*Greetings* have similar components in most cultures – touching, mutual gaze, bowing, head nods, smiling. The Indians and Japanese do not touch, and a variety of exotic greetings are found in primitive societies – smelling cheeks and rubbing noses, taking off some or all clothes, kissing beards, and so on (Argyle, 1988). Pike (1967) reports the case of a missionary girl who got into difficulties with a cannibal chief because she tried to throw him on the floor (shook hands) and laughed at him (smiled).

*Etiquette* All cultures have their social rules; when these are elaborate and rigid they are referred to as 'etiquette'. In Western countries it is only in old-fashioned upper-class circles that these rules are made into explicit codes of conduct. In the Far East, especially in Japan, formal etiquette is more widely followed, but this only applies to certain traditional social situations, and not apparently to getting on buses and trains. In Britain, in polite circles, there are rules about seating people at table; in Boston, USA, there were once rules about who to speak to during each course.

*Establishing rapport* Americans are able to establish a certain, rather superficial, contact very quickly, whereas the British are experienced as more 'standoffish', 'closed' or simply difficult to get to know. This may be due to differences in affiliative motivation, or to differences in the social techniques which are acquired.

*Self-presentation* occurs in all cultures. However, in Britain there is a taboo on direct, verbal self-presentation (pp. 213ff.), while in India and Japan it is quite normal to speak highly of oneself. In most of the East 'face' is of great importance and must not be lost.

### SOCIAL CLASS

Most societies, and all modern industrial ones, are stratified into classes. These are groups of people who regard members of the other groups as inferior or superior, and who share a common culture. The higher groups have more money, property and power. Members of each social class mix freely and can form intimate relationships with other members of their own class, but are much less likely to do so with people from other classes. Class is really a continuous variable, and boundaries are hard to define, though groupings and barriers appear from time to time. A development in the British class system during the 1950s was the emergence of an upper working class, whose members shared much of the material culture of the middle class but did not mix socially with that class or have the same pattern of social behaviour (Goldthorpe et al., 1969).

Social class is shared by families, and depends mainly on the husband's occupation, income and education, and on the size and location of the home. Social scientists in Britain usually assess class from occupation; the Registrar General for a long time used this scale:

1   Professional, higher management
2   Intermediate
3n  Skilled, non-manual
3m  Skilled manual
4   Semi-skilled
5   Unskilled

Members of the public do not assess each other's class in this way but use other criteria, such as accent, area of residence, friends, education, clothes, income and lifestyle (Reid, 1989).

Members of different classes in Britain have quite different accents. People in Norwich drop 'h's at the beginnings and 'g's at the ends of words, though much less if they are speaking carefully, as when reading lists of words (Fig. 3.1). There are also class differences in the way language is used. Bernstein (1959) suggested that working-class people used a 'restricted code', consisting of short and simple sentences, often uncompleted, with a lot of slang and idiom, many personal pronouns, and recurring rhetorical questions of the type 'didn't I?' Middle-class people also use a restricted code, but they can use an 'elaborated' one which is more impersonal, complex and grammatical. Research shows that middle-class people do use more complex syntax and a larger vocabulary, and are more effective at communicating impersonal information. However, these class differences occur as matters of degree, and working-class people can use the elaborated code if necessary, though they find it more difficult.

It has sometimes been suggested that middle-class people are more socially skilled than working-class people. However, their goals are probably different: middle-class behaviour is directed more to the accurate communication of information, working-class behaviour to the maintenance of social ties, if Bernstein is right. Most middle-class jobs involve dealing with people and therefore require a lot of social skill – managers, lawyers, doctors and politicians for example.

When members of different classes meet, it is like a meeting between members of an organizations that has different ranks, like the army or a hospital. Each recognizes the other's rank, from speech or clothes, and treats him or her accordingly. When juries elect a foreman, or when clubs elect their officers, those of higher social class are often appointed. This is not exactly deference, but it does show an acceptance of the class hierarchy. There is often a sense of discomfort and social distance unless those concerned are in some established role relationship. Nurses of different ranks, as we have seen, accommodate to each other's speech style with no difficulty (p. 69).

It is in public places, on purely social occasions and between strangers that inter-class difficulties appear. Mary Sissons arranged for an actor to stop eighty people in Paddington Station and ask them the way to Hyde Park. For half of them he was dressed and behaved as if upper middle-class, for half he appeared to be working-class. The interviews were filmed and tape-recorded, and the social class of the respondents was obtained by subsequent interview. It was found that the middle-class–middle-class encounters went most smoothly compared with the other three combinations of social class; there was instant rapport, the encounters lasted longer, respondents smiled more and there was a definite ending (Sissons, 1971).

Social mobility is widely desired and many individuals do move to another class; in Britain 34 per cent cross the manual/non-manual line in one direction or the other. Upward mobility is greater for those who are intelligent, well-educated and have high achievement motivation. It is also more likely for men who are tall, and for women who are thin and physically attractive. As Sorokin said, 'There is permanent recruiting of beautiful women into the upper social strata' (1964); a number of ingenious experiments have confirmed this by varying the attractiveness of interview candidates (p. 85). Downward mobility is more likely for those who are less intelligent, attractive or hard-working, or who are mentally disturbed.

We described class differences in relationships in Chapter 6, and showed how middle-class people have happier marriages and make more use of their friends, while working-class people see more of their kin. Most friendships and other relationships are with others of the same class, but not all, and cross-class relationships are important for the integration of society. Forty per cent of friends are from other classes; contacts with kin are reduced for men, but not for women, when class differences develop. Leisure groups are a major source of social integration, especially sports groups, church and evening classes (Argyle, 1994).

## INTER-GROUP CONTACT AND CONFLICT

We saw earlier that groups often form negative stereotypes about one another (p. 85). These negative attitudes sometimes lead to violence between people of different races, religions or nationalities. Sherif thought this was because of real conflicts of goals between groups. In a famous study he and colleagues (1961) divided eleven- to twelve-year-old boys at a summer camp into two groups. It was found that competitive sports, and an occasion when one group frustrated the other, led to a dangerous level of hostility. Peace was restored by getting the groups to work together for shared goals, such as restoring the · deliberately interrupted water-supply. Other studies have shown that realistic conflict is often the source of hostility between groups, and that co-operation is successful in reducing it in the case of small groups. However, superordinate goals often do not work with larger groups, like the factory departments studied by Rupert Brown (1988). One way of tackling inter-group conflict would be to work harder at the introduction of shared goals, to persuade the two sides to co-operate.

Tajfel (1970) and co-workers found that negative attitudes to an out-group can occur without any conflict of interests. Subjects in their 'minimal group experiments' chose to give larger rewards to in-group members, where the group was defined vaguely in terms of similar aesthetic choices. The explanation put forward was that the self-image is partly based on the success of the group to which a person belongs. This theory has been supported by experiments showing that self-esteem is enhanced by making favourable allocation of rewards to the in-group (Oakes and Turner, 1980). Low-status groups may enhance their self-esteem in various ways, such as emphasizing features on which they are superior to other groups. Brown (1978), with real industrial groups, found that all preferred a wage settlement where they were paid £1 per week more than a rival department even if this meant they themselves were paid £2 per week less than they might otherwise have been paid. However, a laboratory experiment found that such self-sacrifice in pursuit of group status only happened when there had been competition with the other group. Mann (1963) found that South African Hindus accept their economic inferiority but believe they are superior in spiritual, social and practical fields. On the other hand, these ideas only seem to work with certain kinds of group, such as sports teams and competing ethnic groups, but not with leisure groups for example (Hinkle and Brown, 1990). And as yet this theory has had no application in the resolving of actual conflicts between groups.

Another approach to resolving conflicts between groups is the 'contact hypothesis', which said that sheer contact between two groups is enough to remove hostile attitudes to one another. This was first demonstrated in the US army in World War II, when mixed white and black regiments were formed, and this had dramatic effects on the racial attitudes of those concerned. Unfortunately it doesn't always work: in a recent study in Amsterdam it was found that the Dutch came to like Indonesians more if they lived next door, but the opposite happened for Turks living next door (Dijker, 1987). The conditions of contact must be exactly right; these conditions include equal status, co-operation and some degree of intimacy. Another problem is that favourable experiences with pleasant members of the other group may fail to generalize, so that they can be regarded as 'exceptions'. Wilder (1986) found general attitude change to members of a rival college if subjects met pleasant and 'typical' members of it; Hamburger has recently found that meeting elected representatives has similar effects; this is important because sometimes one meets leaders who are of course not 'typical'. In our leisure groups research (Argyle and Lu, 1992) the greatest degree of social-class integration was reported for sports groups, church and evening classes; these groups probably provide the optimum conditions for the contact hypothesis to work.

Aronson et al. (1978) devised the 'jigsaw classroom', intended to create such optimum conditions for improving attitudes to another group. Groups of six children are formed, including Anglo, Mexican-American and black. Each pupil is taught part of the materials needed for a group project, and then teaches the others; the teachers just help. The results of several follow-up studies were that the jigsaw pupils increased in liking for the other ethnic groups more than those in ordinary classes.

When people from different cultures meet, there is infinite scope for misunderstanding and confusion. This may be a matter of misinterpreting the other's communications, verbal or non-verbal. There is the Englishman who depreciates his own abilities in what turns out to be a highly misleading way; there is the Arab who starves at a banquet because he is only offered the dishes once; there is the African who puts his hand on a western knee. There may be difficulties in setting up a stable pattern of interaction – Americans and Europeans have been seen retreating backwards or gyrating in circles at international conferences, pursued by Latin Americans trying to establish their habitual degree of proximity (Hall, 1955). Westerners are perplexed by Japanese who giggle when hearing or delivering bad news. American businessmen find it difficult to adjust to the more hierarchical pattern of relationships in their overseas branches, where subordinates do not speak their mind to their superiors.

The result of these cross-cultural misunderstandings is likely to be that each person rejects the other as one who has failed to conform to the standards of civilized society, and regards him as impossible to get on with. There are several solutions to this problem. One is to find out the cultural patterns of the other, and either conform oneself or at least use them to interpret the other's behaviour properly; the difficulty here is that many of these patterns of behaviour are very subtle, and it takes a long familiarity with the culture to know them all. Another approach is to be far more flexible and tolerant when dealing with people from other cultures, and to make a real effort to understand and to control one's reactions to the unusual aspects of their behaviour.

Several research groups have been engaged in developing methods of training people to function effectively in alien cultures. It is common nowadays for those going to work abroad to receive some training in how to cope in the new culture; in the past, there had been a failure rate of 60 to 70 per cent in those sent abroad by the Peace Corps and some other organizations, especially to certain countries, like Japan and Saudi Arabia. The training may take various forms:

*Booklets* The simplest way of preparing people for a visit abroad is to give them a well-informed booklet describing some of the important differences of behaviour, and giving warnings of how visitors may get into trouble.

*Education* A lot has been done in schools, especially in the USA, to teach white children about blacks, sometimes using role-playing. In some versions children role-play various cross-cultural encounters, or quite complex roles such as that of a black policeman at a race riot. These methods have been used to give greater insight into cultural differences and the problems of people in other groups.

*The Culture Assimilator* A critical-incident survey is carried out, in which a large number of individuals who have visited a certain country are asked to describe difficulties which they have had. This locates the forty to sixty main problem situations in the culture in question, which leads to the construction of a do-it-yourself 'tutortext'. The Arab Culture Assimilator developed at the University of Illinois consists of fifty-five problem episodes for trainees to solve, which are intended to teach them about such matters as the role of women, dealing with subordinates, entertaining guests and the importance of religion. It has been found that this kind of training produces some improvement in interaction with Arabs and Thais (Fiedler, Mitchell and Triandis, 1971).

*Workshop methods* Another approach has been used by Peter Collett at Oxford. Englishmen were taught the interaction styles known to be used by Arabs – standing closer, touching, etc. These trainees got on better with Arabs and were liked better than untrained subjects (Collett, 1971). Where new social skills need to be learnt such techniques are very desirable. La Framboise and Rowe (1983) taught American Indians the skills they need to cope with encounters with white Americans. Standard social skills training methods were used – modelling and videotape playback – and training in non-verbal communication was included.

*The BAFA-BAFA game* is intended to prepare people to cope with any other culture. A group of about twenty is divided into two, and each group learns the rules of an imaginary, arbitrary culture, e.g. only special gestures may be used, a conversation may only start if the senior person present has agreed, etc. Visitors are exchanged, who at first get on very badly and are rejected. However, later visitors know what to expect, and eventually each group learns the culture of the other.

*Integrated schemes* Most serious programmes of inter-cultural training have used a combination of methods. For example the Peace Corps established a centre in Hawaii for those going to south-east Asia, with a replica Vietnamese village complete with water buffaloes. The training included (Guthrie 1966):

1 Basic linguistics, so that trainees could pick up local dialects quickly; later this was replaced by teaching specific dialects.
2 Lectures by experts on different aspects of the new culture.
3 Physical and survival training at the Puerto Rican jungle camp; later this was replaced by training in the culture itself.

In Britain training for diplomats and other high-level visitors abroad is given at Farnham Castle. In addition to educational materials such as books and films, there are meetings with returned expatriates and, where possible, natives of the area to be visited. Similar schemes for managers include case studies of typical management problems likely to be encountered.

## FURTHER READING

Argyle, M., *The Social Psychology of Work*, 2nd edn, Penguin Books, Harmondsworth, 1989.

Baron, R. A., and Byrne, D., *Social Psychology: Understanding Human Interaction*, 6th edn, Allyn and Bacon, Boston, 1991, ch. 6 and 10.

Bochner, S., ed., *Intercultural Communication*, Pergamon, Oxford, 1982.

Brown, R., *Group Processes*, Blackwell, Oxford, 1988.

Myers, D. G., *Social Psychology*, 3rd edn, McGraw-Hill, New York, 1993.

## CHAPTER 8

# SELF-IMAGE AND SELF-PRESENTATION

We showed in Chapter 4 how people categorize each other in order to know how to behave towards them. When a person is constantly categorized and treated in a particular way he acquires a *self-image*. Depending on how far others treat him with approval and respect he will acquire some degree of *self-esteem*. The self affects behaviour in a number of ways, of which the most important is *self-presentation*, that is, behaviour intended to create certain impressions for others.

It was postulated in Chapter 1 that people have a need for a distinct and consistent self-image and for self-esteem. This may result in attempts to elicit responses from others which provide confirmation of these images of and attitudes towards the self. The self-image is one of the central and stable features of personality, and a person cannot be fully understood unless the contents and structure of his self-image are known.

### THE DIMENSIONS OF SELF AND THEIR MEASUREMENT

*The self-image* This term, like 'ego-identity', refers to how a person consciously perceives himself. The central core usually consists of his name, bodily feelings, body-image, sex and age. For a man the job will also be central, unless he is suffering from job alienation. For many women, the family and husband's job may also be central. The core will contain other qualities that may be particularly salient, such as social class, religion, particular achievements of note or anything that makes a person different from others. The self-image contains some enduring aspects and others which vary with the situation and the role being played.

The same person occupies a number of roles; he may be a lecturer, a father and a member of various committees and clubs. He plays these roles in a characteristic style; the way he sees himself in these roles is a part of his ego-identity. He may perceive himself vaguely or clearly. The more he has discussed his personal problems with others the more clearly he is likely to see himself. During psychotherapy the therapist may provide the concepts which the patient can use to talk about himself. Some aspects of the self-image are more important to a person than others, and it is more upsetting if these are challenged or lost. Where an important aspect of the self-image involves the playing of a role (e.g. scientist, orator), a person will try hard to develop the necessary skills (Rosenberg, 1981).

One method of finding the contents of a person's self-image is the Twenty Statements Test. Subjects are asked to give twenty answers to the question 'Who am I?' The first answers are usually roles – sex, social class, job, etc., together with a number of relationships – parent, spouse, friend, worker, etc. (Thoits, 1992). The rest consists of personality traits or evaluations – happy, good, intelligent, etc. (Kuhn and McPartland, 1954). This test gives some measure of the importance of each item to the subject, but it has not yet been shown to be particularly reliable or valid.

Another method of assessing the self-image is by seven-point scales such as the Semantic Differential. Subjects are asked to describe 'the kind of person I actually am' along a series of seven-point scales such as:

| | |
|---|---|
| cold | – warm; |
| attractive | – unattractive; |
| stupid | – clever; |
| strong | – weak; |
| kind | – cruel. |

(Osgood, Suci and Tannenbaum, 1957)

However, the original scales of the Semantic Differential need to be modified for measuring the self-image.

The body-image is an important part of the self-image, especially for girls and young women. Males are most pleased with their bodies when they are large, females are most pleased when their bodies are small but with large busts (Jourard and Secord, 1955). This, at any rate, was the situation in the USA in the

1950s; the most desired male and female physiques vary quite a lot between cultures and historical periods.

How far does a person's self-image correspond with the way he is viewed by others? As will be seen, people present a somewhat improved, idealized and censored version of themselves for public inspection, and may come to believe it themselves. On the other hand, reality in the form of others' reactions prevents the self-image from getting too far out of line. It is no good thinking you are the King of France if no one else shares this view. However, some people succeed in insulating themselves from the views of others so that they are simply unaware of how they are regarded.

*Self-esteem* A person's self-esteem is a measure of the extent to which he approves of and accepts himself, and regards himself as praiseworthy, either absolutely or in comparison with others. Like ego–identity, self-esteem has a stable core, together with a series of peripheral esteems based on different role-relationships, and it varies quite a lot between situations (Gergen and Morse, 1967). One complication about self-esteem is that some people develop an exaggerated self-regard in compensation for basic feelings of inferiority. In these cases it is difficult to decide whether they 'really' have high or low self-esteem – it depends on whether this is measured by direct or indirect means.

One of the most widely used measures of self-esteem is Rosenberg's (1965), with self-rating scales like 'I take a positive attitude to myself' and 'At times I think I am no good at all' (reversed), on a four-point scale from 'Strongly agree' to 'Strongly disagree'.

Working-class people, those in low-status jobs or those with little education have much lower self-esteem. This is probably because they are treated with less respect by other people (Argyle, 1994).

*The ego-ideal* This term refers to the kind of person one would most like to be; it is a personal goal to be striven for, and it may also be the image that is presented to others. It may be based on particular individuals who are taken as admired models, and who may be parents, teachers, film stars or characters from literature. It may consist of a fusion of desired characteristics drawn from various sources. The ego-ideal may be remote and unattainable, or it may be just a little better than the self-image in certain respects. The gap between the two can be assessed by means of the measures described already. The Semantic Differential can be filled in to describe 'the kind of person I actually am' and 'the kind of person I would most like to be'. The average discrepancy between scale scores is then worked out thus:

$$\text{(ego–ideal) (self)}$$

$$\text{attractive} ———\overset{\times}{———}———\overset{\times}{—} \text{unattractive}$$

Discrepancy between self and ideal self has been found to be linked to depression, while conflict between self and 'ought' self (i.e. what a person thinks he ought to be like) is correlated with anxiety (Higgins, 1989). On the other hand, happiness and satisfaction are greater when such conflicts, or the 'goal–achievement gap', are smaller (Argyle, 1987). A number of studies have found that neurotics have greater self/ego-ideal conflict than normals, and that the discrepancy gets smaller during psychotherapy – and this is mainly because of changes in self-ratings. People suffering from anorexia (who are usually middle-class girls) are found to have a lot of conflict between actual and 'ought' self over bodily shape (Strauman et al., 1991).

When much conflict is present, it contributes to low self-esteem. It may also lead to efforts to attain the ego-ideal; when there is actually movement in this direction there is said to be 'self-actualization'. There may be efforts to actually change the personality, i.e. some aspects of behaviour, in some way; or there may be efforts to persuade others to categorize one differently, by better self-presentation. A curious feature of the ideal self is that a person who attains it does not necessarily rest on his laurels, enjoying the self-esteem, but may revise his goals upwards – like a high-jumper who moves the bar up a notch.

*Social identity* The self-image and self-esteem of an individual depends partly on the characteristics, and the success, of groups to which he belongs. This is part of the explanation for people thinking highly of in-group members and devaluing members of out-groups: it keeps up their self-esteem. Experiments in which subjects have the opportunity to make these biased judgements have revealed that this raises self-esteem, though these effects only really work for groups in competition with each other (p. 194).

In China and Japan self-images are primarily based on group memberships. On the Twenty Statements Test, American subjects mention individual traits far more often than do people in Japan. Chinese and Japanese subjects see the self as interdependent with others, so that self-esteem is based on maintaining harmony with other people – group members or those in close relationships. The self is seen as less distinctive, and much more similar to others, than it is by Western subjects (Markus and Kitayama, 1991).

A similar difference has been found between American males and females. For women, career is often less salient, relationships more so. Josephs, Markus and Tatarod (1992) found that men with high self-esteem think they have distinctive properties which make them superior to other people; women with high self-esteem do not think this, but are very happy about their relationships with close friends and within social groups. In one experiment men set compensatory raised goals after evidence of failure at independent thinking, women after failure at interdependent thinking.

*Integration of the self* (achievement of identity) A child may admire saints and soldiers, poets and financiers, but eventually he has to decide in which direction he really wants to go. The degree of integration or diffusion of ego-identity is an important aspect of personality. At one extreme are the completely dedicated, single-minded fanatics, at the other are those adolescents who do not yet know 'who they are or where they are going'. The more integrated the self-image, the more consistent a person's behaviour will be; one effect of the self-image on behaviour is the suppression of behaviour that is out of line. This 'consistency' may take various forms, depending on whether the self-image is based on the attributes of some person, on a set of ethical or ideological rules of conduct, or on an occupational or social-class role.

THE ORIGINS OF THE SELF

*The reactions of others* The main origin of self-image and self-esteem is probably the reactions of others – we come to see ourselves as others categorize us. This has been called the theory of the 'looking-glass self': to see ourselves we look to see how we are reflected in the reactions of others. There is experimental evidence that others' reactions affect self-ratings. In one experiment subjects were asked to read poems; some were evaluated favourably, others unfavourably, by a supposed speech expert, and self-ratings on ability to read poems and on related activities shifted accordingly (Videbeck, 1960). If parents tell a child he is clever, or treat him as if he is untrustworthy, these attributes may become part of the ego-identity. The whole pattern of reactions is important here, the spoken and the unspoken.

Parents and teachers do not hesitate to give full descriptive feedback to children, but amongst older people there is something of a taboo on such direct verbal feedback, especially in its negative aspects, and it has been suggested that it would be helpful to provide people with rather more of such information than is currently regarded as polite. On the other hand this can be a very traumatic way of finding out about oneself, and information should be delivered with tact, or indirectly by the use of subtle hints and non-verbal reactions.

The impact of the reactions of others is greatest when we care about their opinions and respect their judgement, when they are expert on the field in question, when we think they are sincere and unbiased, when there is a consensus of such views and when we have not yet crystallized our self-image (Rosenberg, 1981).

An interesting example of the effects of others' reactions is the 'gloried' self of American college basketball heroes, who bask in the admiration of their fans and forget about other parts of their self, such as the work self (Adler and Adler, 1989).

*Comparison with others*  Self-perception may include concepts such as 'tall' or 'clever'; however, these only have meaning in comparison with the height or cleverness of others. An important source of the emergent self-image is the comparison of oneself with brothers, sisters, friends or others who are constantly present and are sufficiently similar to invite comparison. If other families in the neighbourhood are wealthier than his own, a child will regard himself as poor; if his brothers and sisters, or those in the same school form, are more intelligent, he will come to see himself as not clever, and so on. Robinson, Taylor and Piolat (1990) found that the bottom 20 per cent of children in comprehensive schools had low self-esteem and low self-confidence. In a study of a large number of adolescents in New York State, Rosenberg (1965) found that those with the highest self-esteem tended to be of higher social class, to have done better at school and to have been leaders in clubs – all of which could be bases for favourable comparisons of self with others.

People compare their abilities or fortunes with others who are similar: an ordinary tennis-player does not compare himself either with Wimbledon champions or with hopeless beginners, manual workers do not compare their wages with those of the managing director or of Indian peasants. Subjects in experiments are most interested to know about those who are slightly better than themselves (Latané, 1966), as if they were trying to do better by small instalments.

*Social roles*  An important source of the self-image is simply the roles a person has played in the past or is playing in the present. These include sex, age, social class, occupation, religion, race, marital status and other categories. People see themselves as doctors, criminals, etc., ascribe to themselves the properties of such roles and evaluate themselves accordingly. This is partly a result of actually playing the roles. Medical students come to look upon themselves as doctors during their

The Psychology of Interpersonal Behaviour

training – 31 per cent in the first year, 83 per cent in the fourth year and nearly all when dealing with patients (Merton et al., 1957). Adults often see themselves primarily in terms of the job they do, although roles of particular importance or excitement in their past may be even more salient (e.g. 'When I was in the Navy . . .').

There are individual differences in role performance, and a person may come to see himself as an *intelligent* juvenile delinquent, i.e. as combining a role and a trait. Goffman (1956a) suggested that, in order to perform a role effectively, the newcomer has to put on a mask to act the part; however, when he has acted the part for long enough and others have accepted the performance this becomes a real part of his personality and is no longer a mask.

*Identification with models* Children identify with a succession of people – parents, teachers and others; that is, they admire and want to be like them. The ego-ideal is mainly based on a fusion of these models. However, it has been found in a number of experiments that identification also modifies the self-image, i.e. people feel that they *already* resemble the model.

*The adolescent identity crisis* There are important developments in identity-formation during adolescence. Blasi and Milton (1991) gave open-ended interviews to adolescents and then rated the answers given. At eleven to twelve years of age the self consisted of a number of external attributes, mainly of body and behaviour, but with no inner self or unity. At seventeen or eighteen, however, a distinction was made between an inner, private or psychological self – the 'real me' – and the publicly observed self. Between the ages of sixteen and twenty-four there is often an 'identity crisis' for those who have not yet arrived at an inner unity, when a person is forced to make up his mind about which of all these bits and pieces of identity to hang on to and which to suppress (Erikson, 1956). The basis of this is partly the need to choose one job rather than another, a marital partner, a political and religious outlook, and a lifestyle. In addition, the development of greater powers of abstract thought probably makes it more important than before to be *consistently* vegetarian, radical, intellectual or whatever it may be.

The state of an individual's identity can be established by an interview assessing whether he has gone through a crisis period and how far he is committed in two main spheres – occupation and ideology. Four main kinds of identity are found among students in the USA and Canada (Marcia, 1966). In the most highly developed, an integrated identity has been achieved, which is to have 'a feeling of being at home in one's body, a sense of knowing where one is going, and an inner assuredness of anticipated recognition from those who count' (Erikson, 1956). The four kinds of identity are:

1 *Identity achievement* Here the individual has been through a decision-making period, or crisis, and has made occupational, religious and political commitments.

2 *Moratorium* The individual is in a period of crisis, trying to make up his mind between alternative careers, having religious doubts and feeling confused about politics.

3 *Foreclosure* Although occupationally and ideologically committed, the individual did not go through a period of crisis, rebellion or exploration of alternatives; he has accepted parental guidance on his occupation and typically shares his parents' views on religion and politics.

4 *Identity diffusion* Here a person may or may not have passed through a crisis, but in either case he has not decided upon, nor is he much concerned about, his occupational, religious and political orientation.

Integrating different interests into a career choice may require some ingenuity. The author met a young man who couldn't decide whether to go into the Church or whisky distilling. He thought of solving the problem by going into the manufacture of sacramental wine.

*The need for self-esteem* We have seen that there are forces in the personality acting to achieve a *unified* identity, and that this is controlled by outside forces acting to keep it *realistic*. There is another force acting to produce a *favourable* self-image, which provides sufficient self-esteem. We have seen that self-ratings are usually somewhat more generous than ratings given by others. However, the self-image depends on the reactions of others; this is why such a lot of effort is put into self-presentation and the manipulation of others' perceptions. What happens if others' evaluations are *more* favourable than self-evaluation? Experiments show that such evaluations are neither believed nor remembered (Shrauger, 1975).

The need for self-esteem is usually limited by reality; if this is not the case behaviour becomes absurd and preposterous, and there is a continual lack of confirmation by others. This happens in the instance of paranoia (pp. 234ff.). In fact people differ widely in their feelings of esteem, from conceit to inferiority. Both extremes usually reflect failure to perceive accurately the present responses of others, and can be regarded as failures of adjustment. A mythical psychotherapist is said to have told a patient who suffered from feelings of inferiority, 'But you really *are* inferior.'

Is it possible to increase self-esteem? One reason for people feeling inferior is that they were earlier rejected by their parents, and they can't do much about that. Another reason is having too elevated an ideal self, creating a large gap between attainment and aspirations. Or they may be comparing themselves with too elevated a comparison group. These last two conditions can be changed, and this sometimes happens in cognitive therapy. It is quite possible to select prestigeful items out of a long list of self-attributes and roles once played, and these often become favourite (though boring) topics of conversation. Perhaps women have less trouble sustaining their self-esteem, if it is based mainly on harmonious relations with others.

It is interesting that self-esteem is *not* any lower among members of racial or other minority groups subjected to discrimination, probably because it depends on the evaluation of, and comparisons with, individuals in the same group (Wylie, 1979). However, the self-esteem of such people is reduced if they live in mixed communities, and, as we have seen, self-esteem does vary with social class.

## CONDITIONS UNDER WHICH THE SELF IS ACTIVATED

The self is not at work all the time; people are not continually trying to discover, sustain or present a self-image. For example, when at home rather than at work, in the audience rather than on the stage, the self-system is not very active.

Most people feel self-conscious when appearing in front of an audience, and some feel very anxious. It has been found that these effects are greater when the audience is large and of high status (Fig. 8.1, Latané, 1981). As this figure shows, audience anxiety can be intense, for young or inexperienced people, even with small audiences. The performer is the centre of attention for a number of people and his performance will be assessed, so there is the danger that he will receive disapproving reactions, and self-esteem may be damaged.

When a person addresses an audience of any kind, it is no good his speaking in the informal 'familial' style: he won't be heard properly. It is inevitable that he must put on some kind of 'performance'. Once he does so he is accepting a certain definition of the situation and presenting a certain face: he is someone who is able to perform before this audience and is worth attending to. It is this implicit claim which creates the risk of loss of face. We shall discuss later the social skills of dealing with audiences, including how stage fright can be reduced (pp. 275ff.).

There are many social situations where other people can be regarded as a kind of audience and where one's performance may be assessed. Argyle and Williams (1969) asked subjects, 'To what extent did you feel mainly the observer or the observed?' after they had been in a variety of situations. It was found that they felt more observed (a) when being interviewed rather than interviewing, (b) when with an older person, especially in the case of seventeen-year-old subjects, and (c) when a female with a male. Individuals differ in the extent to which they see themselves as observers of others or as being observed by others. It is found that some people consistently see themselves as observed, particularly males who are insecure and dependent. It is interesting to find that females feel observed, especially by males; they

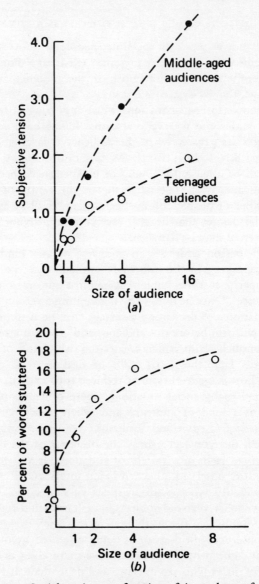

Figure 8.1     Social tension as a function of size and age of audience
(from Latané, 1981).

tend to wear more colourful and interesting clothes and to take more trouble about their appearance than males.

The self can be activated in other ways. Duval and Wicklund (1972) called this 'objective self-awareness' – the awareness of oneself as an object, as seen from outside. They produced this state simply by placing people in front of mirrors. An individual will be more self-conscious if he or she is different in some obvious way from everyone else in the room, for example by wearing distinctive clothes or by being the only female or black present. Conversely 'de-individuation' can be brought about by dressing everyone up in white lab coats or other uniforms; this produces a loss of individual responsibility and people even forget who said what. Self-awareness is produced by 'penetration' of territory or privacy – being discovered with too few clothes on, or when one has not been able to arrange one's appearance, or when awkward private facts are disclosed.

There are individual differences in self-consciousness and audience anxiety, that is, a feeling of nervousness when appearing in public or when made the centre of attention. The personality trait Public Self-consciousness (PSC) predicts audience anxiety quite well. In one experiment subjects were paid one cent for each second they could keep singing in front of a small audience. Those high on PSC sang for a much shorter time in front of a stranger – only about nineteen seconds each (Froming, Corley and Rinker, 1990). People who are very self-conscious and worried about disapproval behave in a cautious, protective manner, playing safe, taking no risks; they may succeed in avoiding rejection but are unlikely to attract many positive reactions either. We shall see in the next chapter that such self-attention is high in mental patients.

Being, or feeling, shy is very common; 30 to 40 per cent of young people think they are shy. They lack self-confidence, especially in meeting strangers, are awkward and inhibited, blush, stammer and perspire on social occasions, and think afterwards that they have made a hash of it. In our terms they have poor social skills and are preoccupied with themselves and their performance. Surveys show that many Japanese and

Americans, but few Israelis, consider themselves to be shy (Crozier, 1990).

## THE EFFECTS OF THE SELF-IMAGE ON BEHAVIOUR

What happens when the self is activated, by audiences, mirrors or in other ways? In the first place there is a heightened level of physiological arousal, which results in greater effort, greater productivity if some task is being performed, as well as disruption of that performance if arousal is too great. Secondly, attention is directed towards the self rather than to others, and the self is seen as from outside. Duval and Wicklund (1972) suggest that this makes people aware of the discrepancies between self and ideal self, and self-image and the perception by others. They found that subjects who had been made aware of such discrepancies, and were placed in front of a mirror, left the mirror as soon as they could; in other experiments it was found that subjects gave lower self-ratings when in front of a mirror (Wicklund, 1975). On the other hand, Carver (1979) suggests that, while self-awareness leads to a comparison between aspects of the self and certain external standards, the outcome is not always negative.

*The motivation for self-presentation* People want to project a self-image for several reasons. To begin with, for interaction to occur at all it is necessary for the participants to be able to categorize one another – they need guidance on how to respond to each other. In other words, selves have to be not only presented but *negotiated*, perhaps modified to what others will accept. People also use self-presentation for immediate social and material goals – to be liked, to get a job, and for professional purposes. There is a good reason for this: clients are more likely to respond in the desired way if they have confidence in the expertise of the practitioner. There is widespread evidence that pupils learn more if they think their teachers are good, and that patients in psychotherapy recover faster if they believe that the therapist can cure them. A third motive for self-presentation is simple self-esteem; the approval or admiration of others enhances it. A fourth, more subtle, motivation is the construction, extension or affirmation of the self-image: if other people accept the identity offered, you can believe in it yourself. Tice (1992) asked subjects to role-play a personality different from their own, for an experiment. If this was done with an audience (of one) the self-perceptions of subjects shifted towards the role-played personality.

Goffman (1956a) observed that undertakers, salesmen, waiters and other professional and service workers engage in a lot of deception and impression manipulation (see p. 218). The stage is set in the 'front regions' of premises, and may involve collusion between team members; members of the public are kept out of the back regions, which are dirtier and less impressive, and where behaviour is more vulgar and informal. Goffman maintains that a similar degree of deception occurs in many other non-professional situations, such as a family receiving guests. Part of this theory has been confirmed by Canter's finding (lecture at Oxford) that the main division seen in the spaces of houses is between the public and private rooms.

*Verbal self-presentation and 'face-work'* How do people project an identity? The easiest way would be simply to tell other people how nice, important or clever we are. It is fairly obvious why this doesn't work: everyone would like to make such claims, but are they true? Verbal self-presentation appears to be acceptable only if it is very indirect; if such messages are too direct they can easily become ridiculous, as in name-dropping. Stephen Potter has given a satirical account of indirect ways of claiming a prestigeful identity in his book *One-Upmanship* (1952). For example:

LAYMAN: Thank you, Doctor. I was coming home rather late last night from the House of Commons . . .

M. D.-MAN: Thank you . . . now if you'll just let me put these . . . hair brushes and things off the bed for you . . . that's right . . .

LAYMAN: I was coming home rather late. Army Act, really . . .

M. D.-MAN: Now just undo the top button of your shirt or whatever it is you're wearing . . .

LAYMAN: I say I was coming . . .

M. D.-MAN: Now if you've got some hot water – really hot – and a clean towel.

LAYMAN: Yes, just outside. The Postmaster-General . . .

M. D.-MAN: Open your mouth, please.

E. E. Jones has carried out a series of experiments on ingratiation, in which subjects were motivated to give a good impression, for some purpose (1964). He found that people were very careful over their self-presentation; for example, mentioning their good points in unimportant areas only, subjects in a high-status role being particularly modest. Gove et al. (1980), in a large American survey, found that as many as 26.5 per cent of people admitted to having pretended to be less intelligent or knowledgeable than they really were – men more than women, though wives had often played dumb in this way with husbands. This is almost the reverse of self-presentation, and evidently it too can be advantageous.

Another aspect of verbal self-presentation is what Goffman (1961) called 'face-work', to describe the strategies used to repair the damage after a blunder had led to a potential loss of self-esteem. The methods he described were making excuses, giving justifications (e.g. it didn't matter) or apologizing. Holtgraves (1992) found that apologies were judged to be the most effective, justifications least. He extended the concept of face-work to other situations: disagreements threaten the other person's face, and are usually wrapped up in a lot of polite verbiage; self-disclosure is potentially face-threatening, since the other may disapprove of what is disclosed (this will be discussed below). Interactors are also concerned with the face of others, and this has been regarded as the central aim of politeness (Brown and Levinson, 1978). The Japanese are very concerned with face, including others' face, so that it is rude to say 'no' for example. We discussed politeness earlier, in Chapter 3.

*Non-verbal self-presentation* Self-presentation is done most efficiently by non-verbal communication. Signals like clothes, hair, voice and general style of behaviour have more impact than words. Sometimes these NV signs are actually part of what is symbolized – like upper-class speech or football-fan clothes.

Sometimes they symbolize aspects of the self which cannot be easily displayed in the course of interaction, like being honest or intelligent.

Clothes can indicate social classes, membership of groups (e.g. punks), some occupations (the Church, nursing) and certain aspects of personality. Gibbins (1969) found that English grammar-school girls were agreed as to what kind of girl would wear various sorts of clothes – whether she would be promiscuous, go to church, drink, etc.; the clothes they themselves preferred had images which resembled both their actual and ideal self. A number of experiments have shown how clothes affect the reactions of others. Wearing a uniform leads to people obeying orders; the news is not believed if the TV newscaster is not 'properly' dressed; putting a confederate in different clothes affects whether they are successful if they ask for help in the street; and of course people are more or less likely to get jobs at interviews – women have to be particularly careful to project the right degree of femininity for the occasion (Argyle, 1988).

Accent is widely used for self-presentation. When people are asked to speak carefully, for example to read word lists, their accent shifts towards a more educated style, for example not dropping initial 'h's or final 'g's. In the USA lower middle-class people were found to go beyond the upper middle class to a non-existent accent (Labov, 1966). On the other hand, when members of different classes meet they often 'accommodate' to each other's speech style (p. 68).

Of course people do wear the clothes, speak with the accent and in others ways keep to the ways of their own social group, not necessarily for self-presentation but simply because these are the norms of their group.

*Embarrassment* is a special form of social anxiety, in which the person affected blushes, smiles, laughs, averts gaze or touches the body. It is not quite the same as anxiety, since the physiology is different, for example the appearance of blushing. This is a puzzling phenomenon, whose evolutionary origins are obscure; possibly it is an appeasement signal to avert trouble from the group. It is produced by threats to public identity or undesired social attention. It is most common among adolescents and those high in Public Self-consciousness, and, for some reason, in Britain (Crozier, 1990; Leary, Britt, Cutlip and Templeton, 1992).

Goffman (1956b) offered a theory of embarrassment: people commonly present a self which is partly bogus; if this image is discredited in the course of interaction, embarrassment ensues. For example, a person's job, qualifications or social origins may turn out to be less impressive than had been suggested. This theory can be checked against the 1,000 instances of embarrassment collected by Gross and Stone (1964). About a third of these cases involved discrediting of self-presentation, but the rest could not really be classified in this way, and other sources of embarrassment need to be considered. Edelmann (1989) found that there are a number of separate factors here; his first factor corresponded to Goffman's ideas.

Another theory is that embarrassment is due to a failure by an individual to meet certain social expectations, leading to his receiving a fall in public esteem, and hence experiencing a fall in his self-esteem (Modigliani, 1971). This has been confirmed in a study in which subjects judged that people who, for example, knocked over piles of cans or choked on their food would be perceived as be clumsy, incompetent, immature and unintelligent, but that the actors' subjective ratings on such scales would be lower than the way they were actually perceived by others (Semin and Manstead, 1981).

Embarrassment can be produced by forgetfulness, such as not remembering someone's name. Take the case of a man who met Princess Margaret at a party:

Man: The old firm still flourishes, eh?
Princess: You could say that.
Man: Your sister still well, I hope, still flourishing?
Princess: Still Queen.

It can also be caused unwittingly, by ignorance, e.g. of the fact that a person is divorced, is a Jew or has just lost his wife. Accidents can be very embarrassing: Gross and Stone report an extraordinary case of a man at a banquet who got the tablecloth caught in his trouser zip-fastener and pulled everything off the table when he rose to speak. The inappropriate sexual element here makes things worse. Such episodes are more embarrassing at formal occasions since one is to some extent putting on a performance and implicitly making claims of competence. Rule-breaking can be embarrassing, whether through ignorance or the effects of drink, fatigue or insanity. Rule-breaking causes consternation because it is unexpected, breaking the smooth flow of interaction, and because others may not know how to deal with it.

Can embarrassment be avoided? Some people are able to remain poised when embarrassing incidents occur; they 'keep their cool' and prevent the situation from disintegrating. Adolescents often tease and insult one another, perhaps as a kind of training in dealing with embarrassment. Some of the possible causes of embarrassment can be avoided by presenting a face which cannot be invalidated, and it is less likely to happen to those who are not dependent on external confirmation of their self-image and self-esteem. Breakdown of interaction may still occur, however, as a result of accidental errors, as in social gaffes. Rules of etiquette and skills of tact help to avoid such instances. An example of etiquette is the rule not to send invitations too long before the event, when it is difficult to refuse them. An example of tact is knocking on a door or coughing when a couple may be making love on the other side of it.

When a person is embarrassed the others present usually want to prevent the collapse of social interaction, and will help in various ways. To begin with they will try to prevent loss of face by being tactful in the ways described. They may pretend that nothing has happened, make excuses for the offender – he was only joking, was off form, etc. – or in some other way 'rescue the situation'. Finally, if face is irrevocably lost, they may help the injured party to rehabilitate himself in the group in a new guise (Goffman, 1959b; Gross and Stone, 1964).

*Deception and concealment* Another feature of self-presentation is concealment: people are careful not to reveal aspects of themselves which are likely to lead to disapproval. Jourard (1964) surveyed large numbers of students, using a questionnaire asking how much they had revealed about themselves to other people. This varied greatly with content: more was revealed about opinions and attitudes than about sexual behaviour or money, for instance. People will reveal more to those they can trust not to reject them – to their mothers, close friends, people who are similar to themselves and (we may add) to psychiatrists and clergymen. We recently found that a person discloses different things to different others – to his doctor and his bank manager, for example. Students tell their parents about how well they are doing and how hard up they are, but not about their love affairs (Argyle, Trimboli and Forgas, 1988).

Concealment is quite common, as Goffman (1956a) has shown. For example, discreditable episodes or features of the self are concealed. In any group of people who know each other well, there is collaboration in the process of forgetting unfortunate events. Similarly, if someone has a low opinion of a colleague it is probable that the most constructive line of action involves some concealment of these opinions. Some people are 'stigmatized', in that they would be socially rejected if the truth were known: many homosexuals, ex-convicts, mental patients, members of disreputable professions. They conceal these facts from outsiders but can often recognize one another. Deception by undertakers and waiters is not so much about the self as about other features of the professional performance. Sometimes this is to the performer's advantage – as with salesmen and waiters; sometimes it is to the client's advantage – as with undertakers and doctors.

A number of psychologists have come to the conclusion that actual deception is fairly rare; it is more that individuals emphasize different aspects of themselves, for example by wearing different clothes on different occasions (DePaulo, 1992). Jourard and others, however, have argued that behaviour *ought* to be authentic and sincere. Instead of treating the deception versus authenticity debate as a moral issue, it can be seen as a difference between two kinds of personalities. Snyder (1979) devised the Self-monitoring (SM) scale, with items like: 'When I am uncertain how to act in social situations, I look to the behaviour of others for cues' and 'In different situations and with different people I often act like very different persons.' A series of experiments has shown that people high on the SM scale are sensitive to situations and try to present themselves in a suitable way; they see themselves as flexible and adaptable. Those low on the scale have a clear and enduring self-image and want to be true to themselves. High SMs are able to control their emotional expression, give the impression of being friendly and extraverted, not anxious or nervous, whether they really are or not (Lippa, 1978), are less shy, commonly take the initiative and talk more with strangers.

*Problems of self-presentation* What happens when self-presentation is unsuccessful? As we have seen, there are display rules which prevent the expression of negative non-verbal reactions and politeness rules preventing negative verbal ones, so that negative reactions may be difficult to detect. But when A's face has really been lost, by obvious failure or inability to sustain the image presented, there are various strategies open to him. One is simply to ignore what has happened or to laugh it off as unimportant. It would be expected from the analysis given in earlier chapters that a person who had failed to project an image would try alternative ways of doing so. If he is rattled he may fall back on less subtle techniques of the kind 'Look here, young man, I've written more books about this subject than you've read', 'Do you realize that I . . .', etc. What very often happens is that A forms a lower opinion of a person or group that does not treat him properly, and he goes off to present himself to someone else. It has been found that salesgirls in shops preserve their image of competence in the face of customers whom they can't please by categorizing them as 'nasty', or in some similar way (Lombard, 1955); if a low opinion is formed of B, it doesn't matter whether B confirms the girl's self-image of competence or not. A number of experiments show that people withdraw from groups who do not react to them in the desired way, and that they prefer the company and friendship of those who confirm their self-image (Secord and Backman, 1974).

220       *The Psychology of Interpersonal Behaviour*

**FURTHER READING**

Crozier, W. R., ed., *Shyness and Embarrassment*, Cambridge University Press, 1990.
Wylie, R., *The Self-Concept*, vol. 2, University of Nebraska Press, Lincoln, Nebr., 1979.
Yardley, K., and Honess, T., eds, *Self and Identity*, Wiley, Chichester, 1987.

## CHAPTER 9

# SOCIAL BEHAVIOUR AND MENTAL DISORDER

The simplest definition of mental health is 'the absence of anxiety, depression or other symptoms of distress commonly found in mental patients'. However, as well as experiencing distress, mental patients often have social behaviour which is inadequate or peculiar in some way. This topic is of importance for two reasons. Firstly, we can learn a lot about normal social performance by studying the ways in which it goes wrong; each kind of failure in social performance shows us a feature of normal social behaviour which has to be managed properly. Secondly, the study of the social behaviour of mental patients may throw light on the nature of mental disorders and have implications for new forms of treatment. In fact it has already done so: social skills training, the provision of social support and various social preventive measures will be described later. In addition, people are often regarded by others as mentally ill if their social behaviour is abnormal; if their social behaviour is more normal, they are less likely to be labelled as insane. We shall not attempt in this chapter to give a complete or balanced account of mental disorders, and shall only be concerned with the *social* behaviour of mental patients.

In fact the social behaviour of patients is inadequate in a variety of ways. There are several views about how the failure of social behaviour may be related to the other aspects of disorders. One theory is that failure to learn the right social skills in childhood results in later social rejection and failure to cope with life events; this in turn causes anxiety, depression or other symptoms. But another explanation is that general disturbance, e.g. of thinking or emotions, affects social performance. There is evidence from twin studies that mental disorders are partly inherited, and this is particularly true of the psychoses, such as schizophrenia, rather than of the neuroses; this would lend support to the second theory. On the other hand, the psychoses are affected by childhood experiences, are often precipitated by rejection or other social stresses, and some of the main symptoms are in the sphere of social performance, so that the first process may also be operating, and this is even more likely with the neuroses.

THE EXTENT AND DISTRIBUTION OF MENTAL DISORDER

*Extent* Probably the most valid measure of psychological disorder is an examination by a psychiatrist. There is a lengthy standard form used in Britain known as the Present State Examination (PSE) and a shorter version for community studies. For large-scale research purposes, questionnaires are often used, such as the General Health Questionnaire; the short version has twelve items like 'Have you recently felt constantly under stress?' (four-point scale, from strongly agree to strongly disagree).

How many people are mentally disturbed at any given time? There is no clear cut-off point; it is like asking how many people are tall or intelligent. About 14 to 17 per cent of the people who see a GP are diagnosed as having a psychiatric problem. The *General Household Survey* finds that about one person in three reports some kind of psychological distress – severe headaches, exhaustion, sleeplessness, anxiety or depression. Recent American interview surveys have found that 17 to 23 per cent of adults were affected by psychological disorders, 7 to 15 per cent by anxiety, with lifetime prevalence rates of 29 to 38 per cent.

*Social class* Working-class people in Britain have higher rates of mental disorder. The rate of schizophrenia in class V (unskilled) is about five times that in class I (professional); the rate of depression is also much higher. Working-class people have high rates of alcoholism and drug addiction, but there is little difference for anxiety neurosis. Large-scale social surveys in the USA show similar class differences. Kessler (1982) re-analysed the data from eight national surveys, with 16,000 people in all; low income was the strongest predictor for men, low education for women. Mental health is very poor among the unemployed.

What is the explanation for these class differences?

1 Working-class schizophrenia is partly the result of 'downward drift'; that is, many schizophrenics started in other classes but, due to their condition, ended up in low-grade work or unemployment.

2 Are working-class people under more stress? In some ways they are, especially stress caused by loss of jobs, ill-health and certain daily 'hassles'.

3 Working-class people are more upset by the same stress – they are more vulnerable. This is partly due to lack of resources to deal with stress, especially financial resources, but also to lack of social support. There are some class differences in personality which are probably relevant here as well. Working-class people use less active styles of coping, passive rather than active problem-solving, and are low on 'internal control' (the belief that one can control events). These personality differences are in turn caused by child-rearing, which is rigid and punitive, together with the experience that events cannot be controlled (Argyle, 1994).

*Gender* Women report much more depression, anxiety, emotional strain and other kinds of mental distress than men. Women are particularly liable to become depressed (about twice as likely) and suffer more from anxiety neurosis (50 per cent more). On the other hand, men have a slightly higher rate of schizophrenia, are three times as likely to become alcoholics, and break the law far more than women.

Part of the explanation for these differences is that women are more willing to admit to emotional disturbance and to 'take the sick role'; it is more socially acceptable for women. However, women at work are as reluctant as men to go sick, and it has been suggested that work roles keep people going. A second reason for the high rate, especially of depression, for women is that their roles give them less experience of mastery and control; their socialization may also fail to teach them assertiveness and independence, so that they do not use active forms of coping when faced by problems in later life, but slip into 'learned helplessness' (Campbell and Kuipers, 1988).

There is another, rather intriguing, explanation for female depression. Nolen-Hoeksema (1991) asked subjects 'What do you do when you feel depressed?' Women were most likely to have a good cry or a good moan with their friends – a 'ruminating' style which may make things worse. Men said that they engaged in physical activity – such as a run or a game of squash – which distracted them from their troubles.

### STRESS

Mental disorder is partly caused by stressful events in people's lives. I say 'partly' because most people do not become mental patients when becoming bereaved or unemployed; it is only those who are vulnerable, and we shall find out more about who they are later. Stressful life events can be weighted by asking samples of people to give relative weights to different events. Some of the items and weights found by Paykel, McGuiness and Gomez (1976) with a British sample appear in Table 9.1. It can be seen that bereavement, divorce and other losses of relationship score very highly, as does loss of job, which includes the loss of a whole set of social attachments.

A number of studies have shown that those people who have a high score for such events during the past six months are more likely to become ill, mentally or physically. In the case of schizophrenia, it is happenings during the past three weeks which count.

Death of spouse has often been assumed to be the most stressful life event, though the statistics for mental hospital admissions suggest that divorce is worse (Table 9.2).

We know that these events are sometimes precipitated by the individual concerned; for example, neurotic behaviour might lead to divorce. Some studies have used interviews to eliminate such self-induced stresses. It has also been found that repeated daily 'hassles' can be as bad as major one-off events – for example money problems, bad housing, a drunken husband or

| | |
|---|---|
| death of child | 19.53 |
| death of spouse | 19.14 |
| being sent to gaol | 17.76 |
| serious financial difficulties | 17.58 |
| spouse unfaithful | 17.28 |
| divorced | 16.29 |
| fired | 15.93 |
| unemployed for one month | 15.43 |
| serious physical illness (in hospital or one month off work) | 14.67 |
| fail important exam or course | 14.38 |
| begin extramarital affair | 13.70 |
| increased arguments with resident family member (e.g. children) | 13.97 |
| increased arguments with boss and co-workers | 12.28 |
| move to another country | 11.14 |
| retirement | 10.05 |
| child leaves home (e.g. college) | 7.85 |
| wanted pregnancy | 3.70 |

Table 9.1    Ratings of the seriousness of life events (from Paykel, McGuiness and Gomez, 1976).

| Marital status | Mental hospital admissions per 100,000 |
|---|---|
| single | 770 |
| married | 260 |
| widowed | 980 |
| divorced | 1437 |

Table 9.2    Marital status of mental hospital admissions in England in 1981 (Cochrane, 1988).

several young children at home – which partly explains class differences in mental health in British women (Brown and Harris, 1978).

Different kinds of stress produce different kinds of disorder. Bereavement and other kinds of loss of social relationships lead most often to depression, but also to other disorders. Danger, threat and overload, on the other hand, produce anxiety. Continued stress of this kind in air traffic controllers can also result in peptic ulcers.

Interpersonal conflict is a major source of stress, and increased marital arguments are the most frequent life change reported by depressed women. We showed in Chapter 6 that there is more conflict in marriage than in any other relationship (though also more rewards). Work too can be an important source of stress (as well as satisfaction). Job overload, repetitive work, responsibility for others, public performances, competition and conflict are some of the main sources of work stress, and lead to anxiety, psychosomatic symptoms and exhaustion, rather than depression. Doctors, nurses and social workers may suffer from 'burn-out' when their clients prove frustrating and emotionally exhausting. War experience produces various kinds of 'war neurosis' in those who are kept in action too long, and may take several strange forms: talking to dead comrades, waxy immobility, exaggerated jumpiness, blackout and recurrent nightmares. Most of those affected recover on being removed from the scene of battle and allowed to rest, but some are permanently affected.

It should be emphasized that most people do not break down after experiencing stress. In fact most people need a certain level of excitement (and therefore stress) at work and at leisure. Racing motorists and members of the SAS would probably not enjoy working in a museum or library (the least stressful work), or choose to play bowls in the evening. There needs to be a match between personality and stress level.

The best predictor of depression is the degree of depression experienced by an individual at an earlier date (Lewinsohn, Hoberman and Rosenbaum, 1988). The level of depression is increased by stress, but persistent features of personality are actually more important.

*Social support* Stress increases the likelihood of mental disturbance, but the effects of stress can be reduced or eliminated by social support. By social support is meant the availability of family, friends or others who can provide help of a number of kinds. The main kinds of help here are:

1  love, esteem or social acceptance;
2  availability to discuss personal or emotional problems;

3 companionship, simply doing things together; and
4 concrete help, including financial help and provision of information.

The greatest source of support can be the spouse or partner. Table 9.2 showed the massive effects of marriage on mental health. Brown and Harris (1978) found that working-class women in London with husbands who acted as confidants were much less likely to become clinically depressed following stressful life events than those without such husbands. Many other studies have shown similar effects – on the chances of going to mental hospital, committing suicide and getting various forms of cancer and other illnesses (Lynch, 1977). However, it has also been found that the negative features of relationships have a greater effect than the positive ones, i.e. a good marriage has a mild positive effect, but a bad marriage has a larger negative effect (Rook, 1984). An example of this is the effect of expressed emotion (p. 234).

|  | SUPPORT | | |
|---|---|---|---|
|  | high | mid | low |
| women who had stressful life event | 10 | 26 | 41 |
| women with no such events | 1 | 3 | 4 |

Table 9.3 Depression, stress and social support (% depressed) (Brown and Harris, 1978).

The Brown and Harris study (Table 9.3) shows that marital social support is effective mainly when there is a high level of stress. This is known as a 'buffering' effect. Friendship networks, however, have a 'main effect', that is, they are associated with good mental health whether there is stress or not. Friends can provide a different kind of support from spouses, especially companionship in joint leisure activities, which produces a lot of joy and, above all, social integration and acceptance by the community (Cohen and Wills, 1985).

We saw that women may not be helped by talking over their troubles with their friends. However, certain kinds of talk are successful, for example psychotherapy. The sharing of bottled-up traumatic experiences has been found to be beneficial, and conversation can be helpful if it is providing useful information or advice, or is helping to solve problems.

Workmates can provide help with problem where spouse or friends can't. Workmate support can buffer the effects of work stress, and remove the effect of such stresses on physical and mental health. Workmates can provide practical help with the work; they can form mutual-support groups, to co-operate in the face of a difficult boss, for example; their presence can reduce anxiety; and there is a lot of sheer sociability and companionship from workmates. The result of such support is that work stresses are seen as more controllable and less stressful.

There are quite strong sex differences in the benefits received from social support. Women have more intimate relationships, with both family and friends, are more comfortable with intimacy than men, and benefit more from social support. Women also provide more social support, so that in marriage it is husbands who benefit more, because wives are better confidantes and sympathetic listeners (Vanfossen, 1981).

*Vulnerability to stress* We have seen that most people who suffer stress do not become mental patients; it is only some individuals who are vulnerable. The exception is that some very severe stresses, in wartime for example, can cause almost everyone to break down.

The opposite of vulnerability is hardiness, and one predictor of hardiness is the 'assets' or resources that a person can call on. Luborsky, Todd and Kather (1973) drew up a measure of such assets, which included education, occupation, health (e.g. not smoking), economic status (including owning house or car), social networks (friends, marriage, etc.) and good early relations with parents.

Other sources of hardiness and vulnerability lie in the personality. *Neuroticism* is a general dimension of emotionality and negative affect. Individuals with high scores on this dimension are more easily upset, and tend to be anxious, depressed and complain of a variety of minor health problems, such as headaches. It is a predictor of depression or other disturbances following stress. *Interpersonal sensitivity*, which can be assessed by self-report measures with items like 'I worry about what people think of me', is a related vulnerability factor (Boyce et al., 1991). *Internal control* is a general belief that one can control events, as opposed to other people or chance doing so; this helps people resist the effects of stress. *Self-esteem and self-confidence* work in a similar way. *Social interest*, that is, positive concern for others (similar to co-operativeness), leads to stronger social support, and thus greater resources. Optimism and religious beliefs also help people to look at things positively, and enable them to cope better.

There is another very important source of vulnerability and hardiness: *social competence*. People with weaker social skills are more likely to become mentally disturbed. This will be discussed more fully later.

Vulnerability factors in the personality, like neuroticism, are partly inherited, as has been shown by twin studies and adoption studies. For example, children who have been separated from their parents shortly after birth still resemble them as much as or more than they resemble the adoptive parents, in respect of neuroticism and likelihood of becoming schizophrenic. Another source of these personality dimensions is childhood experience. There is extensive evidence that people who come from homes where they were unloved, or received punitive and erratic discipline, or had other bad experiences, are more likely to be disturbed later. However, there is a problem with research on the effects of socialization on mental health. The patient's own early disturbed behaviour may have caused the trouble in the family, rather than the family being the cause of later mental disturbance. Since mental disorder is partly inherited it is quite possible that there would be early manifestations of it in childhood. This direction-of-causation problem has not yet been cracked.

People have different styles of 'coping' with stress. For most situations, where something can be done about them, direct and problem-focused methods of coping are best, while emotional, avoidance, denial or passive methods are not at all good, and create vulnerability. We saw earlier that part of the reason for the poorer mental health of women and working-class people is their less active style of coping (Lazarus and Folkman, 1984).

## SOCIAL SKILLS AND MENTAL HEALTH

Most mental patients have inadequate social skills, and this may be one of their main symptoms. There are a number of common forms of social failure, which are found in a lot of patients, though they take different forms in particular disorders.

1 *Non-verbal communication* Low levels of gaze and smiling; flat, tense or negative tone of voice.

2 *Conversation* Little initiation, can't sustain conversation.

3 *Perception and judgement* Failure to perceive or interpret the behaviour of others correctly; inability to solve interpersonal problems.

4 *Social relationships* Inability to form or sustain relations with friends, family or others, through low rewardingness or other skill failures.

5 *Self-image* Low self-esteem; egocentricity; inability to take an interest in other people, empathize with them or see their point of view.

6 *Social competence* Low rewardingness and assertiveness; performance disrupted by anxiety or fear of negative evaluation; ineffective in social situations.

Does lack of social skill cause or contribute to the development of mental disorder? The model which inspired a great deal of social skills training is as follows. Individuals who are unable to make friends or to deal with relationships at work or in everyday life, or who have difficulty or experience anxiety in common social situations, will experience a lot of stress. They are likely to be rejected and isolated, and this is liable to cause anxiety and depression. The reason that they have poor social skills in the first place lies mainly in socialization in childhood and adolescence; for example, having poor models in the family, being isolated for some reason, or having little contact with the opposite sex (Trower, Bryant and Argyle, 1978). Libet and Lewinsohn (1973) suggested that depressives are so unrewarding that other people avoid and reject them. A number of experiments have been carried out in which subjects met real or role-played depressives, and this is indeed what happens (e.g. Joiner, Alfano and Metalsky, 1992).

Another version of this theory is that people with poor social skills have weaker social support, and this makes them vulnerable to stress. Sarason and Sarason (1985) found that people who had little social support had rigid, authoritarian attitudes, low tolerance for deviance, and a negative, alienated, pessimistic view of life; these authors argue that such views would not be conducive to the formation of close, supportive ties. Jones (1985) found that lonely people lack social skills in a number of ways: they are less rewarding, are shy and unassertive, hostile and pessimistic, and are self-centred, taking little interest in others. This whole negative syndrome is also found in unhappy people.

However, there is another possible explanation of the link between social competence and mental health: other aspects of the disorder may cause the social incompetence. For example, intense anxiety may prevent a person from using his skills. In support of this it has been found that reducing anxiety by desensitization methods can lead to improved social skills (Argyle, Bryant and Trower, 1974). In schizophrenia there are basic disturbances of thought processes and these may well be responsible for the disturbed social performance (see below).

Even if social inadequacy is caused by other aspects of a disorder, it would still be expected to exacerbate the condition, since it would lead to social rejection and loss of social support, as in the previous models. The practical importance of studying the social performance of mental patients is the implication for social skills training (SST): is this likely to be an effective form of treatment for mental patients? If social incompetence is a major cause of mental disorder, or a source of vulnerability, it follows that SST is not only desirable but actually necessary for successful treatment. If social incompetence is an effect of the disorder, it can still make things worse, so that SST could be useful in reducing social rejection and isolation, and increasing social support. How well SST actually works for different disorders we shall see later (p. 245).

SOCIAL BEHAVIOUR IN THE MAIN DISORDERS

In this section a descriptive account will be given of the social behaviour which is observed in the main types of mental disorder. Some of this is commonly reported by clinicians and can be seen in any mental hospital. The more subtle aspects require the use of some of the research methods described earlier, such as the analysis of voice quality, direction of gaze, synchronizing of speech, person perception and so on.

*Schizophrenia* This term is used to cover a wide variety of conditions, but the basic syndrome consists of withdrawal from social relationships, disturbance of thought and speech, hearing voices, a failure of persistent, goal-directed behaviour and a flat emotional state. The disturbance of social behaviour is only one of the symptoms, but it is one of the most characteristic and is a principal reason for patients' inability to deal with everyday life. They simply cannot communicate properly or take part in ordinary social encounters.

Many schizophrenics engage in very little social behaviour; they remain isolated and detached from other people and are engaged with private fantasies and day-dreams. When they are in a group or interview they appear not to be attending to the situation at all, and may make irrelevant remarks, giving a clue to the fantasies with which they are preoccupied.

*Non-verbal behaviour* Their facial expression is usually blank, but with grimaces; there is often gaze aversion; gestures are mainly self-touching rather than communicative; they need a lot of personal space and keep their distance from other people; posture may be immobile or symbolic in some way; voice is monotonous and poorly produced; and their appearance is odd and untidy – schizophrenics do not wear their clothes well (Argyle, 1988).

*Conversation* There may be none, and if there is any it consists of short utterances with bizarre contents, rambling and incoherent, poorly synchronized with another's utterances – perhaps on a different topic – and not synchronized with own bodily movements. There is little acknowledgement of another's utterances and no feedback signals.

*Perception and judgement* It is now known that schizophrenics are able to recognize emotions from videotapes. However, they avoid attending to emotions and do not use emotion words when describing such films (Cramer, Bowen and O'Neill, 1992). It has been found that schizophrenics experience more difficulty in ranking photographs of people consistently than in ranking photographs of physical objects, and that they make no inferences from one dimension to another (Bannister and Salmon, 1966). It looks as if schizophrenics may have a specific cognitive deficiency – of not being able to conceptualize persons or emotions. They may also have delusions – another failure of thinking – and this is more pronounced in paranoia, described below.

*Social relationships* Schizophrenics have very few relationships, consisting mainly of family members. They are very unrewarding and have been described as 'socially bankrupt'. It has been found that schizophrenics report considerably worse symptoms if they are interviewed to see if they should be discharged than if interviewed to see if they should be placed in a closed ward (Braginsky, Braginsky and Ring, 1969). It seems that they want to stay in hospital but on an open ward, and can manipulate their symptoms in order to bring this about. It is found that schizophrenics adjust to the hospital in diverse ways, including avoiding the staff and making full use of the leisure facilities.

Schizophrenia includes a wide variety of patients and a variety of social deficits. The worst cases are deficient in every aspect of social competence; they are virtually incapable of social interaction.

*Causes* The causes of schizophrenia are not yet known, nor is there any known cure, although tranquillizing drugs suppress the symptoms while they are being taken. Since about 0.8 per cent of the world's population suffers from schizophrenia, this is an extremely pressing scientific and social problem. There is evidence for a strong genetic basis, more than for other disorders. This is mediated by biochemical factors, such as increased levels of the neuro-transmitter dopamine; the drugs which suppress schizophrenic symptoms do so by reducing the dopamine level.

There are also social origins of schizophrenia. Sufferers come from families where there is conflict, miscommunication and overprotection, though this may be the result of having a disturbed child. The families are found to be disturbed in certain characteristic ways, such as having dominant and rejecting mothers and various kinds of failure of communication – e.g. one person's remarks are not acknowledged by another, members of the family fail to come to an agreement but then act as if they had – together with a lot of conflict and hostility (Jacob, 1975). The evidence for the effects of 'expressed emotion' is more conclusive: people are more likely to become schizophrenic, or to relapse after release from hospital, if their families are emotionally over-involved, critical or hostile (Campbell and Kuipers, 1988).

Schizophrenia is often triggered by stressful life events, such as death, ill-health or other disasters in the family, or sudden disturbances to the patient's way of life, during the three weeks before onset (Brown et al., 1973).

*Paranoia* This consists of delusions about the self and others. In cases of personality disintegration accompanied by strongly held delusions, the condition is termed paranoid schizophrenia; when the personality is more intact it is called paranoia. Paranoid reactions are commonest in the middle-aged and elderly, while other kinds of schizophrenia occur in the young. Paranoids, it is found, are secretive and seclusive, not trusting or confiding in people, but are generally able to communicate and develop rapport better than schizophrenics. They are always found to be suffering from thought disturbance, but this is invariably focused on relations with other people. Paranoids feel that they are being plotted against, spied upon or otherwise victimized, and that this is the explanation for their other failures. They may believe that their behaviour is being controlled from a distance, by TV, laser beams or whatever is the latest technology, sent by the Brazilian railways or the secret police. Their perception of the world is disturbed in that they think the behaviour of others is orientated primarily towards themselves. They may also have delusions of grandeur, believing that they have an important mission or that they carry a special message or discovery.

While perfectly capable of normal interaction, they are extremely sensitive to minor slights, insults and rejections, and are quite unable to receive or profit by feedback from others concerning their ideas or self-image. At the first hint of negative feedback their defences become rigid, and other people are blamed instead. Paranoids often cause annoyance by their touchy, hostile, arrogant and dominating behaviour, in which they constantly want to demonstrate their superiority. They think that there is a conspiracy against them and that people are talking about them behind their back; as they become gradually excluded from the community this becomes the case (Lemmert, 1962).

Paranoia can be regarded as mainly a disturbance of the self-image, made possible by the tendency to form false beliefs in order to reduce anxiety. For example, a child may explain his failure in an examination by saying that the teacher was not fair; if the parents support this view they could be encouraging paranoid thinking. This is more likely to happen to children who are isolated from the healthy ridicule of the peer group.

Paranoia is precipitated by social stresses such as failure, competition or loss of a supporting social relationship.

*Depression and mania* These illnesses consist mainly of disturbances of mood, but there are also characteristic styles of social behaviour. Some alternate between the two, indicating that the states are probably closely related. Manics are euphoric, self-confident and full of energy; depressives are overwhelmed by feelings of misery, guilt and inadequacy, and are lacking in motivation. Many depressives (known as 'reactive') are greatly affected by stressful life events and show disturbances of social behaviour, so I shall concentrate on them rather than on the 'endogenous' depressives, whose condition is more the result of biochemical processes and whose main symptoms are withdrawal and loss of motivation (Robins and Luten, 1991).

A number of careful experiments have shown that depressives produce an alienating effect on other people, who as a result avoid them; but which are the cues that have this effect?

*Non-verbal communication* Some studies have not found any differences here, although an overall depressive effect was produced. Sometimes the following differences are found: depressed facial expression; crying; low levels of gaze and gaze directed downwards; self-touching gestures; drooping posture, with head down; quiet and slow voice, with low and falling pitch, dead and listless tonal quality; drab and sombre appearance.

*Conversation* The alienating effect of depressives can be produced by the contents of conversation – the discussion of personal problems, together with self-blame and hopelessness – and has this effect especially on opposite-sex interactions (Williams, 1986). In addition, many depressives rarely initiate conversation, and speak little, slowly and with long pauses.

*Perception, judgement and thinking* Depressives have some distortion of perception – they exaggerate the extent to which they are rejected by others (e.g. Siegel and Alloy, 1990). On the other hand, normal people err in the opposite direction, and have an unrealistically positive view of themselves compared with how others see them (Taylor and Brown, 1988). In some studies depressives made more accurate assessments of themselves than normals did. Depressives also feel helpless and think that they are unable to control events, making the future appear black. Marx, Williams and Claridge (1992) found that depressives were worse than normals or anxious patients in social problem-solving.

*Social relationships* Reactive depressives seek support, sympathy and reassurance. Experiments with actors playing depressives, and studies of the room-mates of depressives, find that this behaviour is partly successful, in that some sympathy is elicited; but, as we have seen, they are also rejected and avoided. Joiner and colleagues (1992) found that rejection only occurred if reassurance had been sought. A further part of the story is that depressives exaggerate the amount of rejection received, as we have seen.

Neurotic, reactive depressives are far more able to interact than schizophrenics, but they too are very unrewarding, passive, egocentric and ineffective.

*Self-image* One of the most striking features of depressives is their low self-esteem, together with guilt and other negative feelings. Some of the most influential theories of depression have proposed that it is caused by this negative view of the self, or the tendency to blame the self for bad things that happen. However, longitudinal studies have shown that these cognitive factors do not cause depression; it is more likely the other way round (Haaga, Dyck and Ernst 1971).

*Manics* Manics wear smart, striking but rather loud clothes, look extremely well and very pleased with themselves, are smiling and alert, and have a loud, confident voice of robust, resonant quality. They talk incessantly and tend to monopolize the conversation with their hilarious jokes and outrageous stories, but are easily distracted and move rapidly from topic to topic. Their excitement and jollity are infectious, and they are good at being the life and soul of the party. Manics have a self-confidence and self-esteem for which there is no adequate basis, and they will not take criticism from others. They enjoy making speeches and writing letters to important people. On the other hand they are quite good at handling people. This, together with their energy and self-confidence, often leads to a successful career in one of the more colourful occupations, such as politics or show business. Their chief failings in social competence are an inability to perceive themselves accurately and annoying others by their dominance and unsuitable jokes. Their delusional self-importance, their constant talking and a tendency to bizarre behaviour may lead to their becoming a public nuisance.

Depression and manic illness are partly inherited, especially in the case of endogenous depression, which occurs with little evidence of stress. Early loss of parents was once believed to be a major cause. It is now known to be a fairly minor factor: McLeod (1991) carried out a large study which showed that parental divorce had more effect than death of parents; this worked for women only, and did so by leading to poor marriages.

Depression is one of the disorders in which social skill failure is likely to be a major cause. Cole (1990), in a study of 750 nine- to eleven-year-olds, found that lack of social competence (as rated by peers) and academic failure both correlated highly, and independently, with depression at that age. This kind of study gives support to the Lewinsohn model that depression is caused by rejection, with rejection occuring as a result of poor social skills. A depressed social style then leads to further rejection, as we have seen.

*Neuroticism* Neuroticism occurs as a matter of degree, everyone experiencing anxiety and stress at some time. However, between 5 and 8 per cent of the population are unduly anxious, can stand very little stress, have reduced energy, function below their true capacity, have headaches or other aches and pains, can't sleep and find other people difficult to deal with.

People with anxiety neurosis may have a general 'free-floating' worry about nothing in particular, a phobia for height, travel or other situations, and obsessions, such as a concern with dirt and cleanliness. Agoraphobia – fear of open spaces or being away from home – is a common form; it includes fear of having panic attacks and is common in those who have previously had 'social phobia'. In 'social phobia' there is fear or avoidance of social situations, especially public situations where the sufferer may be observed by others. In some cases there is fear of eating, drinking, working, writing or speaking in front of others; in some there is global fear and avoidance of all social situations; and there can be a vicious circle of being afraid of being seen to be anxious or embarrassed, which produces further symptoms like shaking or sweating (Nicholas Argyle, personal communication). It can be measured by self-report scales of 'fear of negative evaluation', or self-ratings of the amount of fear or avoidance associated with a range of common situations.

*Non-verbal communication* Blushing, trembling, shaking violently, sometimes vomiting, strained face, tense posture; there is a low level of smiling, gaze, gestures and shifts of posture.

*Conversation* Neurotics are usually very bad conversationalists in one way or another. Some of them talk very fast, nervously and rather indistinctly, and tend to speak first in an encounter; however, their utterances are short, they make many speech errors and they may lose control of the quality of their speech. Others are very silent, showing little interest in others, speaking very briefly and in a slow and rather monotonous voice, rarely taking over the conversation, sitting very still and rigid, and assuming a dull, fixed expression.

*Social relationships* Not all neurotics are socially inadequate. Bryant et al. (1976) observed the social behaviour of out-patients diagnosed as neurotic. It was found that, of ninety-two patients studied, 27 per cent were judged to be socially inadequate, 46 per cent of the males (mostly unmarried) and 16 per cent of the females; 21 per cent were thought to be suitable for social skills training.

Neurotics are often socially isolated. Henderson et al. (1978) found that they had far fewer friends than comparable non-neurotics. Lack of friends is one of the commonest complaints on the part of those seeking social skills training. Neurotics may engage in queer, destructive social techniques, whose effects are highly disturbing. The motivation may be aggression, or relief of inner tensions in complex ways, as described by Berne (1966). For example, a fraudulent contract may be offered, as in 'Rapo': a female leads a male on until he makes an advance, whereupon she indignantly rejects him. In 'Why don't you – Yes, but' someone appears to be seeking advice about a problem; whatever solution is offered, he is able to point out the obvious objections to it.

Neurotics with other phobias may be competent at social interaction, and are often very sensitive to the responses of others, but they get into difficulties as a result of their other symptoms. An obsessional who is worried about the smell of bad breath, and a person with a phobia of closed or open spaces, will have difficulties in taking part in many encounters. Like other neurotics, people with anxiety neurosis tend to be self-centred, demanding and more concerned with their own needs and problems than with those of others. In addition, anxiety neurotics are tense, irritable and easily upset; they are often found annoying and unrewarding by others, and so can become gradually isolated.

In our study (Bryant et al., 1976) we found that the socially inadequate group were significantly less extraverted, sociable, dominant and confident, and they reported more difficulty in social situations. They appeared colder, less assertive, happy, controlling or rewarding, and more anxious than the socially adequate group. They were also significantly more likely to have had in adolescence a history of solitariness and difficulty in making friends, and of unsuccessful attempts at 'dating'. In terms of elements of behaviour, they tended towards the 'inactive' or unassertive side, being on the whole rather silent.

*Self-image* Social phobics have low self-esteem and little self-confidence, but are very egocentric, with heightened 'self-attentionism'.

*Causes* The origins of anxiety neurosis lie partly in the genes, partly in a traumatic and disturbed childhood. The origins of phobias, social and otherwise, lie in negative experiences with the object of the phobia, producing anxiety by conditioning or by some more complex process. People suffering from anxiety neurosis are found to have been socially inadequate in childhood, as well as at the present time. But does social inadequacy cause social anxiety (via rejection etc.) or does social anxiety cause social incompetence? The theory that social inadequacy is primary is supported by the findings that SST can cure this condition while drug treatment only alleviates it temporarily, and that social inadequacy is found before the neurosis develops. The argument for social anxiety being primary is that drugs can alleviate the symptoms, and behaviour therapy to reduce anxiety can cure it, including improving social competence without any SST. The latter suggests that anxiety is simply suppressing skills which are already there. Trower et al. (1978) found that socially unskilled patients were helped more by SST than by desensitization; phobics were helped equally by both methods of treatment.

*Hysteria* This consists partly of bodily complaints for which there is no organic basis but which are not under voluntary control, unlike malingering; these include motor blockages (paralyses), sensory blockages (anaesthesias) and failures of memory. This is a form of neurotic breakdown which is more common among extraverts, whereas anxiety neurosis is more common among introverts (Eysenck, 1957). There are also hysterical personalities among normal people, who share some of the same behaviour. There can be hysterical epidemics where, for example, many of the inmates of a girls' school have the same symptoms, such as fainting and dizziness, or more bizarre experiences, such as the 'phantom anaesthetist of Mattoon' (Johnson, 1945). Hysterical breakdown may involve a sudden change of identity, as in the case of the impostor who adopts some high-status role in which he half believes, partly for the material rewards which may be gained, partly for the admiration. Helene Deutsch (1955) describes the cases of a number of people of this type, one of whom made a rapid transition from juvenile delinquent to 'country gentleman'.

*Non-verbal communication* Hysterical symptoms can be interpreted as communications in themselves, in their pretence to being serious physical symptoms. They also help the patient by distracting attention from the real source of distress and enabling him or her to 'take the sick role' (Ziegler and Imboden, 1962), which has benefits for the patient, in getting them out of work or other duties and making other people be considerate to them.

*Conversation* The characteristic social behaviour of hysterics also has a quality of role-playing: they over-dramatize themselves, exaggerate their emotional states and pretend to be more interesting and exciting than they really are.

*Social relationships* Hysterics are very anxious for their self-image to be reinforced and very sensitive to feedback concerning it. They like to be the centre of attention, need to be admired and are often successful as actresses, politicians and public speakers. They are competent interactors, more active than normal people, although not as active as manics. They introduce a superficial sexuality into non-sexual relations (Miller, 1988). Hysterics put on quite an impressive social performance, though in a histrionic, egocentric and annoying way. Basic interaction skills are good, but egocentric demands are made for attention and consideration, by the pretence of intense emotions and imaginary illnesses.

*Causes* Hysteria has not been found to have a genetic basis, except as part of general neuroticism. Hysterics are often females who have been overprotected by their mothers. One theory is that they have been rewarded for minor illnesses, both by avoiding events and by receiving extra maternal care, so that feeling ill becomes the automatic reaction to stress. It is perfectly easy to attend to trivial bodily feelings of discomfort, normally ignored, and decide that one is ill, if this has been reinforced in the past.

*Antisocial personalities and other delinquents* Antisocial personalities, or psychopaths, repeatedly get into trouble with the law, often for inadequately motivated behaviour. This starts at an early age, and includes lying, aggressive sexuality, heavy drinking, stealing and other rule-breaking.

*Non-verbal communication* Emotions are expressed but are very shallow.

*Conversation* Psychopaths sometimes behave with charm and spontaneity. They are thus able to manipulate other people to their own ends, but their relations with others are always a means to ends and never ends in themselves. Psychopaths are rather like some salesmen: they want to interact with people so that they can get their bonus, but have no further interest in the people concerned.

*Perception* A lack of perceptual sensitivity to others has been found (McDavid and Schroder, 1957); this can lead psychopaths into trouble (such as fights) if they fail to realize how they are annoying other people. More serious is an inability to take the role of the other, to see others' point of view.

*Social relationships* Psychopaths are impulsive, egocentric and affectionless, cannot form close or loving relations, and can behave in a callous way towards others. Their marriages break up, they are expelled from schools and sacked from jobs. Despite superficial competence, social performance is fundamentally flawed because of the lack of any concern for others.

*Causes* The origins of antisocial personality lie partly in genetics and partly in disturbed early relations with parents, such as early separation or punitive and inconsistent discipline. The central feature of the psychopathic personality seems to be failure of empathy, of any concern for other people and how they feel. Psychopaths have no remorse for suffering caused to others. There is also a failure of social learning, partly because of the bad examples of their parents and the erratic discipline received, but also because of a failure to learn from punishment (Blackburn, 1988).

There are several different types of delinquent. 'Pseudo-social' delinquents are not abnormal in any clinical sense and are quite different from the impulsive and affectionless psychopaths. They reject adults and others in authority, but behave perfectly well towards members of their group or gang, and indeed may be loyally devoted. Their most interesting feature for present purposes is the total barrier which exists between them and adults – a one-sided barrier in that it is extremely difficult for adults to establish a relationship with them. Various techniques have been suggested for application in institutions, such as the use of young adults who can be seen as suitable models and who work hard to establish rapport.

Groups of football hooligans, drug addicts, violent revolutionaries and others are similar. The behaviour of these and other delinquent groups can partly be explained in terms of learning to be members of an alternative social world, with its own rules, values and beliefs, which gives gratifications that cannot be obtained elsewhere. They are labelled by the outside world as 'football hooligans', for example, and this label becomes part of their self-image, helping to separate them from society, in a process of 'deviance amplification'. There appears to be a failure of social behaviour in dealing with 'straight' society. Sarason and Ganzer (1971), however, have had some success in training delinquents to go for job interviews, for example.

## THE EFFECTS OF TREATING SOCIAL BEHAVIOUR

We must distinguish at this point between the neuroses, such as anxiety and hysteria, and the psychoses, such as schizophrenia and the manic and depressive states. The neuroses have traditionally been treated by psychotherapy, though the recovery rate is very slow – not much faster than the spontaneous rate of recovery for untreated patients; increasingly they are being treated by behaviour therapy and drugs, which do a little better. The psychoses have traditionally been treated by physical methods, though the value of psychological and social techniques is being increasingly recognized. The present position is that schizophrenics can be temporarily improved by means of drugs, but that they deteriorate as soon as they stop taking the drug; some success is claimed for social therapy while the patients are sedated. The outlook for depressives is better, since antidepressant drugs are very successful, and, if these fail, ECT is usually successful.

For both the neuroses and the psychoses there is an urgent need to find better methods of treatment. If the breakdown of social performance is an important element for any of these conditions it is important to know how far it is affected by existing methods of treatment. We may also be able to deduce something about the pattern of causation by seeing whether the social behaviour or the other symptoms are affected first.

*Individual psychotherapy*  Many patients who embark upon psychotherapy suffer from interpersonal difficulties, either over specific problems at work or in the home, or over more general social matters. Some come to the therapist because they have no one else to talk to; he provides a kind of friendship, and may be able to use it to teach them how to get on with other people (Lennard and Bernstein, 1960). Although therapists vary in what they do, certain procedures are common to all (pp. 269ff.).

Some psychotherapists believe that interpersonal problems lie at the root of mental disorder, and they direct their therapy towards the patient's social behaviour and relationships. Rogers (1942) directed his treatment primarily towards the self-system of his patients, to bring about greater self-acceptance, less conflict between self and ideal self, and more commitment to persistent courses of action. We have seen that depressives have very low self-esteem and blame themselves for the bad things that happen to them; neurotics may also have unreasonable beliefs, for example that you can't be happy unless everyone loves and admires you (Beck, 1976). These suggest useful areas for psychotherapists to work on. When the family is deeply involved in a patient's problems, as it often is with adolescents for example, family therapy may be the best form of treatment.

There has been a lot of disagreement over whether psychotherapy actually cures people any faster than they would recover spontaneously; up to 70 per cent recover after two years without treatment. However, a number of carefully controlled studies show that there is more improvement in psychotherapy patients, both in social behaviour and in other respects (see p. 268ff.).

*Behaviour therapy* This consists of a number of training techniques based on learning theory. The most widely used form of behaviour therapy is 'desensitization' for phobias: the patient is lightly hypnotized, relaxes deeply and imagines the least frightening of a hierarchy of fearful stimuli, e.g. connected with heights, flying or spiders, relaxes again and imagines the next stimulus in the hierarchy. Another method is 'flooding', in which the patient confronts the most frightening stimulus, either in reality or imagination, for twenty minutes or so. These methods are very successful with specific phobias, and it is claimed that more general personality disturbance can be helped by dealing with central areas of anxiety. It is recognized by some behaviour therapists that further training in social behaviour may be needed, for certain patients. For example, people with sexual problems may need to be taught heterosexual skills.

*Social skills training (SST) for neurotic patients* This is now a widely used method of treatment for a great variety of patients. The methods used are described in Chapter 11 (pp. 292ff.). Here I shall discuss how well it has been found to work in follow-up studies (see Hollin and Trower, 1986).

*Schizophrenia* is mainly treated with drugs. However, SST can augment the treatment in two ways: it can add to the success of treatment by increasing social skills and producing changes which would not otherwise have occurred, and it is possible to intervene with patients' families to reduce the amount of 'expressed emotion', or to return patients instead to specially designed sheltered environments (Shepherd, 1986).

*Depression* SST does as well as drugs or psychotherapy, and produces greater improvement on all aspects of social behaviour. Furthermore, performance continues to improve after the treatment has ended (Williams, 1986).

*Neuroticism* Assertiveness training and other forms of SST are successful with anxious, neurotic patients, but no more so than various kinds of behaviour therapy. However, socially unskilled patients do better with SST; they need the whole role-play package, including modelling, feedback and homework (see pp. 292ff.).

*Antisocial personalities and criminals* SST has been widely used, especially for disturbed offenders. Sexual offenders have been taught heterosexual skills and aggressive people have been trained in assertiveness, but there has been little focus on training in empathy. A number of follow-up studies have reported positive results, with some generalization to other settings within institutions, but there is little evidence that subsequent criminal behaviour is reduced. Pre-release training has sometimes been given on how to get a job and deal with other problems in the outside world (Howells, 1986).

Alcoholics and drug addicts have been helped by SST, though the effects have not always lasted; SST is now included as part of a more comprehensive treatment package. Disturbed children have also been helped, particularly those who are socially isolated or aggressive.

### SOCIAL PREVENTION OF MENTAL DISORDER

If social factors play an important role in the causation of mental illness, it seems likely that social measures might be useful in preventing it.

*Provision of social support* We saw above the importance of social support for mental health. If this cannot be obtained from family or friends, there are clubs and leisure groups in most neighbourhoods, which usually welcome new members and try to integrate them; in fact these clubs provide a great deal of social support to their members (p. 176). It is possible to improve the mental health of a community by the provision of community centres, places where clubs can meet and groups can form. The design of buildings is also important. Some big apartment blocks had so much vandalism and crime that they were demolished. It is now thought that one of the main factors was the absence of areas where residents could meet, get to know one another and co-operate over keeping order (Newman, 1972).

There are many mutual help groups for those with special problems, like Alcoholics Anonymous and groups for the widowed, gamblers, the obese, and even for women who love the clergy. These groups sometimes have an inspirational, almost religious air about them. About 6.25 million Americans belong to these groups, which threaten to rival psychotherapy as the preferred treatment for a number of problems, partly because they are much cheaper. They can also be seen as a replacement for the family, as a source of social support, and hence of physical and mental health. A curious feature of the groups is that many members never leave (Jacobs and Goodman, 1989).

There have been experiments in the provision of social support by creating networks for long-term psychiatric patients living alone, organized by social workers and linking the patients to local networks (Sorenson, 1985).

*Stress-management training* We have seen that 'coping' style affects vulnerability to stress. Some employers have succeeded in improving the mental health of their workers by teaching them better ways of coping. A form of cognitive therapy has been used, in which employees are shown that a lot of stress is due to the way in which they perceive and interpret situations, and they are taught that stressful situations can be seen in less threatening ways. For example, instead of reacting to overload by feeling incompetent, workers could blame the supervisor for mismanaging the work allocation. Individuals can also be trained in positive imagery, time management and goal-setting (Argyle, 1993).

*Exercise* is very good for physical health; it is also good for psychological health. It is one of the commonest sources of positive emotions, and this may be how it affects mental health. Exercise is often done in the company of other people, and the combination of physical and social activities, as in dancing, tennis and other sports, is a particularly potent source of joy. Some firms have introduced programmes of exercise for their employees, and found that this has paid off: they become less anxious, tense and depressed, especially on exercise days, and have improved work performance (Falkenburg, 1987).

*Stress-reduction in organizations* A number of employers have taken steps to reduce the stresses to which their employees are exposed – and thus to reduce the costs of stress in terms of illness, absence and loss of efficiency. Very often it is possible to alter the working arrangements in various ways: the job can be modified, by reducing physical overload or time pressures, introducing equipment to do dangerous or boring parts of jobs, reducing noise levels, etc.; social support can be increased by the creation of small work-teams; organizations can be changed to produce fewer levels in the hierarchy, more decentralization, better-designed socio-technical systems and more consultation (Argyle, 1989). However, some jobs are intrinsically stressful – those of firemen, police and deep-sea divers for example. There could be periods of less stressful work, selection of people who can cope with stress, and training in stress management.

**FURTHER READING**

Hollin, C. R., and Trower, P., *Handbook of Social Skills Training*, Pergamon, Oxford, 1986.
Miller, E., and Cooper, P. J., *Adult Abnormal Psychology*, Churchill Livingstone, Edinburgh, 1988.
Rosenhan, D. L., and Seligman, M. E. P., *Abnormal Psychology*, W. W. Norton, New York, 1984.

## CHAPTER 10

# SOME PROFESSIONAL SOCIAL SKILLS

Social behaviour has been looked at as a skilled performance which is used to elicit certain desired responses from other people. This approach can be used to give an account of professional social skills; in each of these the performer carries out a task which consists mainly of handling other people in order to get them to react in certain ways. The criteria for success at such professional tasks are clearer in some cases (such as selling) than in others (such as teaching). For some of these tasks there has been a good deal of research into which social techniques, or which kinds of people, are most effective. It is found that there are fairly large individual differences; for example, a ratio of five to one in average takings is not uncommon among salesgirls in the same department, and there are similar variations between the absenteeism and labour turnover rates under different supervisors.

Some social skills for which there is a substantial body of research have been selected for discussion here. Others which might have been included are the skills of the barrister, the negotiator and the social worker. However, the skills discussed are relevant to some of these – barristers use the skills of public speaking and social workers use therapeutic skills, for example. The social skills of everyday life have been covered to some extent in previous chapters. The professional skills which are described below involve rather special techniques which are not necessarily acquired as a result of everyday experience. They also require a certain amount of knowledge – for example, teachers need to know their subject as well as how to teach – and this side of social skills will not be considered here.

We shall start with skills in which one person is handled at a time.

## INTERVIEWING

*The selection interview*  Millions of interviews take place each year to assess the suitability of applicants for jobs. The main purpose is to find out information from the candidate (C), from which the interviewer (Int) can predict how well C would do in the job. In addition Int may provide C with information about the organization, improve its public image and persuade C to take the job; here the situation becomes one of bargaining or negotiation. In fact this often happens at the end of the interviews after one C has been offered the job.

The selection interview can be given by one Int or by a whole panel of them. As will be seen, one of the major problems with this kind of interview is overcoming the anxiety of C, especially with young or inexperienced Cs. This is far worse with a board interview: Cs have been known to collapse physically, and this method gives an advantage to the most self-confident and self-assured Cs, who may not be the best-equipped in other ways. It is far easier to establish a good relationship and to get C talking freely in a one-to-one interview. It is nevertheless valuable for C to be interviewed by several Ints with different personalities, points of view and areas of expertise, so it is probably best for C to have a series of individual interviews.

The behaviour of C during an interview cannot be regarded as a typical sample of his performance, from which a prediction can be made; Int should concentrate on eliciting verbal reports of behaviour in situations resembling the future work situation. Thus an estimate of C's creativity can be obtained by asking him to describe situations in which he might have displayed originality.

Part of the skill of interviewing is being able to deal with awkward Cs. General experience suggests that there are a number of types of awkward C most commonly encountered:

talks too much;
talks too little;
very nervous;
bombastic;

wrong role (e.g. seeks vocational guidance or tries to ask all
the questions);
over-smooth presentation;
unrewarding;
not interested in job;
neurotic;
different class or culture.

There are special ways of dealing with each of these problems.
For example the C who talks too much can be dealt with by (a)
asking more closed questions, (b) using less reinforcement, or (c)
indicating that a short answer is wanted.

'Structured interviews' are more successful than less structured
ones – as was shown in a meta-analysis of 150 studies (Weisner and
Cronshaw, 1988). Structured interviews are based on a job analysis,
selection of up to twenty typical situations, and agreed ratings for
different answers for each, put into an interviewer's booklet. An
alternative strategy is simply to decide on the abilities and traits
needed, such as creativity, ability to cope with stress and positive
attitudes to authority. Each of these dimensions can be assessed
from the answers to suitable questions. For example, attitudes to
authority can be assessed by asking about past relationships with
others of higher or lower status, and attitudes towards traditionally
respected groups and institutions and commonly despised social
groups. In each area several different questions should be asked, in
order to sample the dimension under consideration.

The selection interview has four main phases:

1 welcome, in which the procedure is explained, and C is put
at ease and encouraged to talk freely;
2 gathering information, in which Int goes through the list
of topics, or goes over C's records, with the aid of C's dossier,
and tries to assess C on a number of traits;
3 supplying information, in which C is invited to ask any
questions he may have;
4 conclusion, in which it is explained what happens next.

There may also be a phase of negotiation (in which C is offered
the job), for which the interviewer requires further social skills.

In phase 1, Int establishes rapport with C and reduces C's anxiety. This can be done by a period of a few minutes' relaxed small talk, discovering common friends or interests, or by asking C questions about interesting or successful things he is known to have done recently, accompanied by positive NV signals. In phase 2, Int goes over C's biographical record, asking questions which help in C's assessment. Int should have a definite list of topics to be covered in a certain order: research shows that the interview is more effective when it has a definite plan such as going through the biographical record. These topics will often include C's family and home background, his education at school and later, his past jobs and present employment, his interests and leisure activities, his attitudes and beliefs, his health and adjustment.

There are special skills in asking questions. Each topic is usually introduced with an open-ended question, followed by a series of follow-up questions. Int's questions should be responsive to what C has just said, so that there is a proper dialogue or flow of conversation. The questions on a given topic can be designed to obtain information about different aspects of C's abilities or personality. For example, leisure activities can be pursued to find out about social skills, creativity or emotional stability. Some areas need carefully phrased questions to elicit relevant answers; for example, *judgement* can be assessed from questions about C's opinions about complex and controversial social issues with which he is acquainted.

Int will have some ideas about C from biographical and other data, which he may have in front of him; in fact the more such data he can have before the interview the better. He can then test various hypotheses about C, e.g. that C is lazy, neurotic and so on. It is found that much more notice is taken by Ints of adverse information, and the interview can be regarded to some extent as a search for such information. This is partly justified by C's use of the complementary strategy, i.e. of covering up his weak points. Nevertheless it is useful for Ints to be on the lookout for strong points in Cs as well.

It is important for Int to be able to extract negative information, and he may need to find out, for example, why C left a certain job so quickly or why he was sent down from college. The putting of such questions requires considerable skill. It is partly a matter of careful phrasing of the question; for example, the latter question could be put, 'I gather you had some difficulties with the college authorities; could you tell me about that?' Such questions need to be delivered in a friendly, perhaps slightly humorous manner, and C's face should be saved afterwards by a sympathetic comment.

Ints often use techniques which will increase the amount of C's speech: open-ended questions, agreement and encouragement, and the use of silence. Int should listen carefully to the emotional undertones and implications of C's speech, and respond in a way that shows he understands, accepts and sympathizes. However, he should not take the role of C to the extent of trying to get C the job, because there are other Cs to be considered; Int should remain somewhat detached while at the same time being genuinely sympathetic.

While Int's role is to carry out selection rather than vocational guidance, he may give some vocational advice if it is asked for. The interview should be a rewarding experience for C, and he should feel that he has been properly and fairly assessed.

Although interviewing is universally used as at least a part of selection schemes, there has been some criticism of its validity by psychologists. Part of the problem is that Int has other information about C – biographical, examination and test results, etc. – from which it is possible to make a prediction without any interview at all. However, the results of a number of studies show that the predictions made following the interview are better than those made from background data alone (Ulrich and Trumbo, 1965). It has also been found that some Ints are very much better than others – and that some are unable to predict job success better than chance. The most accurate are those who are similar to the Cs in age and social background, intelligent and well-adjusted, not easily shocked, quiet, serious, introverted, unexcitable and giving an impression of sincerity and sympathy. Further it has been found that certain areas of information can be assessed more accurately by interview than others. C's style of interpersonal behaviour and his likelihood of adjusting to the social aspects of the job situation is one such area; another is C's motivation to work, which can probably be more accurately assessed by interview than in any other way.

There are a number of common sources of error in selection interviews and these were described earlier under person perception (p. 92): being too influenced by first impressions and physical appearance, preferring Cs from certain backgrounds, forming a global favourable or unfavourable impression, and placing more emphasis on negative than positive points. Early impressions about C should be checked by asking further questions.

What social skills should be used by C to make Int more likely to give him the job? It has been found that C stands a higher chance of being accepted when Int does most of the talking, when the interview flows smoothly, with few disagreements being expressed (Sydiaha, 1961), and when C smiles, looks and nods more (Forbes and Jackson, 1980). Ints seem to prefer Cs who are well-washed, quietly dressed, politely attentive, submissive and keen, and they are likely to reject Cs who are rude, over-dominant, not interested or irritating in other ways. There seems to be a definite 'role of the candidate' – he is expected to be nicely behaved and acquiescent – although he may not be expected to be quite like this if he gets the job. There are certain subtleties about being a good C: it is necessary for C to draw attention to his good qualities while remaining modest and submissive. He may need to show what a decisive and forceful person he is, but without using these powers on the selection board. (McHenry, 1981; Ungerson, 1975; Smith, Gregg and Andrews, 1989)

*The social survey interview* The aim of the survey interviewer (Int) is to obtain accurate replies from the respondent (R) about his opinions, attitudes, behaviour or whatever the survey happens to be about. The reliability of survey interviews is not very high: in a number of studies Rs were asked the same questions a second time after a short interval, and it was found that about 80 per cent repeated their previous answers if the same Int was used, while only 60 per cent did so if a different Int was used

(Hyman et al., 1955). It is possible to assess the adequacy of Int's performance by analysing tape-recordings of his interviews, in order to check for errors and biases, though this does not measure validity directly. In several studies, as many as twenty mistakes of various kinds per interview have been found (Brenner, 1981).

The design of the questions can be separated from the actual interviewing; they are done by different people. Designing the questions is a social skill only at second hand, but a very important and sophisticated one. Some points are now familiar and obvious: each question should be on a single topic, should be clear and unambiguous, should not suggest the answer, e.g. invite the answer 'yes'. Other aspects are less obvious; for example, people report twice as much beer-drinking and three times as much masturbation if more familiar words are used (Bradburn and Sudman, 1980). A priest who asked his superior if it was acceptable to smoke while praying received a different answer when he asked about praying while smoking (Zajonc, 1992).

It is important that Int should communicate clearly with R, and this may be difficult because of their different backgrounds. The questions should be appropriate to the level of sophistication of R. If R simply lacks the necessary words or concepts, explanation or examples may be necessary. It is sometimes the practice to alter the wording of questions for use with cultural minority groups so as to make them of 'equivalent meaning'.

There are two main types of question which are used in surveys. One is closed, in which R is invited to choose between 'yes', 'no' and 'don't know', or between some other series of alternatives. The other is open-ended, in which R is invited to talk freely about his behaviour, opinions or experiences in some area. In most surveys both kinds of question are used, though the proportions vary considerably: public-opinion polls use more closed questions, research surveys make more use of open-ended ones. It is found that the answers to open-ended questions are less complete but more accurate; the answer to multiple-choice questions are more complete but less accurate (Dillon, 1986).

The interviewer requires a number of different skills. Firstly he must establish contact with R and persuade him to take part. If rapport is not established R will refuse to co-operate; some Ints have a high rate of failure of this kind, and it leads to error in the results. By rapport is meant a smooth pattern of interaction in which both feel comfortable and there are few pauses and interruptions, together with some degree of mutual trust and acceptance. Int should treat R as an equal and eliminate social barriers. He should show a keen and sympathetic interest, listen carefully, be accepting and uncritical of what is said and indicate that there is plenty of time. For different purposes different degrees of rapport may be needed: to ask intimate questions about income or sex requires more rapport than asking questions about interests or attitudes.

There are a number of rules in which Ints are trained, for example to read each question slowly and exactly as it is written, record answers verbatim, and make sure each answer is correctly understood and adequate. Int should not bias questions by putting vocal emphasis on particular words and should not bias the recorded replies by imputing the usual views of people of the age or social class of R. Int should conceal his own views from R and should not argue with him, no matter how absurd the opinions expressed by the latter. Particular skill is needed with potentially embarrassing issues, such as income or sexual behaviour; Int should adopt a relaxed, matter-of-fact manner, or he can present R with a list of alternatives to check. He can explain to R that he is not concerned with assessing R, and that all answers are equally acceptable, perhaps indicating that a wide range of different answers is commonly obtained. A number of special methods are used in motivation research interviews to get at genuine feelings. R is more likely to be co-operative if he sees how each question is relevant to the main purpose of the interview, and it may be useful to explain the point of certain questions.

When open-ended questions are used, a series of follow-up questions is needed, and Int should react to feedback. When Int has asked an open-ended question on some topic R will often give a reply that is inadequate in one way or another:

1  R refuses to answer the question; Int can explain the purpose of the survey or the particular question.

2  R partly misunderstands the question and talks about the wrong things; Int can then repeat and clarify the question, stressing what is wanted.

3  R doesn't produce enough information; Int can ask him to 'tell me more about this'.

4  R is confused about the issue; Int invites him to talk the topic out to clarify his ideas.

5  R deals only with certain aspects of the problem; Int can ask more specifically about the areas omitted, possibly putting a series of increasingly direct questions in a 'funnel' structure (Kahn and Cannell, 1957).

Often, in social surveys proper, the follow-up questions are drafted from the outset.

A definite sequence of topic areas should be adopted: the easiest and least threatening are taken first, and more difficult ones later, when more confidence has been established. There should also be some sequence of topics so that the interview makes sense to R. Care is taken with the very first questions, and also with the last, so that the interview can end on a pleasant note.

Finally, Int should listen very carefully to what R has to say. He should not be concerned about whether what R says is true or false, but should see it as the expression of his attitudes and way of looking at the world: this is what the interview is trying to find out (Dillon, 1986).

## SELLING

Selling is done all over the world, though in very different ways and at different times and places: compare the endless bargaining with vendors in the markets of the Middle East, the mechanical rigidity of encyclopedia salesmen, the high-pressure methods once common in the USA and the passive role of supermarket attendants. I shall discuss three kinds of selling: retail sales in shops, industrial sales, and salesman-initiated selling of commodities such as insurance.

There are certain principles which are common to all three. The aim in each case is to sell as much as possible, but in addition the salesperson (S) wants to satisfy the customer (C), partly for altruistic motives but also so that C will come again and tell friends about the shop or firm, thus enhancing long-term sales. Ss are often given a bonus, related to the number of sales made. Sales are easier when initiated by C, much more difficult when the contact has to be made by S, as in most insurance sales.

The order of moves varies somewhat between different kinds of selling, but often includes:

S   finding out C's needs;
S   offering one or more items;
C   asking questions;
C   making objections;
S   showing advantages of items and dealing with objections;
S   clinching the sale.

*Retail sales*  It is common to find that some Ss are selling only 20 to 40 per cent of what others in the same department are selling; this is an excellent example of the effects of different degrees of social skills shown in objective and quantitative terms. The use of individual bonus schemes may tempt Ss to use more persuasive methods and to go for the more prosperous-looking Cs; it also causes conflicts among the sales staff. A better scheme is probably to pay a group bonus that is shared between members of a department or counter, though this is inconvenient to administer and many shops manage without a bonus at all. The Ss in a department are supervised by the buyer for that department. Ostensibly C has power over S, and may indeed treat S as a kind of servant; this is particularly true of some upper middle-class Cs, and is much resented by Ss.

According to studies of department stores by myself and Mary Lydall, most sales do not involve a complex sequence of steps: persuasion by S is rare, and Cs spend a lot of time looking by themselves at the goods on display. Some of the briefer sales encounters which we have observed include the following: C selects stockings from the stand, hands them to S, who takes the money and wraps them; C asks for a particular object, naming make, size, price, etc.; C looks through dresses on the rack, selects those she is interested in and S shows C to a changing-room, where she tries them on and decides which to have. What happens is totally different in other departments in the same store; in some C can help himself, in others he has to be served.

We will now try to give an account of the complete possible sequence of events involved in a sale.

1 *Categorization of C by S* This is sometimes in terms of how much money C is likely to spend or what style of clothes C is wearing, the latter being a useful guide to his or her tastes. It has been found in some shops, however, that Ss categorize Cs in terms of a kind of local mythology – 'peppery colonels', 'elderly frustrated females', etc. (Woodward, 1960).

2 *Establishing contact with C* C may ask for help, ask specific questions, ask to see particular objects or stand expectantly at the counter. If C is wandering about or looking at goods on display, S may approach him, but this requires skill and judgement about whether C is ready to be helped.

3 *S finds out C's needs* C may approach S directly or may respond to S's opening by saying, 'I would like to buy a tie', though he may at this point specify his needs in greater detail: 'I would like something fairly bright.' S should listen carefully to whatever C has to say and try to understand what C is really after. Often C's wishes are vague, and S now needs to find out which of a thousand possible ties C would be most interested in. S needs to ask questions, to narrow down the field of choice. The strategies which can be used are similar to those in 'Twenty Questions' (except that direct questions can be asked, e.g. 'Which colour would you prefer?'). However, C may be thinking in terms of all manner of private classification schemes, as indicated by describing ties as 'bright', 'blue', 'terylene', 'with it', etc., and S must attune himself rapidly to C's conceptual structure.

4 *S shows C a variety of items*, if necessary demonstrating them or letting C try them on. There are several different strategies here. In the matter of price, for example, some Ss show the

middle-range item first, others show the most expensive. In either case it is important to make use of feedback, C's reaction providing a hint as to what should be shown next. Similarly, a clearer idea of C's needs can be obtained by studying his reactions to the objects shown. Again it is important to show the right number of objects: if too many are shown C feels confused and can't decide; if too few, C feels coerced. The way S handles the goods can convey a message: in some shops the more expensive goods are handled more reverently.

5 *S gives information and advice* C may ask questions about the goods at this stage, or raise objections. The experienced S will know the answers to questions and the replies to criticisms, and can point to particular advantages of each object. If S has found out C's needs he can point out how various objects would meet these needs. If S really believes in the goods, and wants to help C, this will be a quite genuine argument.

6 *Clinching the sale* This can be done in a variety of ways, different ones probably being suitable for different Cs. Some Cs can be left to decide for themselves, others can be persuaded that a particular object would be the best one for them; for others it can be assumed that they have decided already – 'Will you take it now, or shall we deliver it, Madam?'

7 *After the sale* S can increase C's feelings of satisfaction by providing further information about the object chosen and discussing after-sales service. He attends to payment and delivery, and suggests further related purchases to C.

It is necessary for S to be able to adapt to C's style of interaction, and to be able to handle a variety of Cs. This will affect whether C should be approached or not, whether C should be offered advice and information or not, and what kind of goods should be offered – in terms of price and style. Special techniques are needed with awkward customers; they may be handed over to another, preferably older, S or they may be left with a large assortment of goods to choose for themselves.

S will be more persuasive if he really knows the goods and projects an image of competence. C will be more likely to attend to S if S is friendly and easy to get on with. Observational studies by myself and Mary Lydall found that high-selling salesgirls established good rapport and had a smoother pattern of interaction than others. Chapple and Donald (1947) gave a standard interview to 154 Ss. The best Ss were very active and talked a lot, but were flexible and could adjust well to different styles of interaction. Those who oversold and had goods returned were dominant and made a lot of interruptions.

*Industrial sales* The relationship between S and C is rather different here: C has usually initiated the contact, S has considerable expertise and is in some ways like a consultant, and the problems under discussion are complex. Research by Rackham (1987) and colleagues has found that the most successful industrial salesmen ask about C's needs, and then ask 'need–payoff' questions like 'How much is this problem costing you each year?' S then describes the benefits of the product, showing how it can solve the problem, so that its costs now seem less when set against the costs of the problem (Rackham, 1987).

In addition:

1 S must be acceptable – this depends on his apparent expertise and the reputation of his firm;
2 S provides the right level of technical details for C;
3 S takes C's objections seriously and is able to deal with them without getting into arguments;
4 closing the sale techniques are not successful with expensive products.

(Poppleton, 1981)

*Creative selling* (e.g. of insurance) In this kind of sale it is S who initiates the encounter. Most Cs – perhaps 90 per cent – don't buy, so it is a very unfavourable situation for S, and can be very stressful. One method is for Ss to select people similar to themselves as prospects; another is the use of 'referred leads', one C suggesting others.

Poppleton (1981) found that most Ss do not use standard openings or techniques, and that the use of stories and anecdotes was often successful. One of the main divisions is between the 'hard' and 'soft' sell. There is some evidence that the hard sell is more successful with Cs who are less well educated and informed, the soft sell with the better educated and informed (Poppleton, 1981).

## DOCTORS AND NURSES

*Doctors* The long-term goals of doctors (Ds) are to cure patients (Ps) when they are ill, to alleviate suffering when this is not possible, to prevent people becoming ill and to educate Ps in a better understanding of health and illness. These goals are reached via a number of intermediate ones; for example, curing P involves D first diagnosing the problem, then planning the treatment and finally increasing P's compliance. Still more immediate goals include reducing P's concern and increasing his or her satisfaction with the treatment. Some aspects of D's effectiveness could in principle be measured from the health or recovery rates of his Ps, though this does not entirely include health education activities. In practice Ds are assessed by observation of their performance in the surgery, or videotapes of it, dealing with genuine or role-played Ps. The aspects of D's behaviour which are assessed are those which have been found to contribute to the long-term goals, and which are listed below.

General practitioners (GPs) see Ps on average for six minutes each, hospital doctors for longer. An interview consists of a number of fairly distinct episodes:

(1) relating to P;
(2) discussing the reason for P's attendance;
(3) conducting a verbal or physical examination, or both;
(4) consideration of P's condition;
(5) detailing treatment or further investigation;
(6) terminating.

Byrne and Long (1976) found that all six phases occurred in 63 per cent of interviews, and that sometimes part of the sequence was repeated.

It has been found that quite a lot of Ps are not satisfied with consultations, do not remember what they are told and fail to carry out D's instructions. GPs in turn experience communication difficulties in 21 per cent of consultations, especially with working-class Ps and Ps who have often been before with the same problem (Pendleton, 1981).

*Relating to P* It is important for D to establish and maintain a good relationship with P. There are certain social skills of Ds which have been found to be related to P satisfaction: when D is warm and friendly, gives reassurance, expresses sympathy and understanding, and discovers and deals with P's concerns and expectations, P generally comes away happy.

*Collecting information, history-taking, diagnosis* Ps are more satisfied when they feel that they have been examined thoroughly; however, GPs often stop at the first symptom, and P may not reveal his real worries. Quite a number of Ds fail in this way to spot psychiatric illness, though this can be improved by training. Most important, both GPs and hospital doctors often fail to deal with obvious signs of emotional distress. Giving reassurance is an important source of satisfaction for P.

Some SST for doctors has concentrated on history-taking skills, and produced favourable results in that more information is obtained, more accurate diagnoses are made and psychiatric symptoms are recognized more often (Maguire, 1981); but it has not so far dealt with D's educational role, e.g. in giving explanations.

*Explanation and shared understanding* P is more satisfied if D explains what is the matter simply and clearly. In one study, only 6 per cent of working-class Ps and 18 per cent of class I Ps said that their Ds were good at explaining (Ley, 1977). In fact Ds give less explanation to working-class Ps than to anyone else – the very people who know least about health and whose need for information is greatest. Ps are often given inadequate information before undergoing operations, and Ds sometimes conceal the true situation in cases of serious illness, though this may be the best course of action in some cases.

*Involving P in management, and accepting responsibility* Usually there is a lot which Ps can do for themselves, but they may need to be motivated to do it. It is well established that Ps often forget what they are told and fail to comply with D's instructions.

However, Pendleton (1981) has found that Ps do remember 84 per cent of instructions about medication and 76 per cent of what they were told to do. It is, of course, still worth using techniques to increase compliance with instructions, such as emphasis, repetition and the use of clear and simple language.

There are a number of particular social skill problems for Ds:

1 *Dealing with working-class Ps* Ds see working-class Ps for a shorter time than they do middle- and upper-class Ps, and give them less explanation; subsequently these Ps do not feel Ds explain things well. The same is probably true of patients from ethnic minority groups.

2 *Dealing with emotions* Ds often treat Ps as bodies rather than as persons; the effects of emotional states, social relationships and stressful life events on health are very great, so this is a serious omission. It is interesting that Ds are actually quite good at recognizing Ps' emotions, but unfortunate that they often fail to make full use of this information (Pendleton, Schofield, Tate and Havelock, 1984; Maguire, 1981).

*Nurses* There are a number of special social skills problems for nurses:

1 the uncertainty about how much information to pass on, and the difficulties of exercising discretion here;

2 the difficulty of dealing with unrewarding Ps and the temptation to ignore or punish them;

3 the dangers of over-involvement, especially with dying Ps.

(Davis, 1981; Kagan, Evans and Kay, 1986)

The official goals of nurses (Ns) are to look after Ps' bodies and to administer, or help to administer, treatment. The Ps, however, regard Ns also as sources of information and social support. The effectiveness of Ns can be assessed in terms of P satisfaction, length of recovery time or ratings by sisters.

Patients are often anxious, and in need of social support and information; they depend on nurses for both. Ps often complain that they do not receive enough information about their illness, treatment, progress and tests; 70 per cent said they received no information from nurses (Cartwright, 1964). There appears to be some uncertainty about N's role here and how far it is her job to reveal such facts. Several studies have shown that when Ps are given more of an explanation before an operation they recover faster and need fewer drugs afterwards. It is also unclear whether or not talking to Ps is part of a nurse's job; some Ns think that it isn't, but Ps have a great desire for it. However, Ns appear to be rather poor conversationalists, their chats with Ps lasting on average forty-five seconds. These exchanges are usually ended by Ns, and, although conversation tends to be disease-orientated, Ns often avoid answering questions and frequently change the topic (Davis, 1981). Student nurses in particular are very hesitant to give information, especially to those who are dying.

Ns do think that it is part of their job to give hope and support, if not information. This is done by verbal reassurance and appropriate NV communication. Touching Ps before an operation reduces subsequent recovery time for females but not for males (Whitcher and Fisher, 1979). Ps certainly need this support: in one study 66 per cent were upset by emotional aspects of their stay, including discourteous staff and communication problems (Anderson, 1973). In other studies most Ps have thought that Ns were sympathetic, efficient and thoughtful, Ns need social support too, from their colleagues; where this is available the rate of accidents and errors is reduced (Sheehan et al., 1981). However, Ns get fed up with Ps who complain or express too much suffering, and they react by ignoring them or addressing them sarcastically, and by enforcing the rules strictly. Ns like some Ps more than others, and do more for them. Most Ns prefer male wards to female – there being a jollier atmosphere – and surgical wards to medical – since Ps recover faster in the former (Parkes, 1980).

Social skills training for nurses has often included the following components:

1 Developing rapport and empathy, listening skills, perceiving emotions correctly, communicating understanding.

2 Control and assertiveness, asking questions, giving effective information and instructions to patients.

3 Social problem-solving, dealing with difficult patients and their relatives, persuading patients to do things.

4 Counselling, helping patients in pain or distress with help, sympathy and advice; exploration of the problem, followed by giving understanding and taking action.

In recent years aggression towards nurses, verbal and physical, has increased. Nurses have found that the most effective ways of dealing with threatened physical aggression are:

1  a nurturant attitude, listening and talking softly;
2  assertiveness, standing no nonsense; and
3  persuasiveness, letting the other blow off steam and showing sympathy (Crossland, 1992).

### PSYCHOTHERAPY AND COUNSELLING

These terms will be used fairly broadly to include any situation in which one person tries to solve another's psychological problems by means of conversation. There are many different techniques of psychotherapy, but some of the main varieties can be indicated briefly.

1 *Freudian psychoanalysis* Patients recall dreams and early childhood events, and the psychoanalyst interprets the patient's condition in terms of psychoanalytic theory. The full treatment involves about three sessions a week up to a total of three to six hundred, though many fail to complete the course.

The relationship between therapist (T) and patient (P) is an unusual one. As with other kinds of therapy T is warm, supportive and uncritical, but here T is out of sight, sitting behind P on the couch, so he can use little NVC, and adopts a deliberately neutral role, so that P can project past objects (i.e. imagined others) on to him.

2 *Rogers's non-directive therapy* Here T helps P to understand his emotional reactions by verbally labelling or 'reflecting' what has been expressed, and by giving non-directive encouragement for

further revelations. Treatment requires thirty to fifty sessions. Reflection is used instead of interpretation, and Ps are encouraged to reduce the conflict between actual and ideal self, by valuing the actual self more.

3 *Counselling and brief psychotherapy* This consists of discussion about P's here-and-now problems and what can be done about them. T may use one of a variety of psychological theories or an 'eclectic' combination of them; the number of sessions is typically five to ten. This is the most widely practised kind of psychotherapy; it is given by National Health Service psychiatrists in England, by numerous non-medical psychotherapists and counsellors, and of course by even more numerous clergymen, general practitioners and sympathetic friends.

4 *Cognitive therapy* This form of psychotherapy, which owes its existence to Ellis and Beck, consists of showing the patient that his emotional problems are due to irrational thinking. The therapist acts as a kind of teacher and shows the patient how to think differently about things. Examples of irrational thinking are blaming the self for everything that goes wrong or holding unreasonable beliefs, e.g. I can't be happy unless everyone loves and admires me.

5 *Behaviour therapy* Here T uses techniques based on learning theory to change undesired behaviour or emotional reactions; for example, by desensitization for phobias (see p. 245). It is now recognized that this is a form of psychotherapy, and requires T to be warm and persuasive, and able to build up confidence and positive expectations in P, thus increasing his motivation. In fact cognitive and behaviour therapy have now been combined in 'cognitive behaviour therapy'.

The goals of psychotherapy vary somewhat according to the theories held by T. They usually include:

the removal of feelings of psychological distress or discomfort, such as anxiety and depression;

improving P's functioning at work and in interpersonal relations;

the removal of other symptoms of mental disorder.

The relationship between P and T is affected by the following factors:

P comes voluntarily because he wants to be cured (unless sent by the legal authorities);

traditionally P pays a fee, though this is not the case in the National Health Service;

T has power and prestige based on his medical or other professional standing, his psychological expertise and often his social class. Since P can terminate treatment whenever he wishes, T has no formal power over him, but P may come to see T as the means to the much desired goal of recovery.

The recovery rate for neurotic patients is something like 66 to 70 per cent over two years, although some get worse. However, neurotic patients also recover 'spontaneously', i.e. without any formal treatment. There is considerable controversy as to what the rate of spontaneous recovery is. One view is that the neurotic condition simply waxes and wanes in response to external stresses, so that patients may appear to get either better or worse while being treated (Subotnik, 1972). There have been a number of studies comparing recovery rates of Ps receiving psychotherapy with those of control groups of similar Ps who had no treatment. Smith and Glass (1977) re-analysed the results of 375 such studies, involving over 25,000 patients, and showed that the treated patients improved on average somewhat more than the untreated controls in terms of reduced anxiety, increased self-esteem, and adjustment and achievement at work. The behaviour-oriented therapies did a little better than other forms, but there were no differences between the various types of psychotherapy.

It has been found, however, that some Ts have higher success rates than others, as do certain types of P – so it is evident that under the right conditions psychotherapy can do some good. A lot of therapy is with more than one person – husband and wife, or parents and an adolescent child – and here there is usually no alternative form of treatment. It is clear that some Ts actually make some Ps worse, and that there are considerable variations in social skill here.

We will describe some of the social techniques which are widely used in psychotherapy. The following are common to all forms of treatment:

1 T expresses a warm, accepting and uncritical attitude of interested concern towards P, and creates a strong interpersonal relationship; it is a kind of ideal friendship, in which T participates emotionally, though it is restricted to the therapeutic hour.

2 P is encouraged to talk about his anxieties, conflicts and other bottled-up emotions; the cathartic expression of these feelings, and sharing of them with another person who does not react critically, helps to relieve them and enables P to think about painful problems.

3 T tries to explore P's subjective world of feeling and thinking, to understand P's point of view and to open up communication with him.

4 T tries to give P insight into why he reacts as he does, and thus to change him. This is done by the verbal labelling of P's behaviour; psychoanalysts and others will offer a theoretical interpretation as well, e.g. obsessional hand-washing may be explained as the symbolic cleansing of guilt.

5 T helps P to make plans and positive decisions – to try out new ways of dealing with people and situations and to make positive efforts, thus becoming committed rather than remaining indifferent and passive.

(Sundberg and Tyler, 1962)

Different therapists place different emphases on these common elements, and they vary particularly in their handling of number 4, bringing about emotional or cognitive changes. Much psychotherapy is given in groups, and it is possible that group therapy is beneficial for patients with interpersonal problems.

We have seen that there is no difference in success rate between psychotherapists of different schools, and a number of studies have shown that it is the general social skills of the therapist which are important. There has been widespread belief in the importance of therapist 'warmth, empathy and genuineness', first proposed by Carl Rogers; however, follow-up studies have found only modest effects of these variables. In addition, positive NV signals, expressive voice quality and accurate perception are important. Bad habits include confrontation, anger, disapproval, dealing with emotional issues too soon and failing to provide support (Trower and Dryden, 1981).

In several studies it has been found that briefly trained students and non-graduate housewives have been as successful as highly trained therapists. It has been argued by Schofield (1964) that, at times, everyone experiences unhappiness and distress, and is in need of help, but not so much through any specialized techniques of psychotherapy as through a sympathetic listening and friendship. It is clear that minor degrees of psychological distress are very widespread and that qualified psychotherapists are in short supply. The solution may be for the basic techniques of psychotherapy to be more widely practised on a non-professional and semi-professional basis by members of the social network.

Ts prefer and can establish a better relationship with certain kinds of P – those who are middle-class, keen to recover, intelligent, submissive, friendly and only moderately maladjusted; it is the other Ps who do not recover and are found difficult by Ts, especially by the inexperienced (Luborsky et al., 1971; Bergin and Garfield, 1978; Trower and Dryden, 1981).

### TEACHING

This section will deal with the teaching of children and adults in classes, i.e. in groups between five and forty in number. Teaching seems to have one primary goal and two subsidiary ones: the primary goal is to increase the knowledge, understanding or skills of the pupils (Ps); the subsidiary ones are for the teacher (T) to increase the motivation and interest of Ps, and to maintain order and discipline. They are subsidiary in the sense that the primary goal cannot be attained without them. Further goals could be listed, e.g. that Ps should enjoy the classes and that they should develop in mental health, self-control or other aspects of personality. The most common source of failure in teaching is in maintaining discipline; there is evidence that young Ts, especially women, find this the hardest problem, and this is probably the main reason for their abandoning the profession.

The problems of teaching vary according to the age of the Ps. Younger Ps are usually a captive audience, and are eager to please T; older Ps are less anxious to please but may be highly motivated for other reasons, especially if they have been successful pupils in the past. In between these groups motivation may be lower, and it is with pupils of fourteen or fifteen that keeping order is most difficult. T usually has some formal power, both disciplinary and in controlling the future progress of Ps. T may also have power based on his or her expertise and position to help Ps realize their ambitions.

A lot of research has been done comparing the amount learnt, or the exam results obtained, with different teaching skills (Rosenshine, 1971). Those which have been found to be most effective are as follows:

1 introducing (structuring) topics or activities clearly;

2 explaining clearly, with examples and illustrative materials;

3 systematic and businesslike organization of lessons;

4 variety of teaching materials and methods;

5 use of questions, especially higher-order questions;

6 use of praise and other reinforcement, verbal and nonverbal;

7 encouraging pupil-participation;

8 making use of Ps' ideas, clarifying and developing them further;

9 warmth, rapport and enthusiasm, mainly shown nonverbally.

The teaching of these skills has been built into microteaching programmes (pp. 296–7), one of the best examples of social skills training founded on research to find which techniques produce the best results. The following are some of the main skills which are taught.

*Arousing interest and motivation* A lesson should start by gaining the attention and arousing the interest of Ps. This can be done by asking a challenging or provocative question, related to the interests of the pupils, and by a lively manner on the part of T, especially a dynamic non-verbal style, with expressive voice and gestures and the establishment of mutual gaze. Some Ps may be motivated by the need to be approved by T, a person in authority; some may identify with T and assimilate T's enthusiasm for the subject. If Ps like T they will like the subject (Oeser, 1955). The curiosity drive, to find out new things and to solve puzzles, may be aroused by presenting the material as a set of intriguing and challenging problems. Similarly T can use material or examples that are dramatic, unusual, funny or striking in some other way. Activity methods are one way of doing this, as are videotapes and other visual aids.

*Explanation* This is the central part of the teaching process, and applies to some other social skills too. An explanation should be clear, brief, well organized and fluent, avoiding unfamiliar words and, above all, including examples or analogies; the key points should be emphasized verbally and non-verbally, and repeated. If possible, use should be made of audiovisual aids, maps, charts, models, demonstrations, etc. Feedback from pupils should be studied to make sure they are all understanding.

*Questions* This is a second central activity of schoolteaching: Ts ask up to two questions per minute. These are mainly factual or recall questions, and have not been found to contribute much to teacher effectiveness. Much more important are higher-order questions, which are more open-ended, require pupils to think and thus extend their understanding. These questions may be about evaluation ('why do you think that classical music is better than jazz?') or analysis ('what caused the Gulf War?'). It is important not to let the same Ps answer all the questions, and to be able to cope constructively with wrong answers.

*Interaction sequences* Teaching consists of repeated cycles of interaction. Flanders (1970) has found cycles such as those shown in Figure 10.1. For example:

T: teaches, explains
T: asks question (to which he knows the answer)
P: replies

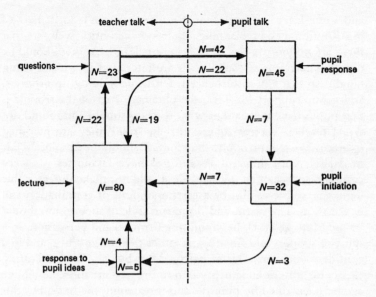

Figure 10.1  Cycles of interaction in the classroom (Flanders, 1970).

Flanders suggests that a lot of the skill of teaching consists of the ability to control such cycles and to move from one to another.

Teaching can also be looked at in terms of episodes. A lesson, or part of a lesson, will have a definite goal and topic; the repeated cycles will be directed towards getting across a particular set of facts or skills. These teaching episodes may take a number of different forms.

*Listening* is an important part of T's performance. He or she should listen attentively to points made by Ps, which may be incoherent, should try to see the speaker's point of view, and should take note of the NV accompaniments. Ts should use strong listening behaviour – head nods, gaze, mm-hmm's – and should usually reinforce pupil contributions – but selectively. It may be necessary to ask probe questions to find out what P really meant. And, while listening, T has to be planning how best to respond to the point made.

*Keeping order* For some young Ts this is the greatest problem, and some leave the profession because they can't do it. Part of the solution lies in planning classroom activities well, so that there are no long pauses or Ps being unclear what they should be doing. There is less trouble if Ps are interested in what is being taught, so that any disturbance is felt to be holding up progress, and group support for T can be obtained. Part of the trouble is that pupils have ideas about what teachers should and should not do; if teachers do not adhere to these 'rules' they are punished (p. 180). To avoid trouble, therefore, T should be absolutely fair in dealing with different Ps and not have favourites — a very common source of annoyance. He should not make unreasonable demands, so there must be a certain amount of consultation and negotiation. The warm-and-dominant style of supervision should be used (pp. 280–81); he should use firmness and persuasion, in a spirit of support and friendliness rather than of hostility, and in a confident manner. This is partly done by NVC — indicating clearly his attitude and intention to control the situation. Discipline can be maintained by punitive and threatening methods, but this creates an anxious and unpleasant atmosphere and makes Ps dislike T, thus hampering the learning process, and discourages a creative, problem-solving approach to the subject under consideration. A study of Canadian university students found the teaching habits which were most disliked were 'ignoring, discouraging and restricting questions; reacting to students' contributions with ridicule, sarcasm, belittlement, hostility, anger and arrogance; squelching students; interrupting students' contributions; or failing to promote discussion or questions' (Crawford and Signori, 1962; Brown, 1975; Dunkin and Biddle, 1974).

## PUBLIC SPEAKING AND LECTURING

There are many kinds of public speaking — political speeches, sermons, lectures, after-dinner speeches. The main goal of a public speaker (PS) is to change the attitudes or behaviour of members of the audience (A), or to increase their knowledge and understanding. Often these two aims are combined, but political and religious PSs and other propagandists emphasize the first, while lecturers in educational establishments emphasize the second. The same person may have different goals on different occasions, for example if he gives both sermons and lectures on theology. There is no doubt that PSs can be very effective in attaining these goals. For example, Billy Graham converted 100,000 people during his first three campaigns in Great Britain – about 4 per cent of those attending; half of these people were still church attenders a year later (Argyle and Beit-Hallahmi, 1975). Graham was exceptionally successful, and many other evangelists are much less effective. In some colleges the public lecture is the main form of instruction, and students acquire most of their education from this source. The main sources of failure in a PS are being inaudible, boring, unconvincing, talking too fast, walking about or having other mannerisms, being nervous, not being able to handle an audience and presenting the material badly.

There are certain problems, requiring special social techniques, which arise with both kinds of PS. Firstly, it is necessary for A to hear him clearly. He should speak loudly and distinctly, with head up, and 'project' his voice to all corners of the audience. He should sound the ends of words, not drop his voice at the ends of sentences avoid saying 'er', and keep pitch, voice quality and breathing under control. Elocution teachers can provide help with difficulties in this sphere. Secondly, the manner of the PS is very important. He will be more effective if seen to be an expert on the subject and well intentioned towards the listeners; this can be indicated by the appropriate NV signals of dress and general demeanour, especially perhaps tone of voice. The speaker should be seen as an expert but also as a member of the group, on equal terms with the audience. Thirdly, many people are anxious when in front of an audience, especially a large and expert audience. However, the level of anxiety usually drops once the performance starts. It can be reduced by preparing the materials carefully so that PS has confidence in them. He should also have decided on his precise relationship with the audience: is he trying to entertain them, to persuade them to do something, to tell them about some new research? Has he the right, and is he in a position, to do this?

PS must start by establishing rapport with A, and getting its attention and confidence. This may include explaining how he comes to be there, outlining what he is going to talk about and why, and indicating his previous contacts with A or the organization in question. PS should also make certain that he can be clearly heard and that he is not speaking too fast or too softly; for this he can usually rely on visual feedback.

PS should keep A under control. He should study its reactions carefully and be on the lookout for people being unable to hear, falling asleep, looking bored, puzzled or cross, or not taking it seriously enough. He should take rapid corrective action, for example speaking louder, explaining points that are not clear, arousing more interest or quietening them down. However, PS should not be dependent on continual positive reactions from A; he is often more concerned with the overall, long-term impact of his presentation.

*Persuasion and propaganda* The successful political or religious speaker does not behave when on the platform in a relaxed, informal and 'familial' style; on the contrary he has 'presence' and dramatizes himself and his message by a certain amount of showmanship. This kind of PS should not allow A to relax but should stir it up into a state of emotional arousal. Many studies show that attitude change takes place more easily when A is emotionally aroused (Sargant, 1957). Some PSs are adept at arousing the emotions of their As. This is done by the dramatic description of emotively arousing events – such as the horrors of hell, the outrages of the enemy or the sufferings of the poor. This is combined with an intense manner, conveyed by facial expression and tone of voice, so that A is unable to treat the matter lightly. The experienced PS discovers which examples or stories are the most effective with particular kinds of audience. Having aroused such an emotional state, the classical social technique used by propagandists is then to show that the A can relieve its anxiety, or satisfy its anger, by acting in certain ways. The nineteenth-century revivalists would make their As terrified of going to hell and then tell them what they must do to be saved; many modern advertisements follow a similar strategy.

Research has shown how persuasive messages should be organized to have the maximum effect. One-sided messages are best, unless the A is initially opposed or well educated, in which case objections should be stated and dealt with. If the message is simple and straightforward the A should be left to draw the conclusions itself; otherwise PS should do this. Overt behaviour is affected most if specific actions are recommended. Earlier arguments have most effect, so the most appealing part of the argument should come first. It is useful to start with statements with which A will agree, in order to win its confidence.

Political speeches have been found to be more effective when certain rhetorical techniques are used. Atkinson (1984) recorded a number of British political speeches and observed that 'spontaneous' applause was often produced by rhetorical devices such as lists of three and 'contrastive pairs', in both cases with appropriate emphasis and pauses. Bull (1987) analysed a speech by Arthur Scargill in which there were twenty-five rhetorical points, of which twenty-two received prolonged applause. The most successful rhetorical devices were contrasts, three-part lists and 'headline-punching' (the speaker proposes to make a declaration or promise, and then makes it). In the sections which produced most applause he used strong hand movements, for example '*they* say . . .' (left-hand gesture), but '*we* say . . .' (right-hand gesture).

*Lecturing* Lectures are not very popular with students, who usually prefer being taught in smaller groups, and they often complain about lectures being badly prepared and presented. However, lectures can be an effective way of conveying information, and in skilled hands they can also arouse interest in the subject and stimulate thought. Common problems are reading from a typed script and turning away from the audience to write extensively on the board; the solutions to these problems are to use notes and an overhead projector, respectively. Successful lecturers have a variety of styles, and it is not possible to prescribe which one is most effective. While lecturers should not arouse the emotions in the same way as propagandists, they should arouse interest, intellectual excitement and curiosity. They should not simply produce a lot of information that nobody wants, so a lecturer should start by stating what problems he is going to deal with and getting A's attention from the outset. He should follow an intelligible plan, which may be built up on the blackboard or shown in a handout, and he should come to clear conclusions. It is important to accompany the statement of principles by concrete examples.

One of the main problems with a lecture is that A can't remember it all. Possible solutions are: not including too much, not making it too long, relating it to A's experience and encouraging A to take notes. Furthermore, a lecture should be made enjoyable and memorable by the use of materials which are of special interest to the audience, dramatic or simply funny. Particular skill is needed when introducing A to novel ideas or ways of looking at things; it may be necessary to use striking and carefully chosen examples, to jolt A out of its previous ways of thinking. Visual aids such as slides, overhead projector, videotapes and charts can help with the presentation and make it more varied and interesting. The lecturer can keep A's interest by adopting a manner which keeps it involved in the situation – use of eye contact, and a striking and pleasant style of behaviour. He should spend as little time as possible looking at notes, writing on the blackboard or otherwise interrupting contact with A. He should show his own enthusiasm for the materials, and a positive attitude towards A, by facial expression and tone of voice. Spatial arrangements are important, especially when visual aids are used; the best room available should be chosen and arranged to best advantage, so that everyone is comfortable and can see and hear. The lecturer should be as near to A as possible and able to see A. During the discussion the contributions of the audience should be taken seriously and sympathetically, and an effort made to understand the points of view expressed. The lecturer should not merely 'deal with' the points made but use them as an opportunity to explain himself further. He should avoid any confrontation with the audience.

There are self-presentation problems here too. Not only is a lecture more than the transmission of a text, it is also more than a performance by PS. As Goffman (1981) says:

The lecturer and the audience join in affirming a single proposition. They join in affirming that organized talking can reflect, express, delineate, portray – if not come to grips with – the real world, and that, finally, there is a real, structured, somewhat unitary world out there to comprehend ... Whatever his substantive domain, whatever his school of thought, and whatever his inclination to piety or impiety, he signs the same agreement and he serves the same cause: to protect us from the wind, to stand up and seriously project the assumption that, through lecturing, a meaningful picture of some part of the world can be conveyed, and that the talker can have access to a picture worth conveying.

(Bligh, 1972; Knapper, 1981)

## SUPERVISION OF GROUPS

We include here not only industrial foremen but directors of research groups and leaders of other groups that have a task to do. The primary goal of the supervisor (S) is to get the work done, but an important secondary goal is to keep the team satisfied – otherwise there will be absenteeism, labour turnover and a general lack of co-operation. Ss may fail in a number of ways, of which the most common are:

relying too much on formal power;
being too authoritative;
not giving enough direction, so that other members of the group assume leadership;
producing high output but low job satisfaction;
producing high job satisfaction but low output.

There is a lot of evidence that the relationship between supervisors and their subordinates is a difficult one. It is often felt, by subordinates, that it is a relationship which generates a lot of conflict but very little satisfaction, and that it is hostile rather than friendly (Argyle and Furnham, 1983). On the other hand supervisors *can* be a major source of job satisfaction and mental health. The way to achieve this is by using the optimum supervisory skills.

In studies of groups of manual workers it is found that groups under certain supervisors may produce 50 per cent more work than under other supervisors; if the work is machine-paced or under wage-incentives these differences are smaller, though with very bad supervision the difference can be greater (Argyle, 1989). The effects on rates of absenteeism and labour turnover are rather greater — ratios of 4:1 or even 8:1 have been found; again the worst supervisors produce the most marked effects (Fleishman and Harris, 1962).

There has been a great deal of research into the social techniques which are most effective, mainly by comparing the behaviour of Ss in charge of high-output and low-output teams. What supervisors actually do varies a lot between different settings, but two dimensions have consistently been found to be important. Both can be measured by a series of ratings by subordinates: the Leader Behaviour Description Questionnaire (LBDQ) (Bass, 1981).

*Initiating structure* It is essential that the supervisor should really supervise, and in the following ways:

1 planning and scheduling the work to be done, and making sure that supplies are available;
2 instructing and training subordinates in how to do their work;
3 checking and correcting the work that has been done;
4 giving subordinates feedback on how well they are doing;
5 motivating subordinates to work effectively.

If he fails to do these things it is likely that the group or some of its members will take over these functions. On the other hand S should do all this with a light hand, since men and women do not like him breathing down their necks and constantly interfering. He should see them frequently, showing interest, giving help where it is needed, but giving as little direction and criticism as possible. In 'job enrichment' schemes some of S's jobs, such as checking, are delegated to members of the group.

*Consideration* Ss are more effective when they look after the needs, interests and welfare of their subordinates. This is particularly true when they are powerful enough really to be able to do something for them. In matters of discipline they should be persuasive rather than punitive, and try to find out the causes of the offending behaviour. It is interesting that foremen who are more concerned with the welfare of the workers than with production usually succeed in getting higher rates of output. On the other hand a number of studies show that S should be somewhat detached and independent: he should do his own job rather than theirs, and not be afraid of exerting influence over them.

Initiating structure on the whole leads to more productivity, but it needs consideration as well. Consideration leads to greater job satisfaction, and lower absenteeism and labour turnover. While the combination of these two dimensions is found to be important, this is difficult to attain; informal groups often have two leaders, one for each of these jobs. Part of the difficulty is that directing the task tends to put a leader at a distance from the group, while getting on well with members means he may lose his authority as a task leader. The solution may lie in a further aspect of supervisory skill.

*Democratic-persuasive style* A democratic leader is usually more effective than an autocratic one. He does not just rely on his formal powers, but on:

1 motivating people, by explanation and persuasion, rather than just giving orders;

2 allowing subordinates to participate in decisions that affect them;

3 using techniques of group discussion and group decision.

By means of these skills the supervisor succeeds in getting the group to set high targets and to internalize the motivation to reach them, without exerting pressure himself. There are of course limits to what the group can decide. It can usually decide about details of administration – who shall work where, how training or holiday schemes shall be implemented. The group can also make suggestions on more far-reaching matters which S can relay to his superiors. He exerts direction and influence but in a way that does not arouse resentment and antagonism. He can still be a real leader, rather than just a chairman for the group.

We now know that the most effective leadership style varies with the circumstances. More initiating structure is required if the job is unstructured, the group large or its members inexperienced. More consideration is needed if the work is unrewarding, while more participation is called for when the leader has insufficient information to make a decision, the subordinates have additional information, or when they might not accept a decision without consultation (Vroom and Yetton, 1973).

Intelligence helps too. Fiedler and Garcia (1987) found that intelligent leaders of a variety of kinds *are* more effective in that their groups have a higher rate of performance. However, this occurs only when the leader is directive and not under stress (especially interpersonal stress from his or her own boss), and when the group members are supportive of the leader.

There is more than one kind of successful leader. The 'charismatic' or 'transformational' leader is one who can communicate a vision or mission, and inspire his group to pursue new goals. Such leaders are particularly effective in times of crises, when a challenging and exhilarating task needs to be done (Howell and Frost, 1989).

## MANAGEMENT

Managers spend a great deal of their time with other people, about 50 per cent of it with subordinates, at scheduled or informal meetings. There have been a number of studies of the effects of the different supervisory styles of second-line leaders on productivity and job satisfaction; these show that they have a greater influence on productivity and satisfaction than first-line leaders (Nealey and Fiedler, 1968). A number of studies have shown that delegation and the use of participatory methods of leadership are effective at both levels. Styles of leadership are often passed down the hierarchy as each person copies his or her immediate superior and may be rewarded by the superior for so doing. This 'falling dominoes' effect has been found for participatory leadership, closeness of supervision, charismatic leadership and amount of interaction with subordinates (Bass, 1981). In recent management methods, like Management by Objectives, managers discuss with their subordinates the tasks to be tackled and the goals to be achieved. Appraisal interviews are carried out every six or twelve months, to evaluate success in reaching these targets.

Managers need the skills used by first-line superiors and the additional skills of managing organizations. These include chairmanship, presenting skills, appraisal and personnel interviewing skills, some of which will be described below (others are described in Argyle, 1989).

Not all managers are socially skilled. Some may have been promoted through their expertise at engineering or accountancy, and these are the people for whom management courses were originally devised. The entrepreneurs who start their own companies are sometimes lacking in social skills too. These people, who may become very rich and successful, are sometimes somewhat deviant personalities, making it difficult for them to fit into large organizations. Case studies have found that some entrepreneurs at least are nonconformist, rebellious, distrust authority, are unwilling to work with others and come from families where they were not appreciated, or from marginal minority groups, giving them a great drive to succeed and establish a new identity (Chell, 1986). They may not be good organization men themselves, and may be quite unlike the socially skilled people who are selected to run the company, and who in turn may get rid of the founder of the company (Argyle, 1989).

*Committee chairmanship* The task of committees and other discussion groups is to solve problems and take decisions in a way that is acceptable to those present and to those they represent. In some cases the emphasis is on problem-solving and creativity, in others the emphasis is on obtaining consensus. Such groups usually have a chairperson, unless there are only three or four people present. The chairperson has a generally accepted social role of controlling discussion and helping the group make decisions.

There has been some research into the skills which are most effective. Maier and Solem (1952) and Hoffman (1965) found, for example, that better and more widely accepted solutions are obtained if minority views can be expressed. Sometimes groups arrive at a solution rather quickly; if the chairman asks them to think of an alternative solution, this is often preferred in the end. The chairman can help the group by focusing on disagreements and searching for a creative solution. Rackham and Morgan (1977) found thirty-one effective chairmen, as judged by others. They had different rates of some kinds of social act, but they all made a lot of procedural proposals, testing understanding, summarizing and information-seeking. They had *low* rates of supporting behaviour, disagreeing and information-giving.

From our knowledge of small-group processes some other principles can be suggested. The formation of an informal status hierarchy in a committee may lead to low-status members not being attended to, however expert they might be on a particular item. The formation of norms may lead to conformity and unwillingness to listen to other ideas. There may be 'risky shifts' to extreme points of view.

It is generally agreed that a chairman should not only prepare the agenda but also discuss it beforehand with key members of the group, such as those being asked to introduce certain items. At the meeting itself the chairman should create the right atmosphere, by the use of appropriate NV signals. There are several phases to the discussion of each item on the agenda. First, the chairman introduces the item by outlining the problem to be discussed, summarizing briefly the main background factors, the arguments on each side and so on. Then the committee is invited to discuss the problem; enough time should be allowed for different views to be expressed, and the chairman should try to keep the discussion orderly, so that different points are dealt with in turn. Now the chairman can help the group to come to a decision, by focusing on disagreements among them and trying to arrive at a creative solution, evaluating different solutions in relation to criteria if these can be agreed, considering sub-problems in turn or asking the committee to consider two possible solutions. Finally, an attempt is made to secure the group's support for a particular solution. If this is impossible it may be necessary to take a vote (Whittington, 1986).

*Negotiation* Managers have to negotiate with trade unions, firms other than their own and government. Negotiation is a kind of joint decision-making between representatives of two sides who are in conflict, though there is joint interest in reaching a settlement. The goal of a negotiator (N) is to reach an agreement quickly which gives his side the best deal obtainable and which will be accepted by all concerned. The success of N can be assessed by ratings from both sides concerning his effectiveness, his record for reaching agreements and the extent to which his agreements stick.

In a sense most social skills have an element of negotiation, since different parties often have different goals, so I shall try to outline the universal principles involved.

A simple kind of negotiation is one where each side makes its case and a series of concessions is made by each side until agreement is reached; selling a car is like this. Usually it is more complicated, since each side has several goals and may not place them in the same order of importance. So one side may give way on one item in return for another which it values more, so that there is an overall advantage – what has been called 'integrative bargaining' (Pruitt, 1976). A further complication is that there is usually a long-term relationship between the two sides, and each has some concern for the other's interests. It has been found that high aspirations on the part of negotiators lead to better outcomes, but only if there is also concern for the other (Pruitt and Rubin, 1986).

Accurate perception of the other side is important, especially perception of their order of priorities. Sometimes negotiators see conflict where there is none, or mistakenly think that the other side has the same goals as themselves (Thompson, 1990).

Negotiations often go through alternating phases of co-operation and competition. During the co-operative phases the negotiators build up their relationship, exchange information and explore possible joint solutions in a problem-solving manner. In the competitive phases there is harder bargaining and decision-taking, over the exact settlement point (Morley, 1986).

Negotiators are often representatives of other groups, which increases the pressure on them, but if anything this improves their performance, unless this pressure is too strong.

Sometimes a professional mediator or chairman is appointed. He may be able to steer Ns towards a more problem-solving approach after a deadlock, and arrive at a solution which is face-saving for both sides. Sometimes informal discussion between junior representatives of the two sides can find a solution when their superiors have failed, since they are freer to explore possible concessions – though their solution may not be accepted in the end by their own sides.

Certain styles of negotiation have been found to be more successful than others, in actual cases or in simulations:

1 N should make a strong case, make strong demands and give small concessions;

2 N should not be too tough, however, or there may be no agreement, and he should not attack or irritate the other side;

3 N should be open to a wide range of alternatives, and not plan a particular outcome in advance;

4 N should adopt a rational, problem-solving approach, in which he explores all the options, finds out a lot about the other side and their problems as well as giving information himself, and communicates clearly and without ambiguity;

5 N should create a reputation for honesty and firmness, and enhance the image of his party.

(Rackham and Carlisle, 1978, 1979)

In addition a number of competitive, non-integrative tactics are sometimes used, and have been studied. These include threats of sanctions and promises of rewards, withholding information and giving misleading information, imposing an agenda of negotiable issues and causing delays or other kinds of annoyance in the tradition of gamesmanship (Greenhalgh, 1987). These are not recommended.

There are also more complex strategies, such as Osgood's GRIT (1960) – Graduated Reciprocation in Tension Reduction

– recommended for disarmament talks. N announces that he will make small concessions, and that if these are matched by the other side he will make more.

### FURTHER READING

Argyle, M., ed., *Social Skills and Health*, Methuen, London, 1981.
Argyle, M., ed., *Social Skills and Work*, Methuen, London, 1981.
Hargie, O., ed., *A Handbook of Communication Skills*, Routledge, London, 1986.

## CHAPTER 11

# TRAINING IN SOCIAL SKILLS

Many jobs consist mainly of dealing with people – teaching, interviewing and selling, for example. All jobs involve communication and co-operation, the giving and receiving of orders, maintaining relationships, and other basic social skills. Most of those in the first group get some training, though others have to pick it up on the job. However, some young teachers are not able to keep order, some interviewers get a lot of refusals, and some salesmen sell very little. For all of these people the training has failed. Perhaps a look at the possible methods of training may show how to improve the training of such people. In the modern world an increasing number of jobs consist more of dealing with people than with things; furthermore the speed of technological change means that many people have to be re-trained for a new job once or even twice in the course of their working lives.

Social skills are also needed in everyday life, to deal with family, friends, neighbours, people in shops and offices, and so on. It is difficult to estimate the proportion of the population whose lives are seriously disrupted by the inability to make friends or deal with other relationships, but our surveys suggest that it is at least seven per cent. Parents implicitly train their children in social skills; perhaps they could do it better. Schools train children in writing and speaking, and sometimes in other aspects of social behaviour; this too could be greatly extended. I believe that it would be possible to train people up to a higher level of sensitivity and competence than is common at present. This could have the effect of making social encounters and relationships far more enjoyable, effective and creative than they often are.

Social skills training (SST) has become widely used in recent years. Doctors, teachers, police, social workers and many others are now trained in the relevant skills. Diplomats, businessmen and others going to work abroad are often trained in the skills needed in another culture. We have seen that several kinds of mental patient can be helped, sometimes with the same degree of success as other psychiatric methods. Heterosexual and assertiveness skills training is available in some quarters. Marital skills training is often part of marital therapy.

The definition of social competence, and the criteria of successful performance of social skills, were discussed earlier (pp. 116ff.). How can it be decided whether or not a particular form of training works? Experience with various forms of training and therapy shows that, while these are often enthusiastically praised by those who have been trained, more careful investigation sometimes shows that there is no real change in behaviour. It is necessary to take measures of performance before and after the training. These measures should not consist just of questionnaires – because people may merely learn what sort of answers to give – but of measures of performance or effectiveness on the job, or objective tests of what they can do. Often ratings by colleagues are used as the criteria; there is a danger that colleagues who believe in a training method will give higher ratings after than before in order to confirm their belief. This can be countered by the use of 'blind' ratings, where the raters do not know which of the individuals they are rating are being trained or belong to a control group. There should be a control group of similar people who are not being trained, in order to allow for improvement with the passage of time and the effects of practice in doing tests. There should be a greater improvement, from before the training to after, for the trained group than for the control group, using some objective index of skill. Wherever possible, studies of this kind will be used below to assess the different methods of training.

### LEARNING ON THE JOB

This is probably the commonest form of training. While manual workers are given carefully designed courses, those who have to deal with people often receive no training at all, because it is so difficult to tell them what they should do. In fact some manual operatives also learn by doing, and learning curves can be plotted which show their rate of progress.

Unfortunately this seems to be a very unreliable form of training. A person can do a job for years and never discover the right social skills; some experienced interviewers have great difficulty with candidates who will not talk, for example. Argyle, Gardner and Cioffi (1958) found that supervisors often learnt the *wrong* things by experience, e.g. to use close, punitive and authoritarian styles of supervision.

The author with Mary Lydall and Mansur Lalljee carried out several studies of the learning of social skills on the job. In one of them an attempt was made to plot the learning curve for selling, this task being chosen because there is an objective criterion of success. Annual fluctuations in trade were overcome by expressing the sales of a beginner as a percentage of the average sales of three experienced sellers in the same department. The average results from three shops are shown in Figure 11.1; it can be seen that there was an overall improvement, especially where there was an individual incentive scheme. However, individuals re-

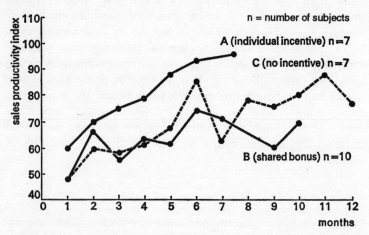

Figure 11.1    Learning curves for selling (Argyle, Lalljee and Lydall, 1958).

sponded in a variety of ways, and while on average most improved, some did not, and others got steadily worse. Again it seems that simply doing the job doesn't always lead to improvement.

McPhail (1967) studied the process of acquiring social competence during adolescence. He gave problem situations to 100 males and 100 females aged twelve to eighteen. Alternative solutions were selected and these were found to change with age in an interesting way. The younger subjects gave a lot of rather crude, aggressive, dominating responses; McPhail classified these as 'experimental' attempts to acquire by trial and error social skills for dealing with the new situations that adolescents face. The older ones on the other hand used more skilful, sophisticated social techniques, similar to those employed by adults (Figure 11.2).

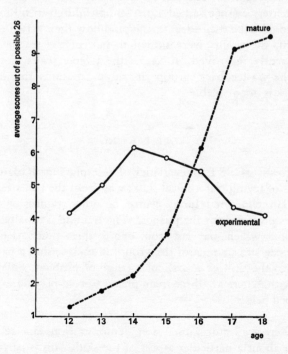

Figure 11.2   Acquisition of social skills in adolescence (McPhail, 1967).

Learning on the job has a great advantage over all other forms of training: there is no problem of transfer from the training situation to real life. A number of studies suggest the conditions under which training on the job can be successful. The most important ingredient is someone who can coach trainees while on the job; this is commonly used in teacher training. Police in some regions are coached by a 'tutor constable' who accompanies trainees on the beat, and can instruct and provide feedback on performance in real-life situations, which cannot be reproduced in the lab. The trainer should be an expert performer of the skill himself, and should be sensitized to the elements and processes of social interaction. The success of such coaching will depend on there being a good relationship between the trainee and the supervisor.

The provision of feedback can also be effective. Gage, Runkel and Chatterjee (1960) asked 3,900 schoolchildren to fill in rating scales to describe their ideal teacher and how their actual teachers behaved; the results were shown to half of the teachers, who subsequently improved on ten of the twelve scales, compared with the no-feedback group. In most situations this kind of feedback is not available.

### ROLE-PLAYING

Most forms of SST are varieties of role-playing. Role-playing consists of trying out a social skill away from the real situation – in the lab, clinic or training centre, on other trainees or on role partners provided for the purpose. The training is usually a series of sessions which may last from one to three hours, depending on the size and stamina of the group. In each session a particular aspect of the skill or a particular range of problem situations is dealt with. There are three main phases to role-playing exercises, described below.

1 There is a lecture, discussion, demonstration, tape-recording or film about a particular aspect of the skill. This is particularly important when an unfamiliar skill is being taught or when

rather subtle social techniques are involved. The demonstration is particularly important; this is known as 'modelling'.

2 A problem situation is defined, and stooges are produced for trainees to role-play with, for seven to fifteen minutes each. The background to the situation may be filled in with written materials, such as the application forms of candidates for interview or background information about personnel problems. The stooges may be carefully trained beforehand to provide various problems, such as talking too much or having elaborate and plausible excuses.

3 There is a feedback session, consisting of verbal comments by the trainer, discussion with the other trainees and playback of audio- or videotapes. Verbal feedback is used to draw attention, constructively and tactfully, to what the trainee was doing wrong and to suggest alternative styles of behaviour. The tape recordings provide clear evidence for the accuracy of what is being said.

There is often a fourth phase, in which the role-playing, phase 2, is repeated. In microteaching this is known as 're-teaching'.

There are two important preliminary steps to this form of training. Firstly it is necessary to draw up a list of the main problem situations to be faced by those being trained; this can be done by 'critical incident' surveys, or more informally by consulting a number of experienced practitioners – of selling, interviewing, teaching or whatever is being taught. Secondly it is necessary to find out the best social techniques for dealing with the problem situations.

Follow-up studies show that role-playing is the most effective form of SST at present available. Experimental comparisons of different procedures show that the full package we described above is the most effective. It is necessary to include:

1 modelling;
2 instructions;
3 role-play practice;
4 an instructor to give the feedback;
5 realistic stooges, e.g. children for microteaching.

*Feedback* is one of the crucial components. It can come from several sources:

1 It may come from the other members of the group, either in free discussion, discussion in smaller groups, questionnaires or behavioural check-lists. These things must be done carefully or they will be disturbing to the recipients of the feedback; on the other hand, they are probably a valuable part of the training process for those observing.

2 It may be given by the trainer, who should be in a position to give expert guidance on the social techniques which are effective and who may be able to increase sensitivity to the subtler nuances of interaction. He may correct errors – such as interrupting, and looking or sounding unfriendly. He can suggest alternative social techniques, such as ways of dealing with awkward clients or situations. This has to be done very carefully: the trainer's remarks should be gentle and kind enough not to upset, but firm and clear enough to have some effect.

3 It may come from a video or, failing that, audio recording which is played back to the trainee after the performance. This directs his attention to the behavioural (facial, bodily and gestural) aspects of his performance, as well as to the auditory. It may be useful to play back the sound tape separately to focus attention on sound.

*Use of homework* The main difficulty with role-playing is that trainees have to transfer what they have learnt in the training centre to the real world. Some of the best results have been obtained when traineees have been persuaded to try out what they have learnt a number of times between sessions.

Morton (1965) used role-playing with mental patients on such domestic problems as disciplining children, keeping a budget and keeping things peaceful. For the role-playing sessions nurses and others were used in the complementary roles. Patients returned home at weekends, after which they reported their progress. This was then discussed by the trainer and the group of trainees.

*Modelling* Modelling can consist of demonstrations by one of the trainers or the showing of films or videotapes. It is used when it is difficult to teach the patient by verbal descriptions alone; this applies to complex skills for neurotic or professional clients, and to simpler skills for more disturbed patients and children. It is generally used in conjunction with role-playing (between sessions) and is accompanied by verbal instructions, i.e. coaching.

Modelling has been found to be most effective under the following conditions:

when the model is similar to the trainee, e.g. in age;

when the model is not *too* expert;

when there is a verbal narrative labelling the model's behaviour;

with a live model and with multiple models;

when the model's behaviour is seen to lead to favourable consequences.

(Thelen, Fry, Fehrenbach and Frautschl, 1979)

*Video playback* has been widely used, especially by trainers who focus on non-verbal communication. The results indicating whether or not SST is more effective when video is used are conflicting, but most studies show that it does make a difference (Bailey and Sowder, 1970). Some people find it mildly disturbing at first, but they soon get used to it. However, it should perhaps not be used with very anxious or self-conscious patients.

*Equipment* Role-playing can be conducted without the use of any specialized equipment, but it is greatly assisted if certain laboratory arrangements are available. An ideal set-up for interviewer training is shown in Figure 11.3. The role-playing takes place on one side of a one-way screen, and is observed by the trainer and other trainees. A videotape is taken of the role-playing. The trainer is able to communicate with the role-player through an ear-microphone; the trainer can give comments and suggestions to the trainee while the role-playing is proceeding. (The author once had to advise an interviewer trainee dealing with an over-amorous 'candidate' to move his seat back three feet.)

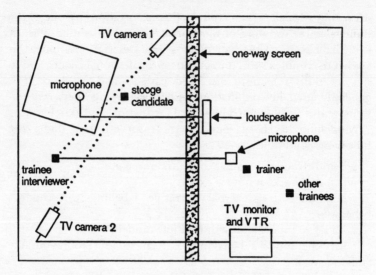

Figure 11.3    Laboratory arrangements for interviewer training.

*Interviewing training* One of the first social skills to be taught by role-playing was selection interviewing. In the course for selection interviewing devised by Elizabeth Sidney and the author, some of the exercises are designed to teach participants how to deal with 'awkward' candidates (p. 250). Trainees interview special stooges who talk too much, too little, are nervous, bombastic, anxious and so on. Each role-playing session on this course begins with a lecture and a film about the problems to be role-played. There is also training in how to assess stability, judgement, achievement motivation, etc., in the interview, and how to avoid common errors of person perception.

*Microteaching* This is now widely used for teacher training. A trainee prepares a short lessons and teaches five or six children for ten to fifteen minutes; this is followed by a videotape playback and comments by the trainer, after which the trainee takes the same lesson again. There are usually a number of sessions, each being devoted to one particular teaching skill – asking higher-order questions, encouraging pupil participation, explaining clearly with examples, etc. (pp. 272ff.). This form of training is found to be faster than alternative forms and is probably the best way of eliminating bad teaching habits (Brown, 1975; Peck and Tucker, 1973).

*Assertiveness training* This was one of the earliest forms of SST; it came from the behaviour therapy tradition, and the rationale was that arousing incompatible (assertive) responses would remove anxious and submissive ones. By assertiveness is meant standing up for your rights, saying no, making requests, initiating conversation and so on. The method of training has consisted of standard role-playing procedures with modelling and VTR playback. It has been widely used with normal adults who think they need it, and with mental patients. Follow-up studies show a considerable degree of success (Rich and Schroeder, 1976). It is a mistake, however, to regard assertiveness as the only goal of SST; control of others is important, but then so is the dimension of interpersonal warmth (pp. 135ff.), which is probably more important for people who complain that they haven't got any friends.

*Heterosexual skills* Many young people suffer from lack of contact with the opposite sex ('minimal dating') or feel anxious in the presence of the opposite sex. This may be due to lack of social skills, which in turn is usually due to lack of experience or to anxiety caused by unsuccessful experiences in the past. Training courses have been devised to teach the necessary skills for making dates and for behaviour during dates. Follow-up studies have found these to be very successful; one, for example, increased the average number of dates per week from 0.8 to 1.9 (Curran, 1977). It has been found that confidence can be increased and anxiety reduced simply by arranging six 'practice dates' between pairs of clients (Arkowitz, 1977).

*Social skills training for mental patients* This has been developed along similar lines. There is usually modelling and role-playing, with videotape playback, of the skills needed by individual patients or of skills needed by several patients if done in groups.

The social performance of mental patients can fail in a great variety of ways, as discussed in Chapter 9; some of these can be corrected by straight role-playing, but others require special techniques, which are described below.

#### SPECIAL TECHNIQUES FOR SOCIAL SKILLS TRAINING

We have shown that a number of quite different processes contribute to social competence; each can go wrong in a number of ways, and training can be focused on one process at a time rather than on social performance in general.

*Expression of NV signals* In training mental patients it is common to coach them in NV communication, since they are often very inexpressive in this sphere or send NV messages which are hostile rather than friendly. Study of a patient's role-played performance in the clinic shows which NV signals require training, though the commonest ones are face and voice. Facial expression can be trained with the help of a mirror and later with a VTR. Trainees are asked to take part in short conversations while expressing certain emotions in the face, such as sadness or happiness. If there is difficulty in producing the correct expression in all parts of the face, the photographs by Ekman and Friesen (1975) can be used as models. The voice can be trained with the help of an audiotape recorder; trainees are asked to read passages from the paper in, for example, friendly, dominant or surprised tones of voice, and these are then played back and discussed.

*Situational analysis* Some mental patients and many adults have difficulty in coping with specific social situations. In the case of a number of professional social skills, the performer has to deal with a variety of situations – for example, in social work and supervising. It is possible to include in the training some analysis of the main situations involved, and especially of those which are found difficult, in terms of goals and goal structure, rules, roles, etc. Situational analysis has also been used in the treatment of obesity, by discovering the situations in which overeating occurs and the series of events leading up to it (Ferguson, 1975). A similar approach is commonly used in the treatment of alcoholics.

*Taking the role of the other* Chandler (1973) succeeded in improving the ability to see another's point of view (and reducing delinquency) by means of exercises in which groups of five young delinquents developed and made video recordings of skits about relevant real-life situations, each member of the group playing a part.

*Self-presentation* In addition to the usual role-playing exercises, trainees can be given advice over clothes, hair and other aspects of appearance. Their voices can be trained to produce a more appropriate accent or tone. There is a correlation between physical attractiveness and mental health, and some therapeutic success has been obtained by improving the appearance of patients. The recidivism of male criminals has been reduced by removing tattooing and scars.

*Perceptual training* It may also be necessary to train people in the perception of NV signals. Some convicts, for example, can't tell when people are becoming upset, so that fights start. For professional skills like social work and psychotherapy it is important to be able to judge the emotional states of others. The Ekman and Friesen photographs can be used to train people to decode facial expression. Trainees can be taught to appreciate tones of voice by listening to tape recordings of neutral messages produced in different emotional states (Davitz, 1964). In each case it is easy to test the subject, for example by finding out the percentage of recordings which they can decode correctly.

*Planning and the use of feedback* The social skills model suggests some further points at which training can be useful. A common problem with mental patients is a failure to pursue goals persistently and a tendency to react passively to others. Assertiveness training is also directed at making the trainees take more initiative and pursue their goals. We have used special exercises for this problem: trainees are asked to carry out a simple skill, like interviewing, which requires that they take the initiative throughout. They can plan the encounter and take notes; the trainer communicates via an ear-microphone during the role-playing if the performer runs out of conversation.

*Conversational sequences* We have seen that socially inadequate people are often very bad conversationalists; they may be incapable of sustaining a conversation, and manage to kill it in one of a number of ways. All social skills use conversation, i.e. a sequence of utterances, and the control of sequences is an important part of the skill. Teachers need to be able to control such cycles of interaction as teacher lectures → teacher asks question → pupil replies (p. 272), and other longer cycles. During repeated sequences of this sort there is also a build-up in the complexity of the topic being taught. The selection interview is similar: there is a certain structure of questions, answers, modified and follow-up questions, and a structure of episodes and sub-episodes, based on topics and sub-topics. Every social skill uses certain conversational sequences, which can be learnt, and in every case there are a number of difficulties, for which the solution can be taught: salesmen may have difficulty in controlling interaction with the client; doctors may find it hard to terminate encounters; and survey interviewers may have to deal with respondents who wander off the point.

### READING, LECTURES, CASE-STUDIES AND FILMS

It may be possible to teach social skills by more traditional methods. It is important to explore these since they are much cheaper and more widely available than those described so far, which need specially qualified trainers or expensive equipment. Early attempts to teach supervisory skills by lectures and discussion were not a success; social skills cannot be learnt without having a go, just as you can't learn to swim by reading books about it. However, most skills require some new knowledge, and this is where educational methods come in.

*Reading* This is one of the most widely used methods of educa- · tion. Many self-improvement books have been produced, particu- larly in the USA, such as that by Carnegie (1936), which has been widely read. More recently there have been a number of books on do–it–yourself assertiveness training, e.g. Bower and Bower (1976), though no follow–up studies have been carried out. 'Bibliotherapy' produces short-term benefits at least in a number of areas, including weight reduction, study behaviour, fear reduction and exercise, though often some minimal therapist contact is needed (Glasgow and Rosen, 1978). One area of social skills where reading is regularly used is inter-cultural communica- tion, where do–it–yourself 'tutortexts' have been used with some success (pp. 196–7). Another area where people are often mis- informed, and would benefit from reading a good book, is that of marital and other relationships (Argyle and Henderson, 1985).

However, reading alone is not enough, and it is normal to combine learning by reading with more active forms of training; self-help manuals usually include guidance on exercises to be carried out. It may be necessary in such cases to have someone who can take the role of trainer and give some feedback on performance.

*Lectures* can be given in which various aspects of skill are explained. They may focus on the basic principles of social behaviour or the details of recommended social techniques, and can be followed by discussion among the trainees. Experience with management training shows that lectures on 'human rela- tions' are often very popular and are a good means of conveying knowledge, and also lead to improved ratings by colleagues when part of management training (Burke and Day, 1986).

There are certain difficulties with lectures. They are effective only when the audience is really interested in what the lecturer has to say, or when he can make them interested by the forcefulness of his presentation, and when he has a manner and status which make him personally acceptable.

*Case-studies* These can provide a good basis for discussion and often do so in management training. They consist of problem situations to which the group has to find the best solution, and may be presented in video or written form. Case-studies are used for general education in management problems, but can also be focused entirely on the human relations aspects. The main weakness is that trainees do not acquire any general principles of social behaviour. It might be possible to design case-studies in such a way that they would illustrate and draw attention to basic principles; perhaps, if a large enough number of cases were used, trainees could be helped to make inductive generalizations from them.

This method has been used for teaching social skills to schoolchildren. A case is presented by the teacher, or from a textbook, which illustrates problems such as dealing with authority, emotional problems at home or moral dilemmas. The case is then discussed by the class under the guidance of the teacher (McPhail, 1972).

*Films and videos* These are sometimes used for modelling in connection with role-playing. A number of suitable films are now available, mainly for management skills. Social skills trainers often make up their own videotapes of modelling behaviour for trainees; however, no follow-up studies are yet available on the use of films for this purpose. Films have been used for training in *manual* skills for some time, and these are found to be successful under certain conditions: if the learner has to try out part of the skill after each piece of film; if there is discussion before or after the film; if the film is shot from the learner's point of view, e.g. over his shoulder; and if appropriate use is made of slow motion, animation and sequences of stills, showing the successive steps in the skill.

### METHODS RECOMMENDED FOR DIFFERENT PURPOSES

*Professional social skills* These were traditionally learnt on the job, but role-playing is now widely used for teachers, interviewers, managers and others. Along the lines described above, it is the most effective form of training available.

How are such courses designed? Some preliminary research is needed to discover what the problems are, e.g. the situations which policemen or supervisors find difficult, and to decide which

are the best skills for dealing with these problems. A course can
then be devised to train employees in the approved ways of
dealing with the problem situations. This will normally be based
on role-playing in groups, but it can also include training on the
job and some educational input from lectures, films and reading.

Further problems arise with those people who suffer from
particularly serious interpersonal difficulties at work. They need
more specialized forms of treatment, as described in the next
section.

*Treatment of individuals with interpersonal difficulties* This includes
people who are quarrelsome and difficult at work, those who
are anxious in social situations and those who are lonely and
isolated, as well as a proportion of mental patients. Some of
them come to psychiatrists and some are given SST; more get
help from friends, family, doctors and clergy. They are difficult
to help, however, without a little knowledge of interpersonal
processes.

A patient's social behaviour first needs to be carefully assessed,
by role-playing exercises, interview and questionnaire, as described before. The patient can then attend a number of role-
played training sessions with other patients who have similar
needs, e.g. for basic social skills. Other patients can act as the
stooges. He or she can then be given a few individual sessions to
deal with any more idiosyncratic problems, such as particular
social situations that present difficulties. At either stage the
training can include laboratory methods other than role-playing,
such as NV exercises. And at the end of each session the patient
can be given written notes about what to think about, and
instructions for homework.

### SOCIAL SKILLS TRAINING – DOES IT WORK?

1 *For the general population* SST is needed by, and to a small
extent provided for, all age-groups. However, adolescents and
young adults are the group for whom the need appears to be
greatest, and where a high rate of success is reported. There are
several varieties.

Assertiveness courses have been found to be very effective, in before-and-after studies, sometimes using realistic but rather unethical role-play tasks with annoying confederates. Compared with anxiety reduction and cognitive therapy, SST has more effect on behaviour, but similar effects on feelings of anxiety and anger.

Heterosexual skills training, mostly with American students, has also been very successful, in terms of number of dates per week, anxiety and behavioural measures of skill. It is not clear whether improved skills or anxiety reduction are more important, and some success has been obtained from simply arranging practice dates, without further training.

Loneliness is mainly caused by social isolation due to poor social skills, and is common among young people. In extreme cases it is a cause of mental disorder. Training in the skills needed is straightforward and very successful (Furnham, 1986).

Adults of all ages have social skills needs too; one of the greatest is for marital therapy. Positive benefits for 65 per cent of clients are reported for SST focusing on rewardingness, improved communication and negotiation skills (Argyle and Henderson, 1985).

SST works for children too. Schneider (1992) recently analysed eighty-five controlled studies of withdrawn, aggressive and unpopular children, and found substantial effects of training overall, equivalent to nearly one standard deviation, though few studies included a follow-up period of more than three months.

2 *Work skills* Most jobs require social skills and most people pick these up on the job. However, some fail completely and give up, e.g. many teachers, while others are very ineffective. Follow-up studies have used before-and-after comparisons of SST to find the effect on objective measures or on rated competence or rated social performance.

Managers, supervisors and leaders of all kinds can be trained successfully, in terms of the effects on productivity, sales, etc., and on the job satisfaction and absenteeism of their subordinates (Burke and Day, 1986); most firms use some kind of

SST for this. About 80 per cent of British teachers receive some 'microteaching', with small classes; all aspects of teaching skills can be improved, including the elimination of errors, both for beginners and the experienced (Brown and Shaw, 1986).

(Argyle, 1993b)

3 *Mental patients* We showed earlier (pp. 245–6) that SST is very useful for depressives and other neurotics, especially those who are socially unskilled, and it can be a useful additional treatment for schizophrenia.

## SOME PROBLEMS OF SOCIAL SKILLS TRAINING

*Prerequisites for successful training* To carry out role-playing or most other forms of training it is necessary to have a working vocabulary of the main elements in the repertoire for the skill being taught. This is needed to communicate with trainees, to label their behaviour, and for them to monitor their own performance. This book has attempted to provide such a vocabulary.

A second prerequisite is knowledge of the skills which are most successful. Without such knowledge the trainer has to fall back on common sense, which is very fallible in this field. A serious problem is that the most effective social skill may vary with situational factors, such as characteristics of the others being handled; this has been studied most in the case of supervisory skills. The best skills may also vary among classes, races or other subcultures. This is a particular problem with the training of mental patients, since the skills which they should be taught may differ considerably with their social class, etc. Very often this kind of knowledge is not available.

*Transfer to real life* Training on the job is the only form of training which does not have to face the problem of transferring the skills which have been learnt in training centre, lab or clinic to the real world. T-groups are very different from the outside world and it has been said that all they train for is other T-groups. Role-playing usually tries to deal with this problem by means of homework (p. 294); however, trainees are often reluctant to try out the new skills or may refuse to do so. Some role-playing uses quite realistic simulations of the real situations; examples are the model villages constructed in the Caribbean and Hawaii for preparing members of the Peace Corps for Latin America and the Far East (Guthrie, 1966). There are other ways of preparing trainees for varied and unexpected incidents in real life. More abstract principles of behaviour may be taught, as opposed to specific skills; an example is 'be rewarding', where this can take a variety of forms. It is also possible to acquire the habit of learning new social skills whenever these are needed, by imitation of successful performers and studying the behaviour which is effective and ineffective.

*The search for more economical methods* If most professional people, many mental patients and 7 to 10 per cent of the normal population need, or could profit by, SST, who is going to administer it? The use of group methods is common, because it saves trainer time and provides role partners. What of do-it-yourself procedures? We have seen that 'bibliotherapy' can be useful, if combined with more active means.

Some microteaching has been carried out without trainers; trainees simply record and play back videotapes of their own role-playing and compare them with films of model teachers. However, microteaching is more successful when there is a trainer (Peck and Tucker, 1973).

*The need for other aspects of personal growth* For several skills it is not enough simply to learn the correct social moves, as it may be impossible to use these skills unless certain emotional problems have been dealt with. Some skill situations commonly arouse anxiety – for example, public speaking, dealing with hostile people or opposing others. Learning effective skills is certainly part of the answer, and practising successfully helps, but it may not be sufficient. Performers may simply lack the self-confidence to take the responsibilities required, for example, by doctors and social workers. This entails a change in self-image, which is usually produced by simply doing the job. Training courses often include an element of guided group discussion, which can help trainees to talk about these matters and receive some social support. Newcomers to a social role often need a set of ideas or principles which will help them to deal with the moral, political or wider (even philosophical) issues at stake; for example, doctors may be concerned about how long to keep patients alive, social workers about conflicts between the demands of law and the interests of clients. Again, this goes beyond social skills and can be tackled by guided group discussion, together with reflection on the experience of performing the skill.

### FURTHER READING

Hollin, C. R., and Trower, P., eds, *Handbook of Social Skills Training*, Pergamon, Oxford, 1986.

Spence, S., and Shepherd, G., *Developments in Social Skills Training*, Academic Press, London, 1983.

Trower, P., Bryant, B., and Argyle, M., *Social Skills and Mental Health*, Methuen, London, 1978.

## CHAPTER 12

# EPILOGUE

I have tried to outline what has been found out, mainly by experimental research, in an important area of human behaviour. Several hundred investigations have been described, and there are several thousand others which have been kept in the background. The main variables have been introduced, and the main processes behind interpersonal behaviour have been described.

Interpersonal behaviour is a centrally important part of human life. Relationships with others are one of the main sources of happiness, but when they go wrong they produce very great distress and are one of the roots of mental disorder. Can our new knowledge of social behaviour help?

## APPLICATIONS OF THE NEW KNOWLEDGE

There are several fields where this new knowledge has already been applied, and where it could be applied more extensively.

1 *Social skills training* It is no longer necessary for a sizeable proportion of the human race to be lonely, isolated, miserable or mentally ill through lack of social skills. Many thousands have already been trained by one technique or another, mainly for jobs which involve dealing with people, such as those of teachers and doctors, and training could easily become available to all. The most useful step would be to include social skills ('human relations') training in the school curriculum, and to make SST available to adults in community centres or elsewhere. Through this sort of training it would be possible to raise the whole *quality* of normal social behaviour so that it is more efficient and enjoyable, and results in help, co-operation and trust rather than rejection, misunderstanding and social barriers. Everyone would be able to find friends and partners more easily, and families would stay together longer.

2 *Redesign of groups and organizations* A lot is now understood about social interaction in various kinds of group and organization. It is known that with certain designs there is alienation, frustration and failure of communication, while other designs work much better. It is recognized, for example, that there should be small, co-operative teams under democratic and employee-centred supervisors, and that there should be few levels in the hierarchy, with delegation and representation of junior members. These are not optional extras which slightly increase job satisfaction, but may be essential if an organization is to survive (Argyle, 1989).

3 *Resolving conflicts between groups* A number of the most important social problems are due to conflicts of interest between groups, but conflict also exists between people of different race, class, age and even sex. Some are due to real differences in wealth or opportunities, but others, numbering among the worst, are between groups of very similar affluence. These conflicts are partly due to the difficulties of interacting with people from another culture, who follow different rules and conventions, use different NV signals and have different ideas. We have seen that a quite short period of training can make people better at dealing with inter-cultural encounters (pp. 193ff.); such training could be a normal part of the school curriculum. Conflicts between management and unions (and other groups) can be resolved faster and more effectively if better negotiating skills are used (pp. 285ff.).

A NEW MODEL OF MAN

Our research shows that previous psychological models of man were mistaken or incomplete through not taking account of man's interpersonal nature. This aspect has, as a result, remained somewhat mysterious, a fitting domain for theologians, moralists and novelists (not to mention the authors of pop songs and *Mad* magazine). These writers have indeed recognized that relations with others are the most important part of human life, and that most of the essential human characteristics cannot be manifested

by a person in isolation. They have rightly been unconvinced of
the relevance to human affairs of experiments with people (or
rats) studied while they perform laboratory tasks in isolation
(Argyle, 1992).

Current models of man held by psychologists portray us as
isolated individuals, whose social behaviour is based on obtaining
the maximum rewards, often at the expense of others. Love, co-
operation, kindness and concern for others are seen as peculiar
phenomena needing explanation in terms of the rewards for self
which they might produce. Unfortunately, much work in social
psychology has been little better – artificial experiments often
on one person, sometimes preventing verbal or non-verbal communication, and often in a laboratory vacuum resembling no
situation in the outside world (Israel and Tajfel, 1972). The form-
ulations of social psychologists have often been highly inadequate;
the importance of NV communication and the roles of gaze are
recent developments, as is most of the research on social relationships. Many social psychologists don't seem to understand that
it takes two to do it, i.e. social behaviour as well as sex.

The model of man we have arrived at is something like this:
For the survival of individuals and their genes, for the satisfaction
of biological needs and for the continuation of the species, co-
operation in groups is necessary; infants are born ready to
interact and relate to others, but these motivations and skills
require experiences in the family to become fully realized; there
is a system of non-verbal signals for communicating interpersonal
intentions and attitudes; there is a means of communication
unique to the species – language; social behaviour is produced as
a stream of closely integrated responses, subject to continuous
correction as a result of feedback, controlled by more or less
conscious plans, and subject to partly verbalized rules derived
from the culture; and social interaction takes place in a limited
range of situations, each with its characteristic structure of rules,
roles and purposes.

There is probably one more essential component: an innate
concern for members of the immediate family and group, resulting in care for others and restraint of aggression. We have seen
that sympathy appears in young children, and that taking account

of the point of view of others is an essential ingredient in interaction. Concern with the views of another takes a second important form: the self-image is largely constructed out of the reactions of others, and this leads to self-presentation behaviour designed to elicit appropriate responses in later social situations.

This basic equipment, partly innate, partly acquired from the culture and developed by socialization experiences, in family and peer group, leads to the formation of interpersonal bonds, small social groups and social structures. Different relationships are formed with spouses, children, friends, workmates and others, in ways partly defined by the culture. Interaction patterns in small groups (families, circles of colleagues and friends) tend to be complex, involving norms of behaviour and differentiation of roles. In larger groups the roles become formalized and the pattern of interaction follows a regular pattern, which is learnt by new members; this is called a social structure.

Some developments in therapy have been directed towards increasing the individual's power of self-control, i.e. freeing him from lower-level causal processes (Meichenbaum, 1977). It is hoped that the knowledge of, and the language for describing, social behaviour contained in this book, in conjunction with the training techniques described, will increase understanding in this field. This in its turn can contribute to the process of self-growth, consisting of a build-up of skills, control over emotions and the elaboration of cognitive constructs.

### POSSIBLE DANGERS OF THE NEW KNOWLEDGE

It has been suggested that the knowledge of interpersonal behaviour might have some undesirable consequences, as well as desirable ones.

1 It is possible that, when people become trained to interact better, their behaviour may become more contrived and insincere, more like acting. This is a complex and controversial issue; while authenticity and sincerity are attractive, it may also be argued that civilization depends on the restraint of many interpersonal feelings – aggressive, sexual and disapproving in particular.

The most effective and desirable kind of behaviour does not necessarily consist of the direct outward expression of inner feelings.

2 It is objected that people will become self-conscious, awkward and unspontaneous in their social behaviour. As we have seen, much social behaviour has the characteristics of a motor skill. When a person learns a new skill, such as handling the gears of a strange car, he goes through a period when the behaviour is awkward, requires full conscious attention and is accompanied by actual or silent speech. This phase rapidly comes to an end as the skill is learnt and becomes habitual.

3 It has been suggested that the discovery of better ways of performing in social situations creates a danger that people may be 'manipulated' by practitioners of the new skills. All scientific discoveries can be used for good or ill, and findings in the field of social interaction are no exception. It need not be assumed that the skilled performer will spend his time outwitting other people and controlling situations to his own advantage. On many occasions it is in the interests of all that people should be socially competent – for example, that a schoolteacher should be good at teaching. It is in situations of conflict that the more socially skilled person is at an advantage – though the same is true of whoever is most verbally or technically skilled.

### RULES AND MORALS

In a previous book it was suggested that the social scientist may,

> from time to time, step outside his role of hard-boiled investigator and play the part of the social reformer or critic. His qualification to do so is the insight he gains into new human goals, and new ways of reaching old ones . . . The social scientist is often the critic and guardian of our highest ideals. He may have a further role to play in sensitizing public opinion to new ideals and standards as yet unthought of. [Argyle, 1964]

What implications does the new knowledge have for how we should conduct our everyday life? The level of social competence could be raised if there were clear social or moral rules indicating which kinds of conduct are to be recommended. There are of course plenty of such rules already, but, as was pointed out earlier, most moral prescriptions are so vague that it is hard to know precisely what to do in a particular situation. How exactly does one love one's neighbour, or treat people as ends in themselves? What precisely does one do about a naughty child, an incompetent employee or an uncooperative colleague? The research which has been discussed does suggest the social techniques and relationships which are most effective in some of these situations, and they do not in general consist merely of being nice to people or behaving in a yielding, unaggressive sort of way. The kinds of behaviour which may be regarded as morally most desirable have to be found out by means of detailed research for each situation. Some of these can be recommended because they enhance the welfare of others, or because they bring about a mutually satisfying relation, or simply because they lead to the efficient execution of co-operative tasks. Several examples have been reported earlier and will be mentioned briefly once more.

1 People are often in trouble and distress, and in need of help. It has been found that much can be done by those who are untrained and unskilled in psychotherapy, provided they can establish a helping relationship. This involves an acceptance of the other, a sympathetic appreciation of his problems and the provision of a warm and supporting relationship (pp. 269ff.).

2 Those who are in charge of others can bring about the greatest satisfaction and productive effort by establishing a particular kind of relationship. This relationship is not obvious to common sense and goes beyond traditional moral ideas in some ways. Subordinates should be consulted and their ideas about the work used as far as possible; they should be helped to set their own goals and evaluate their own progress; when disciplinary action has to be taken it should be more a matter of discussing such goals and evaluations in a sympathetic, therapeutic but firm manner. A leader should exercise influence and control, as he thinks right, in a persuasive way (pp. 281ff.).

3 Parents, teachers and anyone else in charge of children will be faced by special problems. To exercise effectively the guidance

and help the children need requires a combination of warmth and firmness; without warmth the relationship collapses, without control there is no influence. Adults must maintain a certain distance or aloofness, in that they do not share the children's values or points of view and can only share their activities to a limited extent.

4 How can we love our enemies? Research has come up with a number of suggestions such as: try to see their point of view and find common goals – this may lead to co-operation; use negotiation skills; and positive NVC can feed back and cause a change of heart.

# REFERENCES

*Place of publication is London unless otherwise specified*

Adams, B. N. (1967), 'Interaction theory and the social network', *Sociometry*, vol. 30, 64–78.

Adams, B. N. (1968), *Kinship in an Urban Setting*, Markham, Chicago.

Adler, P. A., and Adler, P. (1989), 'The gloried self: the aggrandizement and the constriction of self', *Social Psychology Quarterly*, vol. 52, 299–310.

Ajzen, I. (1987), 'Attitudes, traits, and actions: dispositional predictions of behavior in personality and social psychology', *Advances in Experimental Social Psychology*, Vol. 20, 1–63.

*The Alternative Service Book* (1980), Oxford University Press and Mowbray, Oxford.

Amir, Y. (1969), 'Contact hypothesis in ethnic relations', *Psychological Bulletin*, vol. 71, pp. 319–42.

Andersen, S. M., and Klatzky, R. L. (1987), 'Traits and stereotypes: levels of categorization in person perception', *Journal of Personality and Social Psychology*, Vol. 53, 235–46.

Anderson, E. R. (1973), *The Role of the Nurse*, Royal College of Nursing.

Argyle, M. (1964), *Psychology and Social Problems*, Methuen.

Argyle, M. (1969), *Social Interaction*, Methuen.

Argyle, M. (1976), 'Personality and social behaviour', in Harré, R. (ed.), *Personality*, Blackwell.

Argyle, M. (1987), *The Psychology of Happiness*, Methuen.

Argyle, M. (1988), *Bodily Communication*, 2nd edn, Methuen.

Argyle, M. (1989), *The Social Psychology of Work*, 2nd edn, Penguin.

Argyle, M. (1991), *Cooperation: The Basis of Sociability*, Routledge.

Argyle, M. (1992), *The Social Psychology of Everyday Life*, Routledge.

Argyle, M. (1993), 'Social skills', in Coleman, A. (ed.), *Companion Encyclopedia of Psychology*, Routledge.

Argyle, M. (1994), *The Psychology of Social Class*, Routledge.

Argyle, M., and Beit-Hallahmi, B. (1975), *The Social Psychology of Religion*, Routledge & Kegan Paul.

Argyle, M., Bryant, B., and Trower, P. (1974), 'Social skills training and psychotherapy: a comparative study', *Psychological Medicine*, vol. 4, 435–43.

Argyle, M., and Dean, J. (1965), 'Eye-contact, distance and affiliation', *Sociometry*, vol. 28, pp. 289–304.

Argyle, M., and Furnham, A. (1982), 'The ecology of relationships: choice of situation as a function of relationship', *British Journal of Social Psychology*, vol. 21, pp. 259–62.

Argyle, M., and Furnham, A. (1983), 'Sources of satisfaction and conflict in long-term relationships', *Journal of Marriage and the Family*, vol. 45, 481–93.

Argyle, M., Furnham, A., and Graham, J. A. (1981), *Social Situations*, Cambridge University Press.

Argyle, M., Gardner, G., and Cioffi, F. (1958), 'Supervisory methods related to productivity, absenteeism and labour turnover', *Human Relations*, vol. 11, pp. 23–45.

Argyle, M., Ginsburg, G. P., Forgas, J. P., and Campbell, A. (1981), 'Personality constructs in relation to situations', in Argyle, M., Furnham, A., and Graham, J. A., *Social Situations*, Cambridge University Press.

Argyle, M., Graham, J. A., Campbell, A., and White, P. (1979), 'The rules of different situations', *New Zealand Psychologist*, vol. 8, pp. 13–22.

Argyle, M., Graham, J. A., and Kreckel, M. (1982), 'The structure of behavioral elements in social and work situations', in Key, M. R. (ed.), *Nonverbal Communication Today: Current Research*, Mouton, The Hague.

Argyle, M., and Henderson, M. (1985), *The Anatomy of Relationships*, Penguin.

Argyle, M., Henderson, M., Bond, M., Contarello, A., and Iizuka, Y. (1986), 'Cross-cultural variations in relationship rules', *International Journal of Psychiatry*, vol. 21, 287–315.

Argyle, M., Henderson, M., and Furnham, A. (1985), 'The rules of social relationships', *British Journal of Social Psychology*, Vol. 24, 125–39.

Argyle, M., and Ingham, R. (1972), 'Gaze, mutual gaze and distance', *Semiotica*, vol. 6, pp. 32–49.

Argyle, M., Lalljee, M., and Lydall, M. (1958), 'The social skills of retail sales', unpublished.

Argyle, M., and Lu, L. (1990a), 'The happiness of extraverts', *Personality and Individual Differences*, vol. 11, 1011–17.

Argyle, M., and Lu, L. (1990b), 'Happiness and social skills', *Personality and Individual Differences*, vol. 11, 1255–61.

Argyle, M., and Lu, L. (1991), 'Happiness and cooperation', *Personality and Individual Differences*, vol. 12, 1019–30.

Argyle, M., and Lu, L. (1992), 'New directions in the psychology of leisure', *The New Psychologist*, vol. 1, 3–11.

Argyle, M., and McHenry, R. (1970), 'Do spectacles really increase judgments of intelligence?', *British Journal of Social and Clinical Psychology*, vol. 10, pp. 27–9.

Argyle, M., Salter, V., Nicholson, H., Williams, M., and Burgess, P. (1970), 'The communication of inferior and superior attitudes by verbal and non-verbal signals', *British Journal of Social and Clinical Psychology*, vol. 9, pp. 221–31.

Argyle, M., Shimoda, K., and Little, B. (1978), 'Variance due to persons and situations in England and Japan', *British Journal of Social and Clinical Psychology*, vol. 15, pp. 335–7.

Argyle, M., Trimboli, L., and Forgas, J. (1988), 'The bank manager/ doctor effect: disclosure profiles in different relationships', *Journal of Social Psychology*, vol. 128, 117–24.

Argyle, M., and Williams, M. (1969), 'Observer or observed? A reversible perspective in person perception', *Sociometry*, vol. 32, pp. 396–412.

Aries, R. (1987), 'Gender and communication', in Shaver, P., and Hendrick, C. (eds), *Sex and Gender: Review of Personality and Social Psychology*, vol. 7, 149–76.

Arkowitz, H. (1977), 'Measurement and modification of minimal dating behavior', in Hersen, M. (ed.), *Progress in Behavior Modification*, Academic Press, New York, vol. 5.

Aronson, E., et al. (1978), *The Jigsaw Classroom*, Sage, Beverly Hills.

Asch, S. E. (1952), *Social Psychology*, Prentice-Hall, New York.

Asch, S. E., and Zukier, H. (1984), 'Thinking about persons', *Journal of Personality and Social Psychology*, vol. 46, 1230–40.

Atkinson, J. M. (1970), *Social Isolation and Communication in Old Age*, unpublished report to the G.P.O., Essex University.

Atkinson, M. (1984), *Our Master's Voices*, Methuen.

Austin, J. (1962), *How to Do Things with Words*, Oxford University Press.

Bailey, K. G., and Sowder, W. T. (1970), 'Audiotape and videotape self-confrontation in psychotherapy', *Psychological Bulletin*, vol. 74, pp. 127–37.

Bales, R. F. (1953), 'The equilibrium problem in small groups', in Parsons, T., Bales, R. F., and Shils, E. A. (eds), *Working Papers in the Theory of Action*, Free Press, Glencoe, Ill.

Bannister, D., and Salmon, P. (1966), 'Schizophrenic thought disorder: specific or diffuse?', *British Journal of Medical Psychology*, vol. 39, pp. 215–19.

Baron, R. A., and Byrne, D. (1991), *Social Psychology*, 6th edn, Allyn and Bacon, Boston.

Bass, B. M. (1981), *Stodgdill's Handbook of Leadership*, Collier Macmillan.

Batson, C. D. (1991), *The Altruism Question*, Erlbaum, Hillsdale, NJ.

Beattie, G. W. (1981), 'A further investigation of the cognitive interference hypothesis of gaze patterns in interaction', *British Journal of Social Psychology*, vol. 20, 243–8.

Beck, A. T. (1976), *Cognitive Therapy and the Emotional Disorders*, International Universities Press, New York.

Bell, C. R. (1968), *Middle-Class Families*, Routledge & Kegan Paul.

Bem, S. L. (1974), 'The measurement of psychological androgeny', *Journal of Consulting and Clinical Psychology*, vol. 42, 155–62.

Bergin, A. E., and Garfield, S. L. (1978), *Handbook of Psychotherapy and Behavior Change*, Wiley, New York.

Berkowitz, L. (1993), *Aggression: Its Causes, Consequences and Control*, McGraw-Hill, New York.

Berne, E. (1966), *Games People Play*, Deutsch.

Bernstein, B. (1959), 'A public language: some sociological implications of a linguistic form', *British Journal of Sociology*, vol. 10, pp. 311–26.

Bernstein, B. (1961), 'Social structure, language and learning', *Educational Review*, vol. 3, 163–76.

Berry, D. S., and McArthur, L. Z. (1986), 'Perceiving character in faces: the impact of age-related craniofacial changes on person perception', *Psychological Bulletin*, vol. 100, 3–18.

Berscheid, E., et al. (1971), 'Physical attractiveness and dating choice: a test of the matching hypothesis', *Journal of Experimental Social Psychology*, vol. 7, 173–89.

Blackburn, R. (1988), 'Psychopathy and personality disorder', in Miller, E., and Cooper, P. J. (eds), *Adult Abnormal Psychology*, Churchill Livingstone, Edinburgh.

Blakar, R. M. (1985), 'Towards a theory of communication in terms of preconditions: a conceptual framework and some empirical explorations', in Giles, H., and St. Clair, R.N. (eds), *Recent Advances in Language, Communication and Social Psychology*, Erlbaum, Hillsdale, NJ.

Blasi, A., and Milton, K. (1991), 'The development of the sense of self in adolescence', *Journal of Personality*, vol. 59, 217–42.

Bligh, D. A. (1971), *What's the Use of Lectures?*, Penguin.

Bochner, S., McLeod, B. M., and Lin. A. (1977), 'Friendship patterns of overseas students: a functional model', *International Journal of Psychology*, vol. 12, 277–94.

Borgatta, E. F., and Bales, R. F. (1953), 'Interaction of individuals in reconstituted groups', *Sociometry*, vol. 16, 302–20.

Bornstein, R. F. (1992), 'The dependent personality: developmental, social and clinical perspectives', *Psychological Bulletin*, vol. 112, 3–23.

Bower, S. A., and Bower, G. H. (1976), *Asserting Yourself*, Addison-Wesley, Reading, Mass.

Bowlby, J. (1971), *Attachment and Loss, vol. 1: Attachment*, Pelican.

Boyce, P., et al. (1991), 'Personality as a vulnerability factor in depression', *British Journal of Psychiatry*, vol. 159, 106–14.

Brackman, J. (1967), 'The put-on', *New Yorker*, 24 June, pp. 34–73.

Bradburn, N. M., and Sudman, S. (1980), *Improving Interview Method and Questionnaire Design*, Aldine, Chicago.

Bradbury, T. N., and Fincham, F. D. (1990), 'Attributions in marriage: review and critique', *Psychological Bulletin*, vol. 107, 3–33.

Bradbury, T. N., and Fincham, F. D. (1992), 'Attributions and behavior in marital interaction', *Journal of Personality and Social Psychology*, vol. 63, 613–28.

Braginsky, B. M., Braginsky, D. D., and Ring, K. (1969), *Methods of Madness: The Mental Hospital as a Last Resort*, Holt, Rinehart and Winston, New York.

Braiker, H. B., and Kelley, H. H. (1979), 'Conflict in the development of close relationships', in Burgess, R. L., and Huston, T. L. (eds), *Social Exchange in Developing Relationships*, Academic Press, New York.

Breer, P. E. (1960), 'Predicting interpersonal behaviour from personality and role' (unpublished), Harvard University Ph.D. thesis.

Brein, M., and David, K. H. (1971), 'Intercultural communication and the adjustment of the sojourner', *Psychological Bulletin*, vol. 76, 215–30.

Brenner, M. (1981), 'Skills in the research interview', in Argyle, M. (ed.), *Social Skills and Work*, Methuen.

Brown, G. (1975), *Microteaching: A Programme of Teaching Skills*, Methuen.

Brown, G., and Shaw, M. (1986), 'Social skills training in education', in Hollin, C., and Trower, P. (eds), *Handbook of Social Skills Training*, vol. 1, Pergamon, Oxford.

Brown, G. W., and Harris, T. (1978), *Social Origins of Depression*, Tavistock.

Brown, G. W., Harris, T. O., and Peto, J. (1973), 'Life events and psychiatric disorders, Part 2: nature of causal link', *Psychological Medicine*, vol. 3, 159–76.

Brown, P., and Levinson, S. (1978), 'Universals in language use', in Goody, E. N. (ed.), *Questions and Politeness: Strategies of Interaction*, Cambridge University Press.

Brown, R., and Lenneberg, E. H. (1954), 'A study of language and cognition', *Journal of Abnormal and Social Psychology*, vol. 49, 454–62.

Brown, R. J. (1978), 'Divided we fall: an analysis of relations between sections of a factory workforce', in Tajfel, H. (ed.), *Differentiation between Social Groups*, Academic Press.

Brown, Roger (1986), *Social Psychology*, 2nd edn, Collier Macmillan.

Brown, Rupert (1988), *Group Processes*, Blackwell, Oxford.

Brun, T. (1969), *The International Dictionary of Sign Language*, Wolfe Publications.

Bryan, J. H., and Walbek, N. H. (1970), 'Preaching and practising generosity: children's actions and reactions', *Child Development*, vol. 41, 329–53.

Bryant, B., et al. (1976), 'A survey of social inadequacy among psychiatric outpatients', *Psychological Medicine*, vol. 6, 101–12.

Bull, P. (1987), *Posture and Gesture*, Pergamon, Oxford.

Bull, R., and Rumsey, N. (1988), *The Social Psychology of Facial Appearance*, Springer-Verlag.

Burke, M. J., and Day, R. R. (1986), 'A cumulative study of the effectiveness of managerial training', *Journal of Applied Psychology*, vol. 71, 232–45.

Burman, B., and Margolin, G. (1992), 'Analysis of the association between marital relationships and health problems: an interactional perspective', *Psychological Bulletin*, vol. 112, 39–63.

Buss, A. H., and Perry, M. (1992), 'The aggression questionnaire', *Journal of Personality and Social Psychology*, vol. 63, 452–9.

Buss, D. M. (1988), 'The evolution of human intrasexual competition: tactics of mate attraction', *Journal of Personality and Social Psychology*, vol. 54, 616–27.

Buss, D. M. (1989), 'Sex differences in human mate preferences: evolutionary hypotheses tested in 37 cultures', *Behavioural and Brain Sciences*, vol. 12, 1–49.

Byrne, P. S., and Long, B. E. (1976), *Doctors Talking to Patients*, HMSO.

Campbell, A. (1993), *Men, Women and Aggression*, Basic Books, New York.

Campbell, E. A., and Kuipers, L. (1988), 'Social perspectives on depression and schizophrenia', in Miller, E., and Cooper, P. J. (eds), *Adult Abnormal Psychology*, Churchill Livingstone, Edinburgh.

Capella, J. N. (1992), 'The facial feedback hypothesis in human interaction', *Journal of Language and Social Psychology*, vol. 12, 13–29.

Carnegie, D. (1936), *How to Win Friends and Influence People*, Simon and Schuster, New York.

Cartwright, A. (1964), *Human Relations and Hospital Care*, Routledge & Kegan Paul.

Carver, C. S. (1979), 'A cybernetic model of self-attribution processes', *Journal of Personality and Social Psychology*, vol. 37, 1251–81.

Cassidy, T., and Lynn, R. (1991), 'Achievement motivation, educational attainment, cycles of disadvantage and social competence: some longitudinal data', *British Journal of Educational Psychology*, vol. 61, 1–12.

Chandler, M. J. (1973), 'Egocentrism and anti-social behavior: the assessment and training of social perspective-training skills', *Developmental Psychology*, vol. 9, 326–32.

Chapple, E. D., and Donald, G. (1947), 'An evaluation of department store salespeople by the interaction chronograph', *Journal of Marketing*, vol. 13, 173–85.

Chell, F. (1986), 'The entrepreneurial personality: a review and some theoretical developments', Curran, J., Stanworth, J., and Watkins, D. (eds) *The Survival of the Small Firm*, Gower, Aldershot.

Cialdini, R. B., Cacioppo, J. T., Bassett, R., and Miller, J. A. (1978), 'Low-ball procedure for producing compliance: commitment then cost', *Journal of Personality and Social Psychology*, vol. 36, 463–76.

Cialdini, R. B., Kenrick, D. T., and Bauman, D. J. (1982), 'Effects of mood on prosocial behaviour in children and adults', in Eisenberg-Berg, N. (ed.), *Development of Prosocial Behavior*, Academic Press, New York.

Clark, H. H. (1985), 'Language use and language users', in Lindzey, G., and Aronson, E. (eds), *Handbook of Social Psychology*, Random House, New York.

Clark, M. S. (1986), 'Evidence for the effectiveness of manipulation of communal and exchange relationships', *Personality and Social Psychology Bulletin*, vol. 12, 414–25.

Clark, M. S., and Reis, H. T. (1988), 'Interpersonal attraction and communal relationships', *Annual Review of Psychology*, vol. 39, 609–72.

Clarke, D. D. (1975), 'The use and recognition of sequential structure in dialogue', *British Journal of Social and Clinical Psychology*, vol. 14, 333–9.

Clarke, D. D. (1983), *Language and Action*, Pergamon, Oxford.

Clarke, R. V. G., and Mayhew, P. (eds) (1980), *Designing Out Crime*, HMSO.

Cline, V. B. and Richards, J. M. (1960), 'Accuracy of interpersonal perception – a general trait?', *Journal of Abnormal and Social Psychology*, vol. 60, 1–7.

Cochrane, R. (1988), 'Marriage, separation and divorce', in Fisher, S., and Reason, J. (eds), *Handbook of Life Stress, Cognition and Health*, Wiley, Chichester.

Cohen, S., and McKay, G. (1984), 'Social support, stress, and the buffering hypothesis: an empirical and theoretical analysis', in Baum, A., Singer, J. E., and Taylor, S. E. (eds), *Handbook of Personality and Health*, vol. 4, Erlbaum, Hillsdale, N. J.

Cohen, S., and Wills, T. A. (1985), 'Stress, social support, and the buffering hypothesis', *Psychological Bulletin*, vol. 98, 310–57.

Cole, D. A. (1990), 'Relation of social and academic competence to depressive symptoms in childhood', *Journal of Abnormal Psychology*, vol. 99, 422–9.

Collett, P. (1971), 'On training Englishmen in the non-verbal behaviour of Arabs: an experiment in intercultural communication', *International Journal of Psychology*, vol. 6, 209–15.

Collett, P. (ed.) (1977), *Social Rules and Social Behaviour*, Blackwell, Oxford.

Cook, M. (1979), *Perceiving Others*, Methuen.

Cotton, J. L. (1981), 'A review of research on Schachter's theory of emotion and the misattribution of arousal', *European Journal of Social Psychology*, vol. 11, 365–97.

Cottrell, N. B., et al. (1968), 'Social facilitation of dominant responses by the presence of an audience and the mere presence of others', *Journal of Personality and Social Psychology*, vol. 9, 245–50.

Coupland, N. (1984), 'Accommodation at work: some phonological data and their implications', *International Journal of the Sociology of Language*, vol. 46, 5–32.

Cramer, P., Bowen, J., and O'Neill, M. (1992), 'Schizophrenics and social judgement: why do schizophrenics get it wrong?', *British Journal of Psychiatry*, vol. 160, 481–7.

Crawford, D. G., and Signori, E. I. (1962), 'An application of the critical incident technique to university teaching', *Canadian Psychologist*, vol. 3a, no. 4.

Crook, J. H. (1970), 'The socio-ecology of primates', in Crook, J. H. (ed.), *Social Behaviour in Birds and Mammals*, Academic Press.

Crossland, J. (1992), 'Training nurses to deal with aggressive encounters with the public', Oxford D. Phil. thesis.

Crozier, W. R. (1990), *Shyness and Embarrassment*, Cambridge University Press.

Curran, J. P. (1977), 'Skills training as an approach to the treatment of heterosexual-social anxiety', *Psychological Bulletin*, vol. 84, 140–57.

Davis, B. (1981), 'Social skills in nursing', in Argyle, M. (ed.), *Social Skills and Health*, Methuen.

Davis, M. H., and Oathout, H. A. (1992), 'The effect of dispositional empathy on romantic relationship behaviours: heterosexual anxiety as a moderating influence', *Personality and Social Psychology Bulletin*, vol. 18, 76–83.

Davitz, J. R. (1964), *The Communication of Emotional Meaning*, McGraw-Hill, New York.

Dawkins, R. (1976a), *The Selfish Gene*, Oxford University Press.

Dawkins, R. (1976b), 'Hierarchical organization: a candidate principle for zoology', in Bateson, P. P. G., and Hinde, R. A. (eds), *Growing Points in Ethology*, Cambridge University Press.

Dawson, J., Whitney, R. E., and Lan, R. T. S. (1971), 'Scaling Chinese traditional–modern attitudes and the GSR measurement of "Important" versus "Unimportant" Chinese concepts', *Journal of Cross-Cultural Psychology*, vol. 2, 1–27.

DePaulo, B. M. (1992), 'Nonverbal behaviour and self-presentation', *Psychological Bulletin*, vol. 111, 203–43.

Deutsch, H. (1955), 'The imposter: contribution to ego psychology of a type of psychopath', *Psychoanalytic Quarterly*, vol. 24, 483–505.

de Wolff, C. J., and van den Bosch, G. (1984), 'Personnel selection', in Drenth, P. J. D., et al. (eds), *Handbook of Work and Organizational Psychology*, Wiley, Chichester.

Dickens, W. J., and Perlman, D. (1981), 'Friendship over the life cycle', in Duck, S., and Gilmour, R. (eds), *Personal Relationships 2: Developing Individual Relationships*, Academic Press.

Dijker, A. J. M. (1987), 'Emotional reactions to ethnic minorities', *European Journal of Social Psychology*, vol. 17, 305–25.

Dillon, J. (1986), 'Questioning', in Hargie, O. (ed.), *A Handbook of Communication Skills*, Routledge.

Dion, K. K., and Dion, K. L. (1975), 'Self-esteem and romantic love', *Journal of Personality*, vol. 43, 39–57.

Dodge, K. A., Asher, S. R. and Parkhurst, J. T. (1986), 'Social life as a goal coordination task', in Ames, C., and E. Ames (eds), *Research on Motivation in Education,* vol. 3, Academic Press.

Dominian, J. (1980), *Marital Pathology*, Darton Longman and Todd, and BMA.

Duck, S. W. (1973), *Personal Relationships and Personal Constructs*, Wiley.

Duncan, B. L. (1976), 'Differential social perception and attribution of intergroup violence: testing the lower limits of stereotyping of blacks', *Journal of Personality and Social Psychology*, vol. 34, 590–98.

Dunkin, M. J., and Biddle, B. J. (1974), *The Study of Teaching*, Holt, Rinehart and Winston, New York.

Dutton, D. G., and Aron, A. P. (1974), 'Some evidence for heightened sexual attraction under conditions of high anxiety', *Journal of Personality and Social Psychology*, vol. 30, 510–17.

Duval, S., and Wicklund, R. A. (1972), *A Theory of Objective Self Awareness*, Academic Press, New York.

Eagly, A. H., and Karan, S. J. (1991), 'Gender and the emergence of leaders: a meta-analysis', *Journal of Personality and Social Psychology*, vol. 60, 685–710.

Edelmann, R. J. (1989), *The Psychology of Embarrassment*, Wiley, Chichester.

Ekman, P., and Friesen, W. V. (1969), 'Nonverbal leakage and clues to deception', *Psychiatry*, vol. 32, 88–106.

Ekman, P., and Friesen, W. V. (1975), *Unmasking the Face*, Prentice-Hall, Englewood Cliffs, NJ.

Ekman, P., Friesen, W. V., and Ellsworth, P. (1972), *Emotions in the Human Face*, Pergamon, Elmsford, NY.

Ellis, A., and Beattie, G. (1986), *The Psychology of Language and Communication*, Weidenfeld and Nicholson.

Ellsworth, P. (1975), 'Direct gaze as a social stimulus: the example of aggression', in Pliner, P., Kramer, L., and Alloway, T. (eds), *Nonverbal Communication and Aggression*, Plenum, New York.

Ellyson, S. L., Dovidio, J. F., and Fehr, B. J. (1981), 'Visual behavior and dominance in women and men', in Mayo, C., and Henley, N. M. (eds), *Gender and Nonverbal Behavior*, Springer-Verlag, New York.

Emler, N. (in press), *Secrets and Scandals, Rumours and Reputations*, Harvester, Hemel Hempstead.

Endler, N. S. (1965), 'The effects of verbal reinforcement on conformity and deviant behavior', *Journal of Social Psychology*, vol. 66, 147–54.

Endler, N. S., and Magnusson, D. (eds) (1976), *Interactional Psychology and Personality*, Hemisphere, Washington.

Erikson, E. H. (1956), 'The problem of ego identity', *American Journal of Psychoanalysis*, vol. 4, 56–121.

Etzioni, A. (1961), *A Comparative Analysis of Complex Organizations*, Free Press, Glencoe, Ill.

Exline, R. V. (1971), 'Visual interaction: the glances of power and preference', *Nebraska Symposium on Motivation*, University of Nebraska Press, Lincoln, Nebr.

Exline, R. V., and Fehr, B. J. (1978), 'Applications of semiosis to the study of visual interaction', in Siegman, A. W., and Feldstein, S. (eds), *Nonverbal Behavior and Communication*, Erlbaum, Hillsdale, NJ.

Exline, R. V., and Winters, L. C. (1965), 'Affective relations and mutual glances in dyads', in Tomkins, S., and Izard, C. (eds), *Affect, Cognition and Personality*, Springer, New York.

Exline, R. V., and Yellin, A. (1969), 'Eye contact as a sign between man and monkey', paper to International Congress of Psychology, London, cited in Exline (1971).

Eysenck, H. J. (1957), *The Dynamics of Anxiety and Hysteria*, Routledge & Kegan Paul.

Eysenck. H. J., and Eysenck, M. W. (1985), *Personality and Individual Differences*, Plenum, New York.

Falkenburg, L. E. (1987), 'Employee fitness programs: their impact on the employee and the organisation', *Academy of Management Review*, Vol. 12, 511–22.

Feingold, A. (1988), 'Matching for attractiveness in romantic partners and same-sex friends: a meta-analysis and theoretical critique', *Psychological Bulletin*, vol. 104, 226–35.

Feingold, A. (1992), 'Good-looking people are not what we think', *Psychological Bulletin*, vol. 111, 304–41.

Fellner, C. H., and Marshall, J. R. (1981), 'Kidney donors revisited', in Rushton, J. P., and Sorrentino, R. M. (eds), *Altruism and Helping Behavior*, Erlbaum, Hillsdale, N. J.

Ferguson, J. M. (1975), *Learning to Eat: Behavior Modification for Weight Control*, Hawthorn Books, New York.

Fiedler, F. E., and Garcia, J. E. (1987), *New Approaches to Effective Leadership*, Wiley, New York.

Fiedler, F. E., Mitchell, R., and Triandis, H. C. (1971), 'The culture assimilator: an approach to cross-cultural training', *Journal of Applied Psychology*, vol. 55, 95–102.

Firth, R., Hubert, J., and Forge, A. (1969), *Families and Their Relatives*, Routledge & Kegan Paul.

Fisher, J. D., Rytting, M., and Heslin, R. (1975), 'Hands touching hands: affective and evaluative effects of an interpersonal touch', *Sociometry*, vol. 39, 416–21.

Fiske, S. T., and Taylor, S. E. (1991), *Social Cognition*, 2nd edn, McGraw-Hill, New York.

Flanders, N. A. (1970), *Analyzing Teaching Behavior*, Addison-Wesley, Reading, Mass.

Fleishman, E. A., and Harris, E. F. (1962), 'Patterns of leadership behavior related to employee grievances and turnover', *Personnel Psychology*, vol. 15, 43–56.

Floderus-Myrhed, B., Pederson, N., and Rasmuson, I. (1980), 'Assessment of heritability for personality, based on a short-form of the Eysenck Personality Inventory: a study of 12,898 twin pairs', *Behavior Genetics*, vol. 10, 153–62.

Forbes, R. J., and Jackson, P. R. (1980), 'Non-verbal behaviour and the outcome of selection interviews', *Journal of Occupational Psychology*, vol. 53, 65–72.

Forgas, J. (1992), 'Affect and social perception: research evidence and an integrative theory', in Stroebe, W., and Hewstone, M. (eds), *European Review of Social Psychology*, vol. 3, Wiley, Chichester.

Forgas, J., Argyle, M., and Ginsburg, G.J. (1979), 'Person perception as a function of the interaction episode: the fluctuating structure of an academic group', *Journal of Social Psychology*, vol. 109, 207–22.

Freedman, J. L. (1978), *Happy People*, Harcourt Brace Jovanovich, New York and London.

Freedman, J. L., and Fraser, S. C. (1966), 'Compliance without pressure: the foot-in-the-door technique', *Journal of Personality and Social Psychology*, vol. 4, 195–202.

Fridlund, A. J. (1991), 'Sociality of solitary smiling: potentiation by an implicit audience', *Journal of Personality and Social Psychology*, vol. 60, 229–40.

Friedman, H. S., Prince, L. M., Riggio, R. E., and DiMatteo, M. R. (1980), 'Understanding and assessing nonverbal expressiveness: the affective communication test', *Journal of Personality and Social Psychology*, vol. 39, 333–51.

Froming, W. J., Corley, E. B., and Rinker, L. (1990), 'The influence of public self-consciousness and the audience's characteristics on withdrawal from embarrassing situations', *Journal of Personality*, vol. 58, 603–22.

Furnham, A. (1981), 'Personality and activity preference', *British Journal of Social Psychology*, vol. 20, 57–68.

Furnham, A. (1986), 'Social skills training with adolescents and young adults', in Hollin, C., and Trower, P. (eds), *Handbook of Social Skills Training*, vol. 1, Pergamon, Oxford.

Furnham, A., and Jaspars, J. M. F. (1983), 'The evidence for interactionism in psychology: a critical analysis of the situation-response inventories', *Personality and Individual Differences*, vol. 4, 627–44.

Furnham, A., and Walsh, J. (1991), 'Consequences of person–environment incongruence: absenteeism, frustration, and stress', *Journal of Social Psychology*, vol. 131, 187–203.

Gage, N. L., Runkel, P. J., and Chatterjee, B. B. (1960), *Equilibrium Theory and Behavior Change: an experiment in feedback from pupils to teachers*, Bureau of Educational Research, Urbana, Ill.

Gagnon, J., and Simon, W. (1973), *Sexual Conduct: The Social Sources of Human Sexuality*, Aldine, Chicago.

Geen, R. G. (1990), *Human Aggression*, Open University Press, Milton Keynes.

Geen, R. G. (1991), 'Social motivation', *Annual Review of Psychology*, vol. 42, 377–99.

Gergen, K. J., and Morse, S. J. (1967), 'Self-consistency: measurement and validation', *Proceedings of the American Psychological Association*, pp. 207–8.

Gibbins, K. (1969), 'Communication aspects of women's clothes and their relation to fashionability', *British Journal of Social and Clinical Psychology*, vol. 8, 301–12.

Giles, H., and Coupland, N. (1991), *Language, Contexts and Consequences*, Open University Press, Milton Keynes.

Giles, H., and Powesland, P. F. (1975), *Speech Style and Social Evaluation*, Academic Press.

Giles, H., and Smith, P. M. (1979), 'Accommodation theory: optimal levels of convergence', in Giles, H., and St Clair, R. N. (eds), *Language and Social Psychology*, Blackwell, Oxford.

Glasgow, R. E., and Rosen, G. M. (1978), 'Behavioral bibliotherapy: a review of self-help behavior therapy manuals', *Psychological Bulletin*, vol. 5, 1–23.

Goffman, E. (1956a), *The Presentation of Self in Everyday Life*, Edinburgh University Press.

Goffman, E. (1956b), 'Embarrassment and social organization', *American Journal of Sociology*, vol. 62, 264–74.

Goffman, E. (1961), *Encounters*, Bobbs-Merrill, Indianapolis.

Goffman, E. (1963), *Behavior in Public Places*, Free Press, Glencoe, Ill.

Goffman, E. (1971), *Relations in Public*, Allen Lane.

Goffman, E. (1981), *Forms of Talk*, Blackwell, Oxford.

Goldthorpe, J., et al. (1969), *The Affluent Worker in the Class Structure*, Cambridge University Press.

Goody, J. (1976), *Production and Reproduction*, Cambridge University Press.

Gottman, J. M. (1979), *Marital Interaction*, Academic Press, New York.

Gough, H. G. (1957), *Manual for the California Psychological Inventory*, Consulting Psychologists Press, Palo Alto, Calif.

Gove, W. R., et al. (1980), 'Playing dumb: a form of impression management with undesirable side effects', *Social Psychology Quarterly*, vol. 43, 89–102.

Graham, J. A., and Argyle, M. (1975), 'A cross-cultural study of the communication of extra-verbal meaning by gesture', *International Journal of Psychology*, vol. 10, 57–67.

Gray, J. A. (1982), *The Neuropsychology of Anxiety*, Clarendon Press, Oxford.

Greatbatch, D. (1988), 'A turn-taking system for British news interviewers', *Language in Society*, vol. 17, 401–30.

Greenhalgh, L. (1987), 'Interpersonal conflict in organization', in Cooper, C. L., and Robertson, I. T. (eds), *International Review of Industrial and Organizational Psychology*, Wiley, Chichester.

Gregory, M., and Carroll, S. (1978), *Language and Situation*, Routledge & Kegan Paul.

Grice, H. P. (1975), 'Logic and conversation', in Cole, P., and Morgan, J.L. (eds), *Syntax and Semantics. Vol. 3: Speech Acts*, Academic Press. New York and London.

Griffitt, W., and Veitch, R. (1971), 'Hot and crowded: influence of population density and temperature on interpersonal affective behavior', *Journal of Personality and Social Psychology*, vol. 17, 92–8.

Gross, E., and Stone, G. P. (1964), 'Embarrassment and the analysis of role requirements', *American Journal of Sociology*, vol. 70, 1–15.

Guerrero, L. K., and Anderson, P. A. (1991), 'The waxing and waning of relational intimacy: touch as a function of relational stage, gender and touch avoidance', *Journal of Social and Personal Relationships*, vol. 8, 147–65.

Guthrie, G. M. (1966), 'Cultural preparation for the Philippines', in Textor, R. B. (ed.), *Cultural Frontiers of the Peace Corps*, M.I.T. Press, Cambridge, Mass.


Haaga, D.A.F., Dyck, M. J., and Ernst, D. (1971), 'Empirical status of cognitive theory of depression', *Psychological Bulletin*, vol. 110, 215–36.

Hall, E. T. (1955), 'The anthropology of manners', *Scientific American*, vol. 192, 84–90.

Hall, E. T. (1966), *The Hidden Dimension*, Doubleday, New York.

Halliday, M. A. K. (1978), *Language as Social Semiotic*, Arnold.

Hamburger, Y. (1992), *The Contact Hypothesis Reconsidered*, Oxford D. Phil. thesis.

Hargie, O. (ed.) (1986), *A Handbook of Communication Skills*, Routledge.

Hargie, O., Saunders, S., and Dickson, D. (1987), *Social Skills in Interpersonal Communication*, 2nd edn, Routledge.

Harré, R. (1976), 'Living up to a name', in Harré, R. (ed.), *Personality*, Blackwell, Oxford.

Harris, M. (1968), *The Rise of Anthropological Theory*, Routledge & Kegan Paul.

Hastorf, A. H., and Cantril, H. (1954), 'They saw a game: a case study', *Journal of Abnormal and Social Psychology*, vol. 49, 129–34.

Hatfield, E., Cacioppo, J. T., and Rapson, R. L. (1992), 'Primitive emotional contagion', in *Emotion and Social Behavior: Review of Personality and Social Behavior*, vol. 14, 151–77.

Hatfield, E., and Sprecher, S. (1986), *Mirror, Mirror, on the Wall*, State University of New York Press, Albany, NY.

Hays, R. B. (1985), 'A longitudinal study of friendship development', *Journal of Personality and Social Psychology*, vol. 48, 909–24.

Haythorn, W. (1956), 'The effects of varying combinations of authoritarian and equalitarian leaders and followers', *Journal of Abnormal and Social Psychology*, vol. 52, 210–19.

Hazan, C., and Shaver, P. (1987), 'Romantic love conceptualised as an attachment process', *Journal of Personality and Social Psychology*, vol. 52, 511–24.

Headey, B. W., Holstrom, E. L., and Wearing, A. J. (1985), 'Models of well-being and ill-being', *Social Indicators Research*, vol. 17, 211–34.

Heider, E. R. (1971), 'Style and accuracy of verbal communication within and between social classes', *Journal of Personality and Social Psychology*, vol.18, 33–47.

Henderson, M., and Argyle, M. (1985), 'Social support by four categories of work colleagues: relationships between activities, stress and satisfaction', *Journal of Occupational Behaviour*, vol. 6, 229–39.

Henderson, S., Duncan-Jones, P., McAuley, H., and Ritchie, K. (1978), 'The patient's primary group', *British Journal of Psychiatry*, vol. 132, 74–86.

Henley, N. M. (1977), *Body Politics*, Prentice-Hall, Englewood Cliffs, N.J.

Hewstone, M., Argyle, M., and Furnham, A. (1982), 'Favouritism, fairness and joint profit in long-term relationships', *European Journal of Social Pschology*, vol. 12, 283–95.

Hewstone, M., and Jaspars, J. M. F. (1982), 'Explanations for racial discrimination: the effect of group discussion on intergroup attributions', *European Journal of Social Psychology*, vol. 12, 1–16.

Higgins, E. T. (1989), 'Self-discrepancy theory: what patterns of self-beliefs cause people to suffer?', *Advances in Experimental Social Psychology*, vol. 22, 93–136.

Hill, C. T., Rubin, Z., and Peplau, L. A. (1976), 'Breakups before marriage: the end of 103 affairs', *Journal of Social Issues*, vol. 32, 147–68.

Hinkle, S., and Brown, R. (1990), 'Intergroup comparisons and social identity: some links and lacunae', in Abrams, D., and Hogg, M. A. (eds), *Social Identity Theory: Constructive and Critical Advances*, Harvester Wheatsheaf, New York.

Hoffman, L. R. (1965), 'Group problem-solving', *Advances in Experimental Social Psychology*, vol. 2, 99–132.

Hofstede, D. (1984), *Culture's Consequences*, Sage, Beverly Hills.

Hollander, E. P. (1958), 'Conformity, status and idiosyncrasy credit', *Psychological Review*, vol. 65, 117–27.

Hollin, C. R., and Trower, P. (eds) (1986), *Handbook of Social Skills Training*, Pergamon, Oxford.

Holtgraves, T. (1992), 'The linguistic realization of face management: implications for language production and comprehension, person perception, and cross-cultural communication', *Social Psychology Quarterly*, vol. 55, 141–59.

Homans, G. C. (1950), *The Human Group*, Routledge & Kegan Paul.

Howell, J. M., and Frost, P. J. (1989), 'A laboratory study of charismatic leadership', *Organizational Behaviour and Human Decision Processes*, vol. 43, 243–69.

Howells, K. (1986), 'Social skills training and criminal and antisocial behaviour', in Hollin, C. R., and Trower, P. (eds), *Handbook of Social Skills Training*, Pergamon, Oxford.

Hurlock, E. B. (1929), 'Motivation in fashion', *Archives of Psychology*, vol. 3, 1–72.

Huston, A. C. (1983), 'Sex-typing', in Hetherington, E. M. (ed.), *Handbook of Child Psychology*, vol. 4, Wiley, New York.

Hyman, H. H., et al. (1955), *Interviewing in Social Research*, University of Chicago Press.


Israel, J., and Tajfel, H. (eds) (1972), *The Context of Social Psychology: A Critical Assessment*, Academic Press.

Izard, C. E. (1971), *The Face of Emotion*, Appleton-Century-Crofts, New York.

Izard, C. E. (1975), 'Patterns of emotions and emotion communication in "hostility" and aggression', in Pliner, P., Kramer, L., and Alloway, T. (eds), *Nonverbal Communication of Aggression*, Plenum, New York.

Jacob, T. (1975), 'Family interaction in disturbed and normal families: a methodological and substantive review', *Psychological Bulletin*, vol. 82, 33–65.

Jacobs, M. K., and Goodman, G. (1989), 'Psychology and self-help groups', *American Psychologist*, vol. 44, 36–45.

Janis, I. L., and Mann, L. (1977), *Decision Making: A Psychological Analysis of Conflict, Choice and Commitment*, Collier Macmillan.

Jennings, H. H. (1951), *Leadership and Isolation*, Longmans Green, New York.

Johnson, D. M. (1945), 'The "phantom anaesthetist" of Mattoon: a field study of mass hysteria', *Journal of Abnormal and Social Psychology*, vol. 40, 175–86.

Johnson, H. G., Ekman, P., and Friesen, W. V. (1975), 'Communicative body movements: American emblems', *Semiotica*, vol. 15, 335–53.

Joiner, T. E., Alfano, M. S., and Metalsky, G. I. (1992), 'When depression breeds contempt: reassurance seeking, self-esteem, and rejection of depressed college students by their room mates', *Journal of Abnormal Psychology*, vol. 101, 165–73.

Jones, E. E. (1964), *Ingratiation: A Social Psychological Analysis*, Appleton-Century-Crofts, New York.

Jones, W. H. (1985), 'The psychology of loneliness: some personality issues in the study of social support', in Sarason, I. G., and Sarason, B. R. (eds), *Social Support: Theory, Research and Applications*, Nijhoff, Dordrecht.

Joseph, P. L. A., Sturgeon, D. A., and Leff, J. (1992), 'The perception of emotion by schizophrenic patients', *British Journal of Psychiatry*, vol. 161, 603–9.

Josephs, R. A., Markus, H. R., and Tafarodi, R. W. (1992), 'Gender and self-esteem', *Journal of Personality and Social Psychology*, vol. 63, 391–402.

Jourard, S. M. (1964), *The Transparent Self*, Van Nostrand, Princeton, NJ.

Jourard, S. M. (1966), 'An exploratory study of body-accessibility', *British Journal of Social and Clinical Psychology*, vol. 5, 221–31.

Jourard, S. M. (1971), *Self-Disclosure*, Wiley-Interscience, New York.

Jourard, S. M., and Secord, P. F. (1955), 'Body-cathexis and personality', *British Journal of Psychology*, vol. 46, 130–38.

Kagan, C., Evans, J., and Kay, B. (1986), *A Manual of Interpersonal Skills for Nurses*, Harper and Row.

Kahn, R. I., and Cannell, C. F. (1957), *The Dynamics of Interviewing*, Wiley, New York.

Kahn, R. L., Wolfe, D. M., Quinn, R. P., and Snoek, H. D. (1964), *Organizational Stress*, Wiley, New York.

Kalma, A. (1992), 'Gazing in triads: a powerful signal in floor apportionment', *British Journal of Social Psychology*, vol. 31, 21–39.

Katz, D., and Braly, K. W. (1993), 'Racial prejudice and racial stereotypes', *Journal of Abnormal and Social Psychology*, vol. 30, 175–93.

Kellerman, K., and Lim, T-S. (1990), 'The conversation MOP: III The timing of scenes in discourse', *Journal of Personality and Social Psychology*, vol. 59, 1163–79.

Kelley, H. H. (1950), 'The warm–cold variable in first impressions of persons', *Journal of Personality*, vol. 18, 431–9.

Kelly, G. A. (1955), *The Psychology of Personal Constructs*, W. W. Norton, New York.

Kendon, A. (1967), 'Some functions of gaze direction in social interaction', *Acta Psychologica*, vol. 28, no. 1, 1–47.

Kendon, A. (1977), *Studies in the Behavior of Social Interaction*, Indiana University Press, Bloomington, Ind.

Kendon, A., and Ferber, A. (1973), 'A description of some human greetings', in Michael, R. P., and Crook, J. H. (eds), *Comparative Ecology and Behaviour of Primates*, Academic Press.

Kenrick, D. T., et al. (1990), 'Person–environment interactions: everyday settings and common trait dimensions', *Journal of Personality and Social Psychology*, vol. 58, 685–98.

Kephart, W. M. (1967), 'Some correlates of romantic love', *Journal of Marriage and the Family*, vol. 29, 470–74.

Kessler, R. C. (1982), 'A disaggregation of the relationship between socioeconomic status and psychological distress', *American Sociological Review*, vol. 47, 752–64.

Kirchler, E. (1992), 'Adorable woman, expert man: changing gender images of women and men in management', *European Journal of Social Psychology*, vol. 22, 363–73.

Kleinpenning, G., and Hagendoorn, L. (1991), 'Contextual aspects of ethnic stereotypes and interethnic evaluation', *European Journal of Social Psychology*, vol. 21, 331–48.

Knapper, C. K. (1981), 'Presenting and public speaking', in Argyle, M. (ed.), *Social Skills and Work*, Methuen.

Kohn, M. L., and Schooler, C. (1983), *Work and Personality*, Ablex Pub. Corp., Norwood, NJ.

Krauss, R. M., and Weinheimer, S. (1964), 'Changes in reference phrases as a function of frequency of usage in social interaction: a preliminary study', *Psychonomic Science*, vol. 1, 113–14.

Kraut, R. E., and Johnston, R. E. (1979), 'Social and emotional messages of smiling: an ethological approach', *Journal of Personality and Social Psychology*, vol. 37, 1539–53.

Kuhn, M. H., and McPartland, T. S. (1954), 'An empirical investigation of self-attitudes', *American Sociological Review*, vol. 19, 68–76.

Kurtz, J. (1975), 'Nonverbal norm-sending and territorial defense' (unpublished), University of Delaware Ph.D., cited by Exline and Fehr (1978).

Labov, W. (1966), *The Social Stratification of English in New York City*, Center for Applied Linguistics, Washington, DC.

Labov, W., Cohen, P., Robins, C., and Lewis, J. (1968), *A Study of the Non-Standard English of Negro and Puerto Rican Speakers in New York City*, Office of Health, Education and Welfare, Washington, DC.

La Fromboise, T.-D., and Rowe, W. (1983), 'Skills training for bicultural competence: rationale and application', *Journal of Counseling Psychology*, vol. 30, 589–95.

La Gaipa, J. J., and Wood, H. D. (1981), 'Friendship in disturbed adolescents', in Duck, S., and Gilmour, R. (eds), *Personal Relationships, vol. 3: Personal Relationships in Disorder*, Academic Press.

Laird, J. D. (1974), 'Self-attribution of emotion: the effects of expressive behavior on the quality of emotional response', *Journal of Personality and Social Psychology*, vol. 29, 475–86.

Lalljee, M., Lamb, R., Furnham, A., and Jaspars, J. (1984), 'Explanations and information search: inductive and hypothesis-testing approaches to arriving at an explanation', *British Journal of Social Psychology*, vol. 23, 201–12.

Lanzetta, J. T., Cartwright-Smith, J., and Kleck, R. E. (1976), 'Effects of nonverbal dissimilation on emotional experience and autonomic arousal', *Journal of Personality and Social Psychology*, vol. 33, 354–70.

Larson, R. W. (1990), 'The solitary side of life: an examination of the time people spend alone from childhood to old age', *Developmental Review*, vol. 10, 155–83.

Latané, B. (ed.) (1966), 'Studies in social comparison', *Journal of Experimental Social Psychology*, Supplement I.

Latané, B. (1981), 'The psychology of social impact', *American Psychologist*, vol. 36, 343–6.

Latané, B., and Wolf, S. (1981), 'The social impact of majorities and minorities', *Psychological Review*, vol. 88, 438–53.

Lazarus, R. S., and Folkman, S. (1984), *Stress, Appraisal and Coping*, Springer, New York.

Leary, M. R., Britt, T. W., Cutlip, W. D., and Templeton, J. L. (1992), 'Social blushing', *Psychological Bulletin*, vol. 112, 446–60.

Leech, G. N. (1983), *Principles of Pragmatics*, Longman.

Lemmert, E. M. (1962), 'Paranoia and the dynamics of exclusion', *Sociometry*, vol. 25, 2–20.

Lennard, H. L., and Bernstein, A. (1960), *The Anatomy of Psychotherapy*, Columbia University Press, New York.

Lewinsohn, P. M., Hoberman, H. M., and Rosenbaum, N. (1988), 'A prospective study of risk factors in unipolar depression', *Journal of Abnormal Psychology*, vol. 97, 251–64.

Ley, P. (1977), 'Psychological studies of doctor–patient communication', in Rachman, S. (ed.), *Contributions to Medical Psychology*, Pergamon Press, Oxford.

Libet, J. M., and Lewinsohn, P. M. (1973), 'Concept of social skills with special reference to the behavior of depressed persons', *Journal of Consulting and Clinical Psychology*, vol. 40, 304–12.

Lieberman, M. A., Yalom, I. D., and Miles, M. B. (1973), *Encounter Groups: First Facts*, Basic Books, New York.

Linde, C. (1988), 'The quantitative study of communicative success: politeness and accidents in aviation discourse', *Language in Society*, vol. 17, 357–99.

Linville, P. W., Fischer, G. W., and Salovey, P. (1989), 'Perceived distributions of the characteristics of in-group and out-group members: empirical evidence of a computer simulation', *Journal of Personality and Social Psychology*, Vol. 57, 165–88.

Lippa, R. (1978), 'Expressive control, expression consistency, and the correspondence between expressive behavior and personality', *Journal of Personality*, vol. 46, 438–61.

Livesley, W. J., and Bromley, D. B. (1973), *Person Perception in Childhood and Adolescence*, Wiley.

Livingstone, S., and Green, G. (1986), 'Television advertisements and the portrayal of gender', *British Journal of Social Psychology*, vol. 25, 149–54.

Locksley, A., et al. (1980), 'Sex stereotypes and social judgement', *Journal of Personality and Social Psychology*, vol. 39, 821–31.

Lombard, G. G. F. (1955), *Behavior in a Selling Group*, Harvard University Press, Cambridge, Mass.

Long, E. C. J., and Andrews, D. W. (1990), 'Perspective-taking as a predictor of marital adjustment', *Journal of Personality and Social Psychology*, vol. 59, 126–31.

Luborsky, L., et al. (1971), 'Factors influencing the outcome of psychotherapy: a review of quantitative research', *Psychological Bulletin*, vol. 75, 145–85.

Luborsky, L., Todd, T. C., and Katcher, A. H. (1973), 'A self-administered social assets scale for predicting physical and mental health', *Journal of Psychosomatic Research* vol. 17, 109–20.

Lynch, J. J. (1977), *The Broken Heart*, Basic Books, New York.

McAdams, D. P. (1988), 'Personal needs and personal relationships', in Duck, S. (ed.), *Handbook of Personal Relationships*, Wiley, Chichester.

McClelland, D. C. (1987), *Human Motivation*, Cambridge University Press.

McClelland, D. C., and Winter, D. G. (1969), *Motivating Economic Achievement*, Free Press, New York.

McDavid, J., and Schroder, H. M. (1957), 'The interpretation of approval and disapproval by delinquent and non-delinquent adolescents', *Journal of Personality*, vol. 25, 539–49.

McDowall, J. J. (1978), 'Interactional synchrony: a reappraisal', *Journal of Personality and Social Psychology*, vol. 36, 963–75.

McHenry, R. (1981), 'The selection interview', in Argyle, M. (ed.), *Social Skills and Work*, Methuen.

McLeod, J. D. (1991), 'Childhood parental loss and adult depression', *Journal of Health and Social Behavior*, vol. 32, 205–20.

McNeill, D. (1985), 'So you think gestures are nonverbal?', *Psychological Review*, vol. 92, 350–71.

McPhail, P. (1967), 'The development of social skills in adolescents' (unpublished), Oxford Department of Education, paper to B. P. S.

McPhail, P. (1972), *Moral Education in Secondary Schools*, Longmans.

Madsen, M. C. (1971), 'Developmental and cross-cultural differences in the cooperative behavior of young children', *Journal of Cross-Cultural Psychology*, vol. 2, 365–71.

Maguire, P. (1981), 'Doctor–patient skills', in Argyle, M. (ed.), *Social Skills and Health*, Methuen.

Maier, N. R. F., and Solem, A. R. (1952), 'The contribution of a discussion leader to the quality of group thinking: the effective use of minority opinion', *Human Relations*, vol. 5, 277–88.

Mann, J. W. (1963), 'Rivals of different rank', *Journal of Social Psychology*, vol. 61, 11–28.

Marcia, J. E. (1966), 'Development and validation of ego-identity status', *Journal of Personality and Social Psychology*, vol. 3, 551–8.

Markus, H. (1977), 'Self-schemata and processing information about the self', *Journal of Personality and Social Psychology*, vol. 57, 165–88.

Markus, H. R., and Kitayama, S. (1991), 'Culture and the self: implications for cognition, emotion and motivation', *Psychological Review*, vol. 98, 224–53.

Marsh, P., Harré, R., and Rosser, E. (1978), *The Rules of Disorder*, Routledge & Kegan Paul.

Marx, E. M., Williams, J. M. G., and Claridge, G. C. (1992), 'Depression and social problem-solving', *Journal of Abnormal Psychology*, vol. 101, 78–86.

Mead, M. (ed.) (1937), *Cooperation and Competition among Primitive Peoples*, McGraw-Hill, New York.

Mehrabian, A. (1969), *Tactics in Social Influence*, Prentice-Hall, Englewood Cliffs, NJ.

Meichenbaum, S. (1977), *Cognitive-Behavior Modification*, Plenum Press, New York.

Melly, G. (1965), 'Gesture goes classless', *New Society*, 17 June, pp. 26–7.

Merton, R., et al. (1957), *The Student-Physician*, Harvard University Press, Cambridge, Mass.

Milgram, S. (1974), *Obedience to Authority*, Harper & Row, New York.

Miller, E. (1988), 'Hysteria', in Miller, E., and Cooper, P. J. (eds), *Adult Abnormal Psychology*, Churchill Livingstone, Edinburgh.

Miller, N. E. (1944), 'Experimental studies of conflict', in Hunt, J. McV. (ed.), *Personality and the Behavior Disorders*, Ronald, New York.

Miller, P. A., and Eisenberg, N. (1988), 'The relation of empathy to aggressive and externalizing/antisocial behavior', *Psychological Bulletin*, vol. 103, 328–44.

Modigliani, A. (1971), 'Embarrassment, facework and eye contact: testing a theory of embarrassment', *Journal of Personality and Social Psychology*, vol. 17, 15–24.

Morley, I. (1986), 'Negotiating and bargaining', in Hargie, O. (ed.), *A Handbook of Communication Skills*, Routledge.

Morris, D., Collett, P., Marsh, P., and O'Shaughnessy, M. (1979), *Gestures: Their Origins and Distribution*, Cape.

Morris, L. W. (1979), *Extraversion and Introversion*, Wiley, New York.

Morton, R. B. (1965), 'The uses of the laboratory method in a psychiatric hospital', in Schein, E. H., and Bennis, W. G. (eds), *Personal and Organizational Change through Group Methods*, Wiley, New York.

Moscovici, S. (1980), 'Toward a theory of conversion behaviour', *Advances in Experimental Social Psychology*, vol. 13, 209–39.

Mosher, D. L. (1979), 'Sex guilt and sex myths in college men and women', *Journal of Sex Research*, vol. 15, 224–34.

Murray, L., and Trevarthen, C. (1985), 'Emotional regulation of interactions between two-month-olds and their mothers,' in Field, T. M., and Fox, N. A. (eds), *Social Perception in Infants*, Ablex, Norwood, NJ.

Muuss, R. E. (1962), *Theories of Adolescence*, Random House, New York.

Myers, D. G. (1993), *Social Psychology*, 4th edn, McGraw-Hill, New York.

Naegele, K. D. (1958), 'Friendship and acquaintance: an exploration of some social distinctions', *Harvard Educational Review*, vol. 28, no. 3, 232–52.

Nealey, S. M., and Fiedler, F. E. (1968), 'Leadership functions of middle managers', *Psychological Bulletin*, vol. 70, 313–20.

Newcomb, A. F., Bukowski, W. M., and Pattee, L. (1993), 'Children's peer relations: a meta-analysis review of popular, rejected, neglected, controversial and average sociometric status', *Psychological Bulletin*, vol. 113, 99–128.

Newman, O. (1972), *Defensible Space*, Macmillan, New York.

Nicholson, J. (1980), *Seven Ages*, Fontana.

Noesjirwan, J. (1978), 'A rule-based analysis of cultural differences in social behaviour: Indonesia and Australia', *International Journal of Psychology*, vol. 13, 305–16.

Nolen-Hoeksema, S. (1991), 'Responses to depression and their effects on the duration of depressive episodes', *Journal of Abnormal Psychology*, vol. 100, 569–85.

Oakes, P.-J., and Turner, J. C. (1980), 'Social categorization and intergroup behaviour: does minimal intergroup discrimination make social identity more positive?', *European Journal of Social Psychology*, vol. 10, 295–301.

Oeser, O. A. (1955), *Teacher, Pupil and Task*, Tavistock.

Olweus, D., et al. (eds) (1986), *Development of Antisocial and Prosocial Behaviour*, Academic Press, Orlando, Fla.

Osgood, C. E. (1960), *Graduated Reciprocation in Tension Reduction: A Key to Initiative in Foreign Policy*, Institute of Communications Research, University of Illinois, Urbana, Ill.

Osgood, C. E., Suci, G. J., and Tannenbaum, P. H. (1957), *The Measurement of Meaning*, University of Illinois Press, Urbana, Ill.

Paikoff, R. L., and Brooks-Gunn, J. (1991), 'Do parent–child relationships change during puberty?', *Psychological Bulletin*, vol. 110, 47–66.

Palmonari, A., Kirchler, E., and Pombeni, M. L. (1991), 'Differential effects of identification with family and peers in coping with developmental tasks in adolescence', *European Journal of Social Psychology*, vol. 21, 381–402.

Parkes, K. R. (1980), 'Occupational stress among student nurses', *Nursing Times*, vol. 76, 113–16 and 117–20.

Pasmore, W., Francis, C., and Halderman, J. (1984), 'Sociotechnical systems: a North American reflection on empirical studies of the seventies', *Human Relations*, vol. 35, 1179–1204.

Patterson, M. (1973), 'Compensation in nonverbal immediacy behaviors: a review', *Sociometry*, vol. 36, 237–352.

Paykel, E. S., McGuiness, B., and Gomez, J. (1976), 'An Anglo-American comparison of the scaling of life-events', *British Journal of Medical Psychology*, vol. 49, 237–47.

Payne, R. (1980), 'Organizational stress and social support', in Cooper, C. L., and Payne, R. (eds), *Current Concerns in Organizational Stress*, Wiley.

Peck, R. F., and Tucker, J. A. (1973), 'Research on teacher education', in Travers, R. M. W. (ed.), *Second Handbook of Research on Teaching*, Rand McNally, Chicago.

Pendleton, D. A. (1981), 'Doctor–patient communication', D. Phil. thesis, Oxford Department of Experimental Psychology.

Pendleton, D., Schofield, T., Tate, P., and Havelock, P. (1984), *The Consultation: An Approach to Learning and Teaching*, Oxford University Press.

Pervin, L. (1989), 'The stasis and flow of behavior: toward a theory of goals', *Nebraska Symposium on Motivation*, University of Nebraska Press, Lincoln, Nebr.

Phares, E. (1976), *Locus of Control in Personality*, General Learning Press, Morristown, NJ.

Pike, K. (1967), *Language in Relation to a Unified Theory of Human Behavior*, Mouton, The Hague.

Piliavin, I. M., Rodin, J., and Piliavin, J. A. (1969), 'Good Samaritanism: an underground phenomenon', *Journal of Personality and Social Psychology*, vol. 13, 289–99.

Popenoe, D. (1988), *Disturbing the Nest*, Aldine de Gruyter, New York.

Poppleton, S. E. (1981), 'The social skills of selling', in Argyle, M. (ed.), *Social Skills and Work*, Methuen.

Potter, S. (1952), *One-Upmanship*, Hart-Davis.

Pruitt, D. G. (1976), 'Power and bargaining', in Seidenberg, B., and Snadowsky, A. (eds), *Social Psychology: An Introduction*, Free Press, New York.

Pruitt, D., and Rubin, J. Z. (1986), *Social Conflict: Escalation, Stalemate, and Settlement*, Random House, New York.

Rackham, N. (1987), *Making Major Sales*, Gower, Aldershot.

Rackham, N., and Carlisle, J. (1978, 1979), 'The effective negotiator', *Journal of European Industrial Training*, vol. 2, no. 6, 6–11, no. 7, 2–5.

Rackham, N., and Morgan, T. (1977), *Behaviour Analysis and Training*, McGraw-Hill, New York.

Ragins, B. R., and Sundstrom, E. (1989), 'Gender and power in organizations: a longitudinal perspective', *Psychological Bulletin*, vol. 105, 51–88.

Regan, D. T. (1971), 'Effects of a favor and liking on compliance', *Journal of Experimental Social Psychology*, vol. 7, 627–39.

Reid, I. (1989), *Social Class Differences in Britain*, 3rd edn, Fontana.

Reis, H. T., et al. (1990), 'What is smiling is good and beautiful?', *European Journal of Social Psychology*, vol. 20, 259–67.

Rich, A. R., and Schroeder, H. E. (1976), 'Research issues in assertiveness training', *Psychological Bulletin*, vol. 83, 1081–96.

Robins, C. J., and Luten, A. G. (1991), 'Sociotropy and autonomy: differential patterns of clinical presentation in unipolar depression', *Journal of Abnormal Psychology*, vol. 100, 74–7.

Robinson, P. (1978), *Language Management in Education*, Allen and Unwin, Sydney.

Robinson, W. P., Taylor, C. A., and Piolat, M. (1990), 'School attainment, self-esteem, and identity: France and England', *European Journal of Social Psychology*, vol. 20, 387–403.

Robson, R. A. H. (1966), 'Group structure in mixed sex triads' (unpublished), University of British Columbia MS.

Rogers, C. R. (1942), *Counselling and Psychotherapy*, Houghton Mifflin, Boston.

Rommetveit, R. (1974), *On Message Structure: A Conceptual Framework for the Study of Language and Communication*, Wiley.

Rook, K. (1984), 'The negative side of social interaction: impact on psychological well-being', *Journal of Personality and Social Psychology*, vol. 46, 109–18.

Rook, K. (1987), 'Reciprocity of social exchange and social satisfaction among older women', *Journal of Personality and Social Psychology*, vol. 52, 145–54.

Rosa, E., and Mazur, A. (1979), 'Incipient status in small groups', *Social Forces*, vol. 58, 18–37.

Rosenbaum, M. E. (1986), 'The repulsion hypothesis: on the non-development of relationships', *Journal of Personality and Social Psychology*, vol. 51, 1156–66.

Rosenberg, M. (1965), *Society and the Adolescent Self-image*, Princeton University Press.

Rosenberg, M. (1981), 'The self-concept: social product and social force', in Rosenberg, M., and Turner, R. H. (eds), *Social Psychology: Sociological Perspectives*, Basic Books, New York.

Rosenfeld, H. M. (1981), 'Whither interactional synchrony?', in Bloom, K. (ed.), *Prospective Issues in Infancy Research*, Erlbaum, New York.

Rosenshine, B. (1971), *Teaching Behaviours and Student Achievement*, N.F.E.R.

Rosenthal, R., and DePaulo, B. (1979), 'Sex differences in eavesdropping on nonverbal cues', *Journal of Personality and Social Psychology*, vol. 37, 273–85.

Ross, L., Amabile, T. M., and Steinmetz, J. L. (1977), 'Social roles, social control and biases in social perception processes', *Journal of Personality and Social Psychology*, vol. 35, 485–94.

Rotter, J. B. (1966), 'Generalised expectancies for internal versus external control of reinforcement', *Psychological Monographs*, vol. 80 (whole no. 609).

Rubin, Z. (1973), *Liking and Loving*, Holt, Rinehart and Winston, New York.

Runyan, W. (1978), 'The life course as a theoretical orientation: sequences of person–situation interaction', *Journal of Personality*, vol. 46, 569–93.

Rusbult, C. E., et al. (1991), 'Accommodation processes in close relationships: theory and preliminary empirical evidence', *Journal of Personality and Social Psychology*, vol. 60, 53–78.

Rutter, D. R., and Stephenson, G. M. (1977), 'The role of visual communication in synchronising conversation', *European Journal of Social Psychology*, vol. 7, 29–37.

Sarason, I. G., and Ganzer, V. J. (1971), *Modeling: an approach to the rehabilitation of juvenile offenders*, US Department of Health, Education and Welfare, Washington, DC.

Sarason, I. G., and Sarason R. B. (eds) (1985), *Social Support: Theory, Research and Applications*, Nijhoff, Dordrecht.

Sarbin, T. R., and Hardyk, C. (1953), 'Contributions to role-taking theory: role-perception on the basis of postural cues' (unpublished), cited by Sarbin, T. R. (1954), 'Role theory', in Lindzey, G. (ed.), *Handbook of Social Psychology*, Addison-Wesley, Cambridge, Mass.

Sargant, W. (1957), *Battle for the Mind*, Heinemann.

Schachter, S. (1959), *The Psychology of Affiliation*, Stanford University Press, Stanford, Calif.

Schachter, S., and Singer, J. (1962), 'Cognitive, social and physiological determinants of emotional state', *Psychological Review*, vol. 69, 379–99.

Schaffer, H. R., and Emerson, P. E. (1964), 'The development of social attachments in infancy', *Monographs of Social Research on Child Development*, vol. 29, no. 3.

Schatzman, L., and Strauss, A. (1955), 'Class and modes of communication', *American Journal of Sociology*, vol. 60, 329–38.

Scherer, K. R. (1981), 'Speech and emotional states', in Darby, J. K. (ed.), *Speech Evaluation in Psychiatry*, Grune and Stratton, New York.

Schneider, B. H. (1992), 'Didactic methods for enhancing children's peer relations: a quantitative review', *Clinical Psychology Review*, vol. 12, 362–82.

Schneider, D. (1968), *American Kinship: A Cultural Account*, Prentice-Hall, Englewood Cliffs, NJ.

Schofield, W. (1964), *Psychotherapy, the Purchase of Friendship*, Prentice-Hall, Englewood Cliffs, NJ.

Secord, P. F., and Backman, C. W. (1974), *Social Psychology*, McGraw-Hill, New York.

Semin, G. R., and Manstead, A. S. R. (1981), 'The beholder beheld: a study of social emotionality', *European Journal of Social Psychology*, vol. 11, 253–65.

Shanas, E., Townsend, P., et al. (1968), *Old People in Three Industrial Societies*, Atherton, NY.

Sheehan, D. V. et al. (1981), 'Psychosocial predictors of accident/error rates in nursing students: a prospective study', *International Journal of Psychiatry in Medicine*, vol. 11, 125–36.

Shepherd, G. (1986), 'Social skills training and schizophrenia', in Hollin, C. R., and Trower, P. (eds), *Handbook of Social Skills Training*, Pergamon, Oxford.

Sherif, M., et al. (1961), *Intergroup Conflict and Cooperation: The Robbers Cave Experiment*, University of Oklahoma Book Exchange, Norman, Okla.

Shimoda, K., Argyle, M., and Ricci Bitti, P. (1978), 'The intercultural recognition of emotional expressions by three national groups – English, Italian and Japanese', *European Journal of Social Psychology*, vol. 8, 169–79.

Short, J., Williams, E., and Christie, B. (1976), *The Social Psychology of Telecommunications*, Wiley.

Shouby, E. (1951), 'The influence of the Arabic language on the psychology of the Arabs', *Middle East Journal*, vol. 5, 284–302.

Shrauger, J. S. (1975), 'Responses to evaluation as a function of initial self-perceptions', *Psychological Bulletin*, vol. 82, 581–96.

Shure, M. (1981), 'A social skills approach to childrearing', in Argyle, M. (ed.), *Social Skills and Health*, Methuen.

Shute, R., and Howitt, D. (1990), 'Unravelling paradoxes in loneliness: research and elements of a social theory of loneliness', *Social Behaviour*, vol. 5, 169–84.

Siegel, S. J., and Alloy, L. B. (1990), 'Interpersonal perceptions and consequences of depressive significant-other relationships: a naturalistic study of college room mates', *Journal of Abnormal Psychology*, vol. 99, 361–73.

Simon, R. W., Eder, D., and Evans, C. (1992), 'The development of feeling norms underlying romantic love among adolescent females', *Social Psychology Quarterly*, vol. 55, 29–46.

Singer, J. E. (1964), 'The use of manipulation strategies: Machiavellianism and attractiveness', *Sociometry*, vol. 27, 138–50.

Sissons, M. (1971), 'The psychology of social class', in *Money, Wealth and Class*, The Open University Press, Bletchley, Bucks.

Slater, P.E. (1955), 'Role differentiation in small groups', in Hare, A. P., et al. (eds), *Small Groups*, Knopf, New York.

Smith, M., Gregg, M., and Andrews, D. (1989), *Selection and Assessment: A New Appraisal*, Pitman.

Smith, M. L., and Glass, G. V. (1977), 'Meta-analysis of psychotherapy outcome studies', *American Psychologist*, vol. 32, 752–60.

Smith, P. M. (1985), *Language, the Sexes and Society*, Blackwell, Oxford.

Snyder, M. (1979), 'Self-monitoring processes', *Advances in Experimental Social Psychology*, vol. 12, 85–128.

Snyder, M., Tanke, E. D., and Berscheid, E. (1977), 'Social perception and interpersonal behavior: on the self-fulfilling nature of social stereotypes', *Journal of Personality and Social Psychology*, vol. 35, 656–66.

Sommer, R. (1965), 'Further studies of small group ecology', *Sociometry*, vol. 28, 337–48.

Sorenson, T. (1985), 'Social network stimulation as preventive method among psychiatric long-term patients in a neighbourhood in Oslo', *International Journal of Family Psychiatry*, vol. 6, 189–208.

Sorokin, P. A. (1964), *Social and Cultural Mobility*, Free Press, New York.

Spangler, W. D. (1992), 'Validity of questionnaire and TAT measures of need for achievement: two meta analyses', *Psychological Bulletin*, vol. 112, 140–54.

Spielberger, C. A. (ed.) (1972), *Anxiety: Current Trends in Theory and Research*, vol. 2, Academic Press, New York.

Spitzberg, B. H., and Cupach, W. R. (1989), *Handbook of Interpersonal Competence Research*, Springer, New York.

Sprecher, S. (1992), 'How men and women expect to feel and behave in response to inequity in close relationships', *Social Psychology Quarterly*, vol. 55, 57–69.

Sroufe, L. A., Fox, L. E., and Pancake, V. R. (1983), 'Attachment and dependency in developmental perspective', *Child Development*, vol. 54, 1615–27.

Staples, L. M., and Robinson, W. P. (1974), 'Address forms used by members of a department store', *British Journal of Social and Clinical Psychology*, vol. 13, 131–42.

Stein, R. T., Hoffman, L. R., Cooley, S. J., and Pearse, R. W. (1980), 'Leadership valence: Modeling and measuring the process of emergent leadership', in Hunt, J. G., and Larson, L. L. (eds), *Crosscurrents in Leadership*, Southern Illinois University Press, Carbondale, Ill.

Stone, G. C., Gage, N. L., and Leavitt, G. S. (1957), 'Two kinds of accuracy in predicting another's responses', *Journal of Social Psychology*, vol. 45, 245–54.

Strauman, T. J., et al. (1991), 'Self-discrepancies and vulnerability to body dissatisfaction and disordered eating', *Journal of Personality and Social Psychology*, vol. 61, 946–56.

Straus, M. A., and Gelles, R. J. (1990), *Physical Violence in American Families*, Transaction, New Brunswick, NJ.

Subotnik, L. (1972), 'Spontaneous remission: fact or artifact?', *Psychological Bulletin*, vol. 77, 32–48.

Sundberg, N. D., and Tyler, L. E. (1962), *Clinical Psychology*, Appleton-Century-Crofts, New York.

Sydiaha, D. (1961), '"Bales" interaction process analysis of personnel selection interviews', *Journal of Applied Psychology*, vol. 45, 393–401.

Sykes, G. M., and Matza, D. (1957), 'Techniques of neutralization: a theory of delinquency', *American Sociological Review*, vol. 22, 667–89.

Tagiuri, R. (1958), 'Social preference and its perception', in Tagiuri, R., and Petrullo, L. (eds), *Person Perception and Interpersonal Behavior*, Stanford University Press, Stanford, Calif.

Tajfel, H. (1970), 'Experiments in intergroup discrimination', *Scientific American*, vol. 223, no. 5, 96–102.

Taylor, D. A. (1965), 'Some aspects of the development of interpersonal relationships: social penetration processes', Naval Medical Research Institute, Washington, DC.

Taylor, S. E., and Brown, J. D. (1988), 'Illusion and well-being: a social psychological perspective on mental health', *Psychological Bulletin*, vol. 103, 193–210.

Tetlock, P. E., et al. (1992), 'Assessing political group dynamics: a test of the groupthink model', *Journal of Personality and Social Psychology*, vol. 63, 403–25.

Thakerar, J. N., Giles, H., and Cheshire, J. (1982), 'Psychological and linguistic parameters of speech accommodation theory', in Fraser, C., and Scherer, K. R. (eds), *Advances in the Social Psychology of Language*, Cambridge University Press.

Thelen, H., Fry, R. A., Fehrenbach, P. A., and Frautschl, N. M. (1979), 'Therapeutic videotape and film modeling: a review', *Psychological Bulletin*, vol. 86, 701–20.

Thibaut, J., and Riecken, H. W. (1955), 'Some determinants and consequences of the perception of social causality', *Journal of Personality*, vol. 24, 113–33.

Thoits, P. (1992), 'Identity structures and psychological well-being: gender and marital status comparisons', *Social Psychology Quarterly*, vol. 55, 236–56.

Thomas, E. J., and Fink, C. F. (1963), 'Effects of group size', *Psychological Bulletin*, vol. 60, 371–84.

Thompson, L. (1990), 'Negotiation behaviour and outcomes: empirical evidence and theoretical issues', *Psychological Bulletin*, vol. 108, 515–32.

Thorne, A. (1987), 'The press of personality: a study of conversations between introverts and extraverts', *Journal of Personality and Social Psychology*, vol. 53, 718–26.

Tice, D. M. (1992), 'Self-concept change and self-presentation: the looking glass self is also a magnifying glass', *Journal of Personality and Social Psychology*, vol. 63, 435–51.

Trevarthen, C. (1980), 'The foundations of intersubjectivity: development of interpersonal and cooperative understanding in infants', in Olson, D. R. (ed.), *The Social Foundations of Language and Thought*, Norton, New York.

Triandis, H. (1972), *The Analysis of Subjective Culture*, Wiley, New York.

Triandis, H. C. , et al. (1988), 'Individualism and collectivism: cross-cultural perspectives on self-ingroup relationships', *Journal of Personality and Social Psychology*, vol. 54, 323–8.

Trist, E. L., et al. (1963), *Organizational Choice*, Tavistock.

Trower, P., Bryant, B., and Argyle, M. (1978), *Social Skills and Mental Health*, Methuen.

Trower, P., and Dryden, W. (1981), 'Psychotherapy', in Argyle, M. (ed.), *Social Skills and Health*, Methuen.

Trudgill, P. (1974), *Sociolinguistics: An Introduction*, Penguin.

Tse'elon, E. (1989), *Communicating via Clothes*, Oxford D. Phil. thesis.

Ulrich, L., and Trumbo, D. (1965), 'The selection interview since 1949', *Psychological Bulletin*, vol. 63, 100–116.

Ungerson, B. (1975), *Recruitment Handbook*, Gower, Aldershot.

Valins, S. (1966), 'Cognitive effect of false heart-rate feedback', *Journal of Personality and Social Psychology*, vol. 4, 400–408.

Vanfossen, B. E. (1981), 'Sex differences in the mental health effects of spouse support', *Journal of Health and Social Behavior*, Vol. 22, 130–43.

Van Gennep, A. (1908), *The Rites of Passage*, University of Chicago Press.

Van Hooff, J. A. R. A. M. (1972), 'A comparative approach to the phylogeny of laughter and smiling', in Hinde, R. A. (ed.), *Nonverbal Communication*, Royal Society and Cambridge University Press.

VanYperen, N. W., and Buunk, B. P. (1990), 'A longitudinal study of equity and satisfaction in intimate relationships', *European Journal of Social Psychology*, vol. 20, 287–309.

VanYperen, N. W., and Buunk, B. P. (1991), 'Sex-role attitudes, social comparison, and satisfaction with relationships', *Social Psychology Quarterly*, vol. 54, 169–80.

Videbeck, R. (1960), 'Self-conception and the reactions of others', *Sociometry*, vol. 23, 351–9.

von Cranach, M., and Ellgring, J. H. (1973), 'Problems in the recognition of gaze direction', in von Cranach, M., and Vine, I. (eds), *Social Communication and Movement*, Academic Press.

Vroom, V. H., and Yetton, P. W. (1973), *Leadership and Decision-Making*, University of Pittsburgh Press.

Wachtel, P. (1973), 'Psychodynamic behaviour therapy, and the implacable experimenter: an inquiry into the consistency of personality', *Journal of Abnormal Psychology*, vol. 82, 324–34.

Walster, E., et al. (1966), 'Importance of physical attractiveness in dating behavior', *Journal of Personality and Social Psychology*, vol. 4, 508–16.

Watson, D. (1982), 'The actor and the observer: how are their perceptions of causality divergent?', *Psychological Bulletin*, vol. 92, 682–700.

Weiner, B. (1974), *Achievement Motivation and Attribution Theory*, General Learning Press, Morristown, NJ.

Weiner, B. (1980), *Human Motivation*, Holt, Rinehart and Winston, New York.

Weisner, W. H., and Cronshaw, S. F. (1988), 'A meta-analytic investigation of the impact of interview format and degree of structure on the validity of the employment interview', *Journal of Occupational Psychology*, vol. 61, 275–90.

Wellman, B. (1979), 'The community question: the intimate networks of East Yorkers', *American Journal of Sociology*, vol. 84, 1201–31.

Wheeler, L., Reis, H. T., and Bond, M. H. (1989), 'Collectivism–individualism in everyday life: the middle kingdom and the melting pot', *Journal of Personality and Social Psychology*, vol. 57, 79–86.

Wheeler, L., Reis, H., and Nezlek, J. (1983), 'Loneliness, social interaction, and sex roles', *Journal of Personality and Social Psychology*, vol. 45, 943–53.

Whitcher, S. J., and Fisher, J. D. (1979), 'Multidimensional reaction to therapeutic touch in a hospital setting', *Journal of Personality and Social Psychology*, vol. 37, 87–96.

Whittington, D. (1986), 'Chairmanship', in Hargie, O. (ed.), *A Handbook of Communication Skills*, Routledge.

Wicklund, R. A. (1975), 'Objective self-awareness', *Advances in Experimental Social Psychology*, vol. 8, 233–75.

Wilder, D. A. (1986), 'Social categorization: implications for creation and reduction of intergroup bias', *Advances in Experimental Social Psychology*, vol. 19, 291–355.

Williams, J. M. G. (1986), 'Social skills training and depression', in Hollin, C. R., and Trower, P. (eds) *Handbook of Social Skills Training*, Pergamon, Oxford.

Willis, F. N., and Hamm, H. K. (1980), 'The use of interpersonal touch in securing compliance', *Journal of Nonverbal Behavior*, vol. 5, 49–55.

Wilson, E. O. (1975), *Sociobiology: The New Synthesis*, Harvard University Press, Cambridge, Mass.

Wilson, G., and Nias, D. (1976), *Love's Mysteries: The Psychology of Sexual Attraction*, Open Books.

Wilson, K., and Gallois, C. (1993), *Assertion and Its Social Context*, Pergamon, Oxford.

Wilson, T. D., and Linville, P. W. (1982), 'Improving the academic performance of college freshmen: attributional theory revisited', *Journal of Personality and Social Psychology*, vol. 42, 367–76.

Winter, D. G. (1973), *The Power Motive*, Free Press, New York.

Woodward, J. (1960), *The Saleswoman*, Pitman.

Wylie, R. (1979), *The Self-Concept, vol. 2: Theory and Research on Selected Topics*, University of Nebraska Press, Lincoln, Nebr.

Zajonc, R. B. (1965), 'Social facilitation', *Science*, vol. 149, 269–74.

Zajonc, R. B. (1992), 'Lecture at SESP/European Association for Social Psychology', Leuven.

Zebrowitz, L. A. (1990), *Social Perception*, Open University Press, Milton Keynes.

Ziegler, F. J., and Imboden, J. B. (1962), 'Contemporary conversion reactions: II a conceptual model', *Archives of General Psychiatry*, vol. 6, 279–87.

Zigler, E., and Child, I. L. (1969), 'Socialization', in Lindzey, G., and Aronson, E. (eds), *Handbook of Social Psychology*, vol. 3, Addison-Wesley, Reading, Mass.

Zillman, D. (1983), 'Transfer of excitation in emotional behavior', in Cacciopo, T., and Petty, R. E. (eds), *Social Psychophysiology: A Source Book*, Guilford Press, New York.

Zimbardo, P. G. (1969), 'The human choice: individuation and order versus deindividuation, impulse and chaos', *Nebraska Symposium on Motivation*, vol. 17, University of Nebraska Press, Lincoln, Nebr.

Zimbardo, P. G. (1973), 'A Pirandellian prison', *The New York Times Sunday Magazine*, 8 April, pp. 38–60.

Zuckerman, M., DePaulo, B., and Rosenthal, R. (1981), 'Verbal and non-verbal communication of deception', *Advances in Experimental Social Psychology*, vol. 14, 1–59.

# INDEX OF NAMES

References in *italics* are to figures and tables

# SUBJECT INDEX

**PENGUIN ONLINE**

News, reviews and previews of forthcoming books

read about your favourite authors

•

investigate over 12,000 titles

•

browse our online magazine

•

enter one of our literary quizzes

•

win some fantastic prizes in our competitions

•

e-mail us with your comments and book reviews

•

instantly order any Penguin book

'To be recommended without reservation ... a rich and rewarding online experience' *Internet Magazine*

**www.penguin.com**

# READ MORE IN PENGUIN

In every corner of the world, on every subject under the sun, Penguin represents quality and variety – the very best in publishing today.

For complete information about books available from Penguin – including Puffins, Penguin Classics and Arkana – and how to order them, write to us at the appropriate address below. Please note that for copyright reasons the selection of books varies from country to country.

**In the United Kingdom**: Please write to *Dept. EP, Penguin Books Ltd, Bath Road, Harmondsworth, West Drayton, Middlesex UB7 0DA*

**In the United States**: Please write to *Consumer Services, Penguin Putnam Inc., 405 Murray Hill Parkway, East Rutherford, New Jersey 07073-2136.* VISA and MasterCard holders call 1-800-631-8571 to order Penguin titles

**In Canada**: Please write to *Penguin Books Canada Ltd, 10 Alcorn Avenue, Suite 300, Toronto, Ontario M4V 3B2*

**In Australia**: Please write to *Penguin Books Australia Ltd, 487 Maroondah Highway, Ringwood, Victoria 3134*

**In New Zealand**: Please write to *Penguin Books (NZ) Ltd, Private Bag 102902, North Shore Mail Centre, Auckland 10*

**In India**: Please write to *Penguin Books India Pvt Ltd, 11 Community Centre, Panchsheel Park, New Delhi 110017*

**In the Netherlands**: Please write to *Penguin Books Netherlands bv, Postbus 3507, NL-1001 AH Amsterdam*

**In Germany**: Please write to *Penguin Books Deutschland GmbH, Metzlerstrasse 26, 60594 Frankfurt am Main*

**In Spain**: Please write to *Penguin Books S. A., Bravo Murillo 19, 1°B, 28015 Madrid*

**In Italy**: Please write to *Penguin Italia s.r.l., Via Vittorio Emanuele 45/a, 20094 Corsico, Milano*

**In France**: Please write to *Penguin France, 12, Rue Prosper Ferradou, 31700 Blagnac*

**In Japan**: Please write to *Penguin Books Japan Ltd, Iidabashi KM-Bldg, 2-23-9 Koraku, Bunkyo-Ku, Tokyo 112-0004*

**In South Africa**: Please write to *Penguin Books South Africa (Pty) Ltd, P.O. Box 751093, Gardenview, 2047 Johannesburg*

# READ MORE IN PENGUIN

## POLITICS AND SOCIAL SCIENCES

**The Unconscious Civilization**  John Ralston Saul

In this powerfully argued critique, John Ralston Saul shows how corporatism has become the dominant ideology of our time, cutting across all sectors as well as the political spectrum. The result is an increasingly conformist society in which citizens are reduced to passive bystanders.

**A Class Act**  Andrew Adonis and Stephen Pollard

'Will Britain escape from ancient and modern injustice? A necessary first step is to read and take seriously this ... description of the condition of our country. Andrew Adonis and Stephen Pollard here destroy the myth that Britain is a classless society' *The Times Higher Education Supplement*

**Accountable to None**  Simon Jenkins

'An important book, because it brings together, with an insider's authority and anecdotage, both a narrative of domestic Thatcherism and a polemic against its pretensions ... an indispensable guide to the corruptions of power and language which have sustained the illusion that Thatcherism was an attack on "government"' *Guardian*

**Structural Anthropology** Volumes 1–2  Claude Lévi-Strauss

'That the complex ensemble of Lévi-Strauss's achievement ... is one of the most original and intellectually exciting of the present age seems undeniable. No one seriously interested in language or literature, in sociology or psychology, can afford to ignore it' George Steiner

**Invitation to Sociology**  Peter L. Berger

Without belittling its scientific procedures Professor Berger stresses the humanistic affinity of sociology with history and philosophy. It is a discipline which encourages a fuller awareness of the human world ... with the purpose of bettering it.

# READ MORE IN PENGUIN

## POLITICS AND SOCIAL SCIENCES

### Anatomy of a Miracle   Patti Waldmeir

The peaceful birth of black majority rule in South Africa has been seen by many as a miracle – or at least political magic. 'This book is a brilliant, vivid account of this extraordinary transformation' *Financial Times*

### A Sin Against the Future   Vivien Stern

Do prisons contribute to a better, safer world? Or are they a threat to democracy, as increasingly punitive measures are brought in to deal with rising crime? This timely account examines different styles of incarceration around the world and presents a powerful case for radical change.

### The United States of Anger   Gavin Esler

'First-rate . . . an even-handed and astute account of the United States today, sure in its judgements and sensitive in its approach' *Scotland on Sunday*. 'In sharply written, often amusing portraits of this disconnected America far from the capital, Esler probes this state of anger' *The Times*

### Killing Rage: Ending Racism   bell hooks

Addressing race and racism in American society from a black and a feminist standpoint, bell hooks covers a broad spectrum of issues. In the title essay she writes about the 'killing rage' – the intense anger caused by everyday instances of racism – finding in that rage a positive inner strength to create productive change.

### 'Just like a Girl'   Sue Sharpe

Sue Sharpe's unprecedented research and analysis of the attitudes and hopes of teenage girls from four London schools has become a classic of its kind. This new edition focuses on girls in the nineties and represents their views on education, work, marriage, gender roles, feminism and women's rights.

# READ MORE IN PENGUIN

## PSYCHOLOGY

**How the Mind Works**  Steven Pinker

This brilliant and controversial book explains what the mind is, how it evolved, and how it allows us to see, think, feel, interact, enjoy the arts and ponder the mysteries of life. 'To have read [the book] is to have consulted a first draft of the structural plan of the human psyche . . . a glittering *tour de force*' *Spectator*

**The Uses of Enchantment**  Bruno Bettelheim

'Bruno Bettelheim's tour of fairy stories, with all their psychoanalytic connotations brought out into the open, is a feast of understanding' *New Statesman & Society*. 'Everything that Bettelheim writes about children, particularly about children's involvement in fiction, seems profound and illuminating' *Sunday Times*

**Evolution in Mind**  Henry Plotkin
An Introduction to Evolutionary Psychology

Evolutionary theory holds a vital key to understanding ourselves. In proposing a more revolutionary approach to psychology, Professor Plotkin vividly demonstrates how an evolutionary perspective brings us closer to understanding what it is to be human.

**The Man Who Loved a Polar Bear**  Robert U. Akeret

'Six fascinating case histories related with wit and humanity by the veteran psychotherapist Robert Akeret . . . a remarkable tour to the wilder shores of the human mind' *Daily Mail*

**Private Myths: Dreams and Dreaming**  Anthony Stevens

'Its case for dreaming as something more universally significant than a tour across our personal playgrounds of guilt and misery is eloquently persuasive . . . [a] hugely absorbing study – its surface criss-crossed with innumerable avenues into science, anthropology and religion' *Spectator*

# READ MORE IN PENGUIN

## PSYCHOLOGY

**Closing the Asylum**  Peter Barham

'A dispassionate, objective analysis of the changes in the way we care for the mentally ill. It offers no simple solutions but makes clear that "care in the community" is not so easy to implement as some seem to believe' *The Times Educational Supplement*

**Child Behaviour**  Dorothy Einon

Covering the psychology of childcare, this book traces every key theme of child behaviour from birth to adolescence. Dorothy Einon discusses what, at any age, it is reasonable to expect of a child, how to keep things in perspective, and the most interesting and rewarding aspect of parenthood – bringing up a happy, well-adjusted child.

**Bereavement**  Colin Murray Parkes

This classic text enables us to understand grief and grieving. How is bereavement affected by age, gender, personal psychology and culture? What are the signs of pathological grieving which can lead to mental illness? And how can carers provide genuine help without interfering with the painful but necessary 'work' of mourning?

**Edward de Bono's Textbook of Wisdom**

Edward de Bono shows how traditional thinking methods designed by the 'Gang of Three' (Socrates, Plato and Aristotle) are too rigid to cope with a complex and changing world. He recognizes that our brains deserve that we do better with them, and uses his gift for simplicity to get readers' thoughts to flow along fresh lines.

**The Care of the Self**  Michel Foucault
The History of Sexuality Volume 3

Foucault examines the transformation of sexual discourse from the Hellenistic to the Roman world in an enquiry which 'bristles with provocative insights into the tangled liaison of sex and self' *The Times Higher Education Supplement*

# BY THE SAME AUTHOR

### The Social Psychology of Work

In this classic and informative account, Michael Argyle considers every aspect of the social factors influencing our experience of work. He begins with an examination of its historical and sociological origins, goes on to compare the working conditions of several countries, and analyses the role of technology, job design, working groups, and how they relate to job satisfaction and efficiency. Drawing on the latest research, he also examines theories of motivation, leadership, training in social skills and interviewing techniques, with chapters on stress, mental health at work, plus unemployment and retirement. Finally he takes a highly topical look at the future of work.

### The Social Psychology of Leisure

Leisure includes reading and religion, bungee-jumping and bird-watching, running marathons, helping the aged and slumping in front of soap operas. We socialize with family and friends or join clubs devoted to anything from collecting engine numbers to protecting the environment. We set off on holiday in search of self-actualization – or just sun, sea and sex.

In this eye-opening book, a companion volume to *The Social Psychology of Work*, Michael Argyle explores our motivation in all these activities, examines the influence of age, class and gender and considers where we are most likely to find health, happiness, a sense of achievement and other such benefits. As the work ethic is eroded and more leisure time becomes available, the issues raised by this pioneering text will become more and more important.